Politics of Empowerment

Politics of Empowerment

Disability Rights and the Cycle of American Policy Reform

David Pettinicchio

Stanford University Press
Stanford, California

Stanford University Press
Stanford, California

Printed in the United States of America on acid-free, archival-quality paper

Library of Congress Cataloging-in-Publication Data

Names: Pettinicchio, David, author.
Title: Politics of empowerment : disability rights and the cycle of American policy reform / David Pettinicchio.
Description: Stanford, California : Stanford University Press, 2019. | Includes bibliographical references and index.
Identifiers: LCCN 2019010216 (print) | LCCN 2019011746 (ebook) | ISBN 9781503609778 (electronic) | ISBN 9781503600874 (cloth : alk. paper) | ISBN 9781503609761 (pbk. : alk. paper)
Subjects: LCSH: People with disabilities—Civil rights—United States—History. | People with disabilities—Government policy—United States—History. | Social movements—United States—History.
Classification: LCC HV1553 (ebook) | LCC HV1553 .P484 2019 (print) | DDC 323.3/70973—dc23
LC record available at https://lccn.loc.gov/2019010216

Cover design by Rob Ehle

Text design by Bruce Lundquist

Typeset by Newgen in 10/14 Minion

To my brother, family, and friends.
To those who helped make this
book possible.

Contents

Tables and Figures   ix

Preface   xiii

Acknowledgments   xvii

1 The Political Evolution of Disability   1

2 It's Ability, Not Disability, That Counts   19

3 Reshaping the Policy Agenda   49

4 How Disability Advocacy Made Citizens out of Clients   79

5 Politics Is Pressure   105

6 Empowering the Government   136

Appendix   167

Resources   183

Notes   189

Bibliography   227

Index   243

Tables and Figures

Tables

2.1 Average ideological position of select House committees
     in the 1950s   24

2.2 Average voting scores with and against the Conservative
     Coalition, 1959   29

A.1 Disability policy makers of the 1950s   169

A.2 Key disability rights entrepreneurs in Congress,
     1960s–1970s   173

A.3 Estimating attention to the disability civil rights issue,
     using panel data, 1961–2006   176

A.4 Favorable environments for organizational expansion,
     1961–2006   177

A.5 Description of disability protests   179

A.6 Simultaneous equations predicting hearings, public laws,
     and protest, 1961–2006   180

Figures

2.1 Ideological position of the House and House Committee
     on Education and Labor, 1949–1968   25

2.2 Stability and turnover in the House Committee on
     Education and Labor, 1949–1968   25

2.3 Disability issue salience in government, 1950–1965   30

2.4 Organizations testifying before Congress, 1946–1960   34

2.5 Norman Rockwell's *The Paycheck*, 1958   36

2.6 Easter Seals fund-raising campaign magazine advertisement   45

3.1 Expansion of House Committee on Education and
     Labor's informal issue jurisdiction, 1950–1980   52

3.2 Expansion of Senate Committee on Labor and Public
     Welfare's informal issue jurisdiction, 1950–1980   53

3.3 Growth of the welfare state in the 1960s   54

3.4 OASDI spending and disability insurance benefit
     payments, 1957–1980   57

3.5 Expanding venues and issue diversity in disability,
     1961–1980   62

3.6 Disability-related congressional hearings, 1961–1980   63

3.7 Hearing-days and nonbill referral hearings, 1961–1980   63

4.1 Nonprofit organizational density by constituency,
     1961–1985   80

4.2 The rise of advocacy in the disability nonprofit sector,
     1961–1982   85

4.3 Joseph Califano's letter to Congress, introduced into
     testimony at a September 1977 hearing   90

4.4 Letter from attorney Wendell B. Iddings, representing the
     Lebanon School Board, to Congressman John Myers   93

5.1 Disability protest events, 1961–2006   112

5.2 Most active protest groups   112

6.1 A protester being removed by Capitol police, June 2017   140

6.2 Employment and earnings among people with disabilities,
     1988–2014   147

6.3 Demobilization: A shrinking policy agenda,
     declining protest, and contracting organizational field   160

A.1 Table of total expenditures from federal and state funds
     for vocational rehabilitation   170

A.2 Chart of number of rehabilitated people   171

A.3   Conservative voting in the Subcommittee on the
       Handicapped and the Senate   174

A.4   Committee formal proximity to disability   174

A.5   Committees holding disability hearings based on their
       informal jurisdictions   175

A.6   Disability protest size over time, 1961–2006   180

Preface

IT WAS AN EXCEPTIONALLY BEAUTIFUL sunny Seattle December morning in 2012. I was packing up my Capitol Hill apartment, soon to be temporarily back in Montreal before heading off to the University of Oxford. I was reminded by a television news report that the Senate had just failed to ratify the UN Convention on Disability Rights. The convention's language was in effect modeled after the Americans with Disabilities Act (ADA), the so-called emancipation proclamation for people with disabilities. This seemed to fly in the face of the research I had been conducting on the United States as a world leader in disability policy—a fact that did not slip the notice of my academic mentors. But as this book developed over the years, it became clearer to me that this political or policy failure, in fact, was not at all an ironic aberration in American policy making, political institutions, or the political process.

This book, which draws on disability politics and policy making, tells a broader story about the way government lunges forward in producing policy innovations that empower citizens, only to incrementally back-step—a "death by a thousand cuts"—to borrow from liberal Republican and disability rights advocate Lowell Weicker. Indeed, the ADA, a civil rights law second in notoriety perhaps only to the Civil Rights Act itself, was an attempt to restore civil rights enacted years earlier. And it too had to be "restored" eighteen years later with the ADA Amendments Act.

In 2017—more than a quarter century after the ADA was enacted—attempts to roll back rights through, for instance, the ADA Education and Reform Act, were accompanied by efforts to strengthen existing legislation. The Disability Integration Act of 2017, for example, introduced by a man who was no stranger to the disability rights cause, James Sensenbrenner, sought to meet unfulfilled expectations by the ADA in regard to the right to community-based care. In 2018, Democratic senators Bob Casey and Amy Klobuchar (among others) introduced two new bills seeking to bolster the ADA, especially as it relates to undermining economic inequality: the Disability Employment Incentive Act and the Office of Disability Policy Act.

This cyclical nature in US policy making reveals that American political institutions can produce remarkable periods of innovation, but they just as easily allow for devolution, then renewed attempts at restoration, and so on. My book makes a compelling (and troubling) point that something so fundamental as civil rights can remain unsettled despite more than a half century of policy making around the issue.

But much in the way threats of retrenchment during the Reagan years mobilized the disability community, current threats are doing the same. As a 2018 *Time* article so appropriately put it, "Donald Trump inadvertently sparked a new disability rights movement."[1] Longtime activists and long-established disability advocacy groups like ADAPT (Americans Disabled for Attendant Programs Today, formerly Americans Disabled for Accessible Public Transit) have been joined by a new generation of politically savvy disability activists, which may very well constitute a "third wave" of activism protecting and potentially strengthening civil rights for Americans with disabilities.

One cannot fully appreciate where we are today on disability rights without considering the century-old disability policy legacy of incremental shifts within the disability policy domain, punctuated by bursts of creativity within government, the advocacy explosion in the disability voluntary sector, and the rise of disruptive collective action that continues to challenge the state to do what disability rights entrepreneurs intended it to do fifty years ago: to treat citizens with disabilities like any other minority or disadvantaged group entitled to their civil rights.

One of my key objectives in writing the book is to show, within this political context, when, where, and how social movement mobilization and citizen participation matter in promoting and protecting policies meant to improve citizens' lives by guaranteeing basic rights and eliminating inequalities. Activists and organizational leaders are part of a broader social-change field that also includes political elites, institutional activists, and political entrepreneurs working to shape the policy agenda. This is important because policies change how constituencies interact with the state.

The coevolution of institutional contexts and social movements reveals a great deal about how activists and groups recognize and respond to political opportunities to effect change. Organizational advocacy and disruptive action at times supplemented efforts by elite political entrepreneurs and, at other times, supplanted them altogether in an ongoing struggle to firmly incorporate disability rights into American institutions, organizations, and culture.

Acknowledgments

THERE ARE A LOT OF PEOPLE—involved directly and indirectly with this project over the course of many years—whom I want to thank. This project began as an exploration into the political mobilization of a community of individuals often treated as clients of social services. I am forever grateful to two wonderful mentors, Suzanne Staggenborg and Debra Minkoff, who pushed me to systematically think about ways to link rights-based mobilization to the extant service paradigm that dominated disability policy making. I examined the organizational field and the kinds of changes that created a demand for advocacy. It involved a painstakingly lengthy and intense content analysis of all disability voluntary groups over many years, supported in part by a National Science Foundation grant and a grant from the University of Washington's Evans School of Public Policy and Governance.

In developing this line of inquiry through a social movements lens, especially the relationship between policy making, organizations, and protest tactics, I had the pleasure of consulting with David Meyer, John McCarthy, Sarah Soule, Mayer Zald, and so many other scholars, including those I met at the 2011 Young Scholars in Social Movements conference. I am truly grateful for their advice.

I am thankful to have had the support of Robert Crutchfield, Steve Pfaff, and Edgar Kiser in developing the project. They encouraged me to think about the bigger picture and where to place social movements within my explanation of policy reform and social change. I also thank Sharan Brown, who taught me everything I know about disability rights law and the American judicial system. And thanks go to Michael Hechter, who persistently asked me the "so what question" to embrace the book's inherently interdisciplinary contributions to political and social science research.

I also thank Kate Stovel, Karl Dieter Opp, Paul Burstein, Sarah Valdez, and Mo Eger, whom I showed numerous iterations of the project. Their feedback helped generate a richer, more nuanced argument. I thank Becky Pettit, Ross Matsueda, Michelle Maroto, Katie Corcoran, Blaine Robbins, and Jacob Young, who (likely unknowingly) provided insight into how to empirically frame the book. And I am thankful for the opportunity the University of Oxford and Nuffield College provided in allowing me to develop the project into a book proposal and grateful to all my Oxford friends and colleagues who shared their advice on the project, especially Francesco Billari, Michael Biggs, and Olha Onuch.

I very much appreciate the feedback I received from members of the American Sociological Association's Disability and Society Section on different parts of this project as well as informal conversations and e-mail exchanges about the book, especially with Sharon Barnartt and Richard Scotch.

I thank my friends and colleagues in the Sociology Department at the University of Toronto, who provided substantive and practical advice about book writing, as well as moral support, and whose recent books also served as models: Neda Maghbouleh, Clayton Childress, Jenny Carlson, Vanina Leschzinger, and Erik Schneiderhan. In addition, I am grateful to Gregory Lograno, Jordan Foster, and Letta Page for the numerous ways they supported me throughout the process. And, finally, I thank the reviewers and the incredibly helpful and patient people at Stanford University Press, including Frances Malcolm and Jenny Gavacs and especially Kate Wahl and Marcela Cristina Maxfield, who helped see the book to completion.

Politics of Empowerment

1 The Political Evolution of Disability

Government is inescapably responsible to provide leadership which results in citizen solutions.

—Justin Dart, testimony before hearings of the House Subcommittees on Select Education and Employment Opportunities, July 1989

DISABILITY HAS ALWAYS had a place on the American policy agenda. The development of disability policy is so intimately linked to the development of the American welfare state that it is difficult to disentangle the two. While the United States is often considered a welfare laggard,[1] the nature of its political institutions, political process, and legislators' entrepreneurial spirit is reflected in the trajectory of disability rights through piecemeal struggles and setbacks, innovations, and reforms.

In the 1920s, a fairly cozy group comprising members of Congress, the Executive Branch, professional associations, and disability nonprofit and interest groups became the "experts" or, to borrow from Barbara Altman and Sharon Barnartt, "the wise," monopolizing the disability policy agenda.[2] This policy network crystallized in response to a federal mandate to extend rehabilitation services and programs to nonveterans with disabilities.[3]

Driven by the belief that the federal government must do something to "help the disabled help themselves,"[4] policy makers generated an alternative policy pathway to strict medical models of disability that focused squarely on cure.[5] They revised this paradigm by turning patients into social-service clients. Importantly, they were especially critical of the practice of warehousing people with disabilities in asylums and other residential institutions that kept them out of sight and out of mind. These "rehabilitationists," as Edward Berkowitz called them,[6] believed disability could be overcome and that people with disabilities could and should be integrated into the mainstream social and economic life of the nation.

The success of the rehabilitation policy paradigm traces to skilled lawmakers motivated, to varying degrees, by rehabilitation science, the American social

1

welfare mantra of provision for the "deserving poor,"[7] a sense of moral duty toward the least fortunate, and increasing national economic productivity. Political elites—policy makers, organizational leaders, and professionals—defined America's social programs targeting people with disabilities for most of the twentieth century and measured their success in terms of reaching as many new clients as possible. That is, successful disability policy was defined as bringing more Americans into contact with federal programs and creating a lasting interaction between the disabled as clients and the government and nonprofit groups as service providers.

Disability policy was a success story, so members of Congress and established disability nonprofits had little incentive to consider and adopt different approaches. They became invested in the status quo. Yet significant change did occur. Ultimately, the late 1960s and early 1970s emerged as a period of creative ferment in US disability politics. Numerous policy innovations, such as the Architectural Barriers Act, the 1970 Urban Mass Transportation Assistance Act, and Section 504 of the Rehabilitation Act, led institutional, ideological, and cultural transformations in the American civil rights struggle. These policies were largely the work of political entrepreneurs—institutional activists who took advantage of political openings to change the course of disability politics,[8] creatively carving out niches in which a rights agenda might flourish.[9] They continued to push legislation that empowered people with disabilities rather than treated them as dependents of the American welfare state.

The political evolution of disability is inherently about social and political change set against a backdrop of deeply entrenched client-service models. Even in the 1960s, with the black civil rights struggle permeating social policy domains from housing to employment and education, no one urged the government to pursue civil rights for the disabled—not policy makers who worked simultaneously in disability and in civil rights or established disability groups working in the extant disability policy network.

What changed? And who changed it? The answers require knowing not only about the political and organizational history of disability policy making but also about the interplay between shifting institutional settings and the proliferation of political elites who saw Americans with disabilities as more than just clients of federal social programs.

Their efforts, and the policies they pursued, took on new meaning as they sought to break through cognitive and structural barriers informing the government's role in how it should "deal" with disability. Consider, for example,

the pivotal 1973 Rehabilitation Act. Often credited as setting off a rights paradigm for the disabled, the "act to replace the vocational rehabilitation act . . .
with special emphasis on services to those with the most severe handicaps"
was never meant to lay a foundation for disability rights.[10] With the exception
of architectural barriers, nowhere in the act's eleven declarations of purpose
is discrimination or rights mentioned. Yet this hybrid service-provision–civil
rights legislation,[11] precursor to the landmark 1990 Americans with Disabilities
Act (ADA), came to be referred to by rights entrepreneurs like Sen. Bob Dole
(R-KS) as the Handicapped Bill of Rights.[12]

The Rehabilitation Act was reconceived and redesigned by members of
Congress working in the disability policy network. More than just an extension of a half-century-old vocational rehabilitation program, it would forever
change the political landscape. Disability rights entrepreneurs viewed their efforts not only as providing a moral and economic good to their citizens but also
as changing public attitudes about disability. "Emotion and sympathy do not
provide much assistance to the person in a wheelchair seeking access to his post
office, or trying to visit a pigeon-holed local social security office," proclaimed
Rep. Jim Wright (D-TX) at a 1975 architectural barriers oversight hearing. "His
plight can be aided, however, by sensible action programs of government . . .
by sustained commitment, involving both the application of public and private
resources and the reshaping of public attitudes."[13] Wright's point of view was
shared by many: Congress had a role—a *responsibility*, as Justin Dart, cochair of
the Congressional Task Force on the Rights and Empowerment of Americans
with Disabilities claimed—in improving the lives of people with disabilities,
and it went far past vocational rehabilitation.

Former presidential nominee Hubert Humphrey (D-MN) said that the
government brought disabled people out of the "shadows of life" through the
regular policy-making process.[14] Disability rights gained momentum in Congress throughout the 1960s, and in the 1970s increasing attention to the plights
of diverse, historically marginalized groups helped bring disability rights into
the social consciousness as part of "America's rights revolution."[15] Lawmakers
who had experience working on civil rights legislation saw clear parallels, acting to make disability rights enforcement as vigorous as the enforcement of
civil rights for other groups.

Disability rights began as an elite-driven movement. Disability rights entrepreneurs were not challenged by pressure groups or their constituents to
pursue a particular policy trajectory. Instead, their activist spirit was shaped

by their personal and professional biographies, filtered through the institutional and organizational context within which they worked.[16] They were motivated to act by self-interest (e.g., professional and political ambitions), as well as values underpinning their other-regarding interests to do the morally right thing.[17]

Among those with a personal connection to disability, men like Humphrey, Sen. Orrin Hatch (R-UT), and President George H. W. Bush had friends and family members who experienced injustices. Dole, Sen. John McCain (R-AZ), and Rep. Tony Coelho (D-CA) had disabilities and directly confronted social, cultural, and structural barriers in their daily lives. Their experiences influenced their outlook on social policy and the role of government in improving the lives of disabled Americans.

Institutional activism was also motivated by policy makers' belief that the federal government should be a leader in the disability rights struggle, moving beyond compassionate statements to actually improving people's lives. One thing Congress could agree on—at least for a while—was equal rights for the disabled. Working to provide economic opportunities and rights to people with disabilities meant *doing the morally right thing*. Policy elites thus tapped into values at the heart of American society: self-reliance, independence, and citizenship. They made disability rights politically uncontroversial—as "American as apple pie"[18]—creating an attractive, nonpartisan issue readily taken up by freshman members of Congress and ambitious administration officials hoping to develop their policy portfolios and expand policy jurisdictions.

Political elites translated their beliefs about government empowering people with disabilities into action and their professional policy-making experiences into the evolution of disability as a policy issue. Analogizing the plight of the disabled to that of other minority groups and emphasizing their investment in social policy and the Great Society, these actors laid the groundwork for disability rights to expand under new political opportunities.

Institutional changes in the 1970s included the creation of new venues— such as the Senate Subcommittee on the Handicapped—that allowed disability-related issues to expand beyond the rehabilitation-focused policy network. These spaces allowed disability rights entrepreneurs to *proactively* change established ways of interacting with people with disabilities as patients and clients to interaction with them as citizens entitled to their civil rights. Thus, we see the emergence of rights policies such as the 1975 Education for All Handicapped Children Act (later renamed the Individuals with Disabilities Education Act

[IDEA]), among others, which sought to desegregate the educational system by requiring districts to include disabled students in mainstream classrooms.

Outside a bounded political network, however, few people in the government or the public paid much notice to these political entrepreneurs' efforts. President Richard Nixon vetoed the Rehabilitation Act twice, but on the basis of cost (associated with titles involving the expansion of vocational rehabilitation) rather than Section 504, the antidiscrimination and rights provision. Even after the civil rights rollback of the 1980s, when ADA opposition had coalesced around the idea that the legislation "reregulated" the labor market and hurt small business, disability rights were still touted as something that "strikes a chord in all Americans, whatever their political beliefs or geographical backgrounds."[19] Bipartisanship and political compromise continued to mark the framing of disability rights as a righteous cause—perennially noted at anniversary celebrations of the ADA.

Understanding the evolution of disability rights requires linking processes endogenous to the community of actors working in disability policy to broader exogenous forces reshaping American politics. Disability policy evolved incrementally under the stewardship of a disability policy network whose actors meant to extend, not attack, an existing policy area. To them, service provision was not outdated or ineffective; it was just incomplete. They saw accessibility, antidiscrimination, and civil rights efforts as the logical next steps in mainstreaming people with disabilities into social, political, and economic life. After all, what good is vocational rehabilitation if Americans with disabilities are denied employment because of discriminatory attitudes and practices? These efforts ultimately generated, rather than sprang from, a more multifaceted political understanding of disability and had important consequences for the development of the disability rights movement.

Empowering a Constituency

Rights-oriented policies renegotiated the relationship between the state and an already well-established disability nonprofit sector, which had developed in tandem with the welfare state. Institutional activists recast the interaction between the government and its disabled constituents such that the state empowered its citizens to mobilize their civil rights. These institutional transformations were clearly reflected in shifts within the disability nonprofit sector.

The expanding policy focus blending service provision with civil rights generated a demand for political advocacy on both rights and social services. These shifting processes transformed the disability community primarily through the proliferation of advocacy groups in the disability nonprofit sector. Groups like Disabled in Action (DIA) were founded entirely around political and legal advocacy, while established service-provision organizations like the American Association on Intellectual and Developmental Disabilities, Autism Society of America,[20] and United Cerebral Palsy (UCP) adopted political advocacy as part of their core strategy and focused on monitoring, implementing, and expanding newly enshrined civil rights. Advocacy groups gained recognition as actors within the evolving field of disability politics.[21] Advocacy increasingly displaced, but did not supplant, service provision as the legitimate raison d'être for voluntary groups; many organizations adopted rights-based advocacy while simultaneously championing the importance of social services. This reflected the way rights entered into an existing, service-oriented policy area and now provides an example of the endurance of institutional legacies in the face of sociopolitical change.

Institutional transformations led changes in organizational leadership, increasingly reflecting the constituency these groups served and advocated for in the broader social movement sector.[22] Thus, the disability activist network increasingly overlapped with other wide-ranging social movements; from the women's movement to AIDS activism to the pro-life movement, advocacy organizations and activists legitimized disruptive protests. For the disability community, once thought incapable of mobilizing in its own political interests, this was a major cultural transformation.

While the genesis of disability rights policy is not rooted in the demands of a grassroots political movement, organizations served as important mobilizing structures that sustained collective action, particularly as these groups more readily turned to direct action as part of their tactical repertoires. The political evolution of disability rights therefore provides an opportunity for contextualizing—in terms of time and space—the relationship between social movements, political entrepreneurship, policy shifts, and organizational transformations in the broader struggle for civil rights. This is particularly relevant in explaining the back and forth between policy and mobilization, especially how threats of retrenchment generate contention between citizens and the state.[23]

The nascent disability rights movement gained centrality in policy making and implementation as institutional activism encountered ideological and practical hurdles. Neoliberal attitudes about social and economic policy opened a viable path to opposition as well; though disability rights were seen as a peerless political success story of bipartisanship and humanity, policy enforcement was curbed by arguments over the *costs* of reasonable accommodations and equal access. And the courts signaled their conservative position on disability rights, beginning with *Southeastern Community College v. Davis* (1979),[24] in which the Supreme Court ruled in favor of the college that denied a person with a severe hearing disability admission to its nursing program. The decision set a negative precedent regarding how "reasonable accommodations"—the chief mechanism for rectifying inequalities under disability rights law —would be interpreted and implemented.

In the 1980s, President Ronald Reagan's administration halted legislative momentum around accessibility requirements in the public sector, including public transit. This period of retrenchment reveals a shift away from empowerment in which politics allowed the undermining of a community's social, political, and economic well-being. Ironically, bipartisan compromises once heralded as a virtue of disability rights legislation squeezed out progress by generating partial solutions, jeopardizing intended outcomes, and encouraging back-stepping even on something as fundamental as civil rights.

Policies empower activists who in turn empower policy makers to move ahead with legislative projects in the face of political threats. Everyday citizens play a critical role in shaping policy trajectories—especially when detractors threaten to turn *evolution into devolution*. Political opposition as a catalyst in mobilizing everyday Americans into a political movement should not be discounted. To that end, the disability rights movement is best understood within what Andrea Campbell called a "participation-policy cycle" in American politics: the reciprocating relationship between policy innovations, political threats, citizen and elite mobilization, and policy restoration.[25]

Given that civil rights for people with disabilities were achieved through routine politics and policy making, the subsequent rise of a robust grassroots movement—a demand for action *following* legislative victories—points to both the limits of institutional activism and the dynamic relationship between policy and movement mobilization. Reconciling that political institutions can make the United States both a policy innovator and an eventual laggard has generated considerable scholarly work on social movements and the political struggle over civil rights. The evolution of disability policy helps—to use Doug McAdam and Hilary Boudet's phrasing—"put social movements in their place."[26] Throughout this book, we see how activism outside the government can become more central in promoting rights policy agendas as institutional activism is constrained by political exigencies.

A Cycle of Innovation, Retrenchment, and Mobilization

Institutional activism produced policy innovations that made the United States a disability rights policy leader. And the evolution of the disability policy agenda was revolutionary in that it created a newly politicized constituency.

The success of largely service-oriented disability policy making throughout much of the twentieth century rested on self-reinforcing mechanisms via activist policy makers and government bureaucrats as well as incumbent disability service groups working to protect and aggrandize their policy arena. Disability rights entrepreneurs were both constrained and empowered by policy entrenchment. Their incremental institutional work was critical because political opportunities after World War II for social policy or civil rights innovation, including the period following black civil rights activism, remained largely unavailable to people with disabilities. Their approach granted a certain legitimacy to rights and antidiscrimination, which were embedded within an accepted client-service paradigm.

But if political entrepreneurs were counting on the same long-lasting, self-reinforcing mechanisms that made rehabilitation so successful, they would soon have to reckon with the limits of this approach. The persistent struggle to entrench disability rights in part has to do precisely with how disability rights entered into the policy agenda. Although the insertion of rights into the Rehabilitation Act was a political innovation, it meant that disability rights were still excluded from the system that governed rights for other disadvantaged and minority groups.

When the proposed 1971 amendment to include disability in the 1964 Civil Rights Act failed, lawmakers used the Vocational Rehabilitation Act Amendments of 1972 to include Section 504—the civil rights provision. It was entirely the result of behind-the-scenes political entrepreneurship and neatly anticipated problems entrenching disability rights. Political elites sensed a lack of political will—determining that expending political capital on reopening the Civil Rights Act was a fool's errand—and, in their entrepreneurial way, found ways around that.

These early developments saw political entrepreneurs skillfully utilizing their access to power and resources to pursue a policy agenda through a creative combination of new and existing policy tools and ideas. That is, they put disability rights on the policy agenda. Yet this next-best rights trajectory came with unwanted institutional and ideological consequences. Its blend of social welfare and civil rights made disability rights especially vulnerable to social welfare spending cuts, regardless of whether *rights* were directly targeted, just as neoliberal views swept national-level politics. This facilitated opposition and retrenchment under the guise of cost cutting and government efficiency, without the shield (constitutional or otherwise) that might have been provided by the inclusion of disability in the Civil Rights Act.

This period of rapidly collapsing opportunity regarding a disability–civil rights agenda was followed by direct attacks in the 1980s. Rather than "showing leadership" on minority rights, the Reagan administration, according to Rep. George Miller (D-CA), was "hardly a role model."[27] Disability rights entrepreneurs—Republican and Democratic legislators alike—were surrounded by serious obstacles to institutional activism. Among everyday citizens with disabilities, the federal government was seen as having broken its promise and abandoned disability rights as a legitimate principle within the American political and social landscape. Enter the disability rights movement.

With new politics came new political opportunities. In 1973, DIA joined UCP for a Lincoln Memorial vigil, protesting the inability of disabled people to access the site. Policy makers on both sides of the aisle working to secure the civil rights of people with disabilities lauded their demonstration. The following year, DIA sued the city of Baltimore for using federal monies to purchase buses that could not be accessed by people with disabilities. Praising their legal mobilization, Rep. Mario Biaggi (D-NY) called transit companies' practices outright discriminatory.[28] Disability organizations demonstrated an adaptive ability to work with political elites while challenging the state through the use of disruptive protests. The disability rights movement also helped foster a collective identity celebrating disability rather than treating or hiding it—changing social norms rather than asking disabled people to "become normal." The movement became an important vehicle for linking institutional change to cultural change; it made both the notion of minority rights and the policies governing them meaningful for everyday people.

It was soon apparent that rather than political victory, Section 504 was going to be a site of contention over implementation and enforcement. Policy entrepreneurs accused President Jimmy Carter's administration of ignoring its legislative intentions in regard to disability rights, while the administration accused legislators of ignoring so-called practical realities involved in enforcing the law. As President Carter's Health, Education, and Welfare (HEW) secretary Joseph Califano claimed, "It was more fun to be Moses and deliver commandments than to be the rabbis and priests who had to make them work."[29]

Disability movement organizations pushed back and called on legislators seen as champions of rights to do something about the administration's failures. As Sieglinde A. Shapiro of DIA testified, this would be a protracted, uphill battle:

> Five times since 1970, the Congress has enacted legislation to guarantee disabled and elderly people equal access to public transportation. . . . In Section 504 of the Rehabilitation Act of 1973, adopting verbatim the provisions of Title VI of the Civil Rights Act of 1964 . . . the Congress again affirmed its accessibility mandate. . . . The need is not for additional legislation. The Congress' mandate is now and for six years has been, perfectly, patently, crystal clear. You have, if we may presume to say so, done your work well. . . . We ask your continued, renewed and faithful assistance, as individual Senators, as a Committee, and the Congress itself in guiding the new Secretary's decision to the conclusion you have five times mandated. Thank you.[30]

Debbie Kaplan, head of the Disability Rights Center, made a similar argument that same year when she testified before the House Subcommittee on Select Education:

> Recognizing that the HEW regulations for the implementation of Section 504 represent a series of compromises, we are in support of the regulations as they stand and believe that they represent the minimum effort that is required to bring about non-discrimination in the provision of services, benefits, or employment to the disabled. In any discussion of Section 504, I believe it is helpful to bear in mind that we are talking about civil rights, not charity, and that we are talking about ending discrimination, not merely doling out hand outs.[31]

In addition to lobbying Congress, disability activists held sit-ins for nearly two weeks at numerous local HEW offices. They were even encouraged by rights entrepreneurs in the Office of Civil Rights (OCR) who hoped that the protests would help overcome the hurdle in publishing Section 504 regulations—something sympathetic actors in the administration seemed unable to do. Califano eventually signed Section 504's regulations almost five years after the passage of the Rehabilitation Act, revealing the Carter administration as but a false dawn for the disability rights struggle.

Dismayed, Sen. Jennings Randolph (D-WV), chair of the Senate Subcommittee on the Handicapped, held 1979 hearings criticizing the administration's delay in writing regulations. Judy Heumann, founder of DIA and a former intern in Sen. Harrison Williams's (D-NJ) office, spoke for many disability organizations, including the Center for Independent Living and American Coalition of Citizens with Disabilities (ACCD), as she questioned Congress "regarding the manner in which the law is being implemented."[32]

The cautious back-stepping of President Gerald Ford's administration and the Carter administration gave way to the full-on rights rollback of the 1980s. Many policy makers came to see the Rehabilitation Act as an impossible law. The Reagan administration sided with the American Public Transit Association (APTA), which fought against public-transit accessibility regulations, and made access to transportation a continued target of mobilization by nascent disability protest groups throughout the 1980s and 1990s.

The political mobilization of citizens with disabilities arose as an especially important force in protecting new rights from retrenchment, helping generate and sustain momentum around rights and bolstering the work of political entrepreneurs pursuing legislation like the ADA. Movement activists worked with lawmakers to challenge the Reagan administration and the courts. In the years leading up to the ADA, political elites counted on such political advocacy groups for guidance in translating legislative promises into concrete action against persistent inequality and discriminatory attitudes and practices.

The disability rights movement thus relied on the overlapping efforts of political entrepreneurs and social movement activists, on the use of "regular politics" as well as disruptive collective action. By the end of the 1980s, a coalition of new and established disability groups, many having coordinated and participated in protest events throughout the decade, worked closely with policy makers to mobilize disability rights law. With these powerful allies, disability rights entrepreneurs were successful in creating a brief disability rights policy renaissance.[33]

The disability rights struggle seemed to emerge from a destructive period of retrenchment. It was in this context that Justin Dart, Reagan's appointee to the National Council on the Handicapped, so eloquently described government leadership in expanding opportunities for disabled citizens to mobilize rights. Dart worked to convince many in his own Republican Party that a civil rights approach to disability was necessary and that disability rights had to be restored. He and Robert Burgdorf, a law professor and lawyer for the National

Council on the Handicapped, drafted the original ADA, and its primary spon-
sors—Sen. Tom Harkin (D-IA), Sen. John McCain, and Sen. Lowell Weicker
(R-CT)—along with Rep. Silvio Conte (R-MA) and Sen. Tony Coelho, introduced it in Congress in 1988.[34] Addressing members of the House of Representatives that same year, Rep. Robert Odell Owens (D-NY), an ADA cosponsor,
urged Jim Wright, now the Speaker of the House, to focus congressional efforts
on its passage:

> Mr. Speaker, I am here to talk about moving the agenda. Let us not let it get lost.
> . . . This act is on everybody's agenda. Everybody approves, so we would like for
> it not to get lost.
>
> Mr. Speaker, this act represents the next giant step in the American civil
> rights movement.[35] This legislation grants full rights to Americans with dis-
> abilities. This legislation moves our great Nation from a respectable position
> of official compassion for those with disabilities to a more laudable position of
> empowerment for Americans with disabilities.
>
> Beyond basic concern for persons with disabilities, this bill places the moral
> indignation of our just society and the authority of our Government squarely
> behind persons with disabilities who are seeking their full rights. While we take
> great pride in existing Federal legislation which does provide assistance to per-
> sons with disabilities, we are nevertheless anxiously awaiting this great leap for-
> ward into full empowerment.[36]

The ADA directly addressed what activists saw as threats by the administration and the judiciary to rights established by Congress decades earlier. Patricia
Wright of the Disability Rights and Education Defense Fund (DREDF) and
others believed that the Reagan administration's sweeping attack on disability
rights had paradoxically mobilized disability activists, interest groups, and legal
experts and created new political opportunities for the ADA.[37]

For Dart and Owens, the ADA symbolized a government empowering its
people by restoring civil rights and settling the decades-long debate about what
Congress really meant when it added rights provisions to the Rehabilitation Act.
For Republicans and Democrats, activists, and the public, the ADA was a true
policy innovation. Coelho testified that "America and Congress, when it passed
the ADA, proposed a true model to the rest of the world."[38] The issue of disability rights was seemingly a "done deal" at the federal level, so disability rights activists ramped up their protests against the courts, local and state governments,

the transit and nursing home industries, and pity-driven telethons and engaged with complex issues around choice, assisted suicide, and HIV/AIDS.

Meanwhile, disability rights entrepreneurs in the federal government turned their attention to exporting the principles of the ADA, explicitly using the act's rights language as a model for a global human rights initiative: "a chance to use our rich national experience in disability rights to extend the principles embodied in the ADA to the hundreds of millions of people with disabilities worldwide."[39]

A decade later, the House International Relations Committee held hearings regarding the UN Convention on Disability Rights. Rep. Tom Lantos (D-CA) expressed a commonly held view of America's role in disability policy that it is "incomprehensible that the United States would not seize the opportunity in this non-controversial area of common interest, an area in which we are acknowledged world leader, to ensure the best possible Convention that reflects our principles and values we cherish."[40] In a letter to President George W. Bush, Alan A. Reich, president of the National Organization on Disability,[41] requested that the president "continue our nation's world leadership in the area of disability by instructing the U.S. Departments of State and Justice to advance aggressively the work in which our nation and many others are engaged presently at the United Nations to develop a U.N. Convention on Disability Rights." Reich also pointed to the House International Relations Committee's unanimous support of a House concurrent resolution reaffirming the UN Convention.[42] Former George H. W. Bush attorney general Richard (Dick) Thornburgh, whose son has physical and intellectual disabilities, considered disability rights one of America's best exports.[43]

It seemed that people with disabilities would soon enjoy the fruits of a twenty-year period of reform, yet this was not the case. Detractors refocused their efforts on undermining enforcement of disability rights laws. The administrations of Presidents Bill Clinton, George H. W. Bush, and Barack Obama, while not necessarily antagonistic to the cause, were by no means leaders in strengthening disability rights. And Congress—once a bastion of political entrepreneurship in disability rights—dragged its feet. It was stuck in deadlock. Whether discussion was about addressing lax enforcement of antidiscrimination provisions, mainstreaming education, or providing resources for in-home care that allowed disabled people to live in their communities rather than isolating institutions, government stalled on rights.

Not long after the ADA took effect in 1992, rights entrepreneurs in the government, as well as activists, social scientists, and legal scholars, began pointing to the so-called failures of the ADA. It failed, they charged, in its central objectives of improving labor-market conditions, increasing earnings, and undermining economic inequality among people with disabilities.[44] Employment rates among disabled Americans declined in the post-ADA years, and earnings stagnated. By the mid-2000s, advocates were embroiled in a battle to save disability rights law from powerful—mostly judicial—efforts to narrow its scope and enforcement. While they critiqued the law's failures, they also brought attention to the ways its already limited power was being whittled away.

In 2012, the Senate failed to ratify the UN Convention on the Rights of Persons with Disabilities. It was a slap in the face to both Republicans and Democrats who worked on disability-related policy. Sen. Harry Reid (D-NV) proclaimed, with understandable anger, "It is a sad day when we cannot pass a treaty that simply brings the world up to the *American standard* for protecting people with disabilities because the Republican Party is in thrall to extremists and ideologues."[45] McCain said simply that it "was not the Senate's finest hour."[46] Policy makers and activists saw the failure to ratify as just another example of the kinds of partisan conflict and congressional gridlock that leads to an ineffective, unproductive, and, in the words of Bill Moyers and Michael Winship, "do-nothing" Congress.[47]

This was not the Congress Harkin, Weicker, Coelho, and Owens knew. Their "do-something Congress" was a place in which disability rights entrepreneurs aggressively worked to bulwark the disability policy community from threats. It helped lead the way in addressing the needs of specific "vulnerable" groups such as people with disabilities.[48] Lawmakers, along with a large disability organizational sector, helped establish a policy trajectory whereby its partial successes have generated, in a cyclical fashion, episodes of political backlash and mobilization. Today's political struggle over disability rights continues to revolve around the unfinished business of solidifying a nearly half-century-old mandate to safeguard and promote the rights of disabled Americans.

From Disability Rights Policy to Disability Rights Movement

Acts of creative ferment generating political innovations, followed by backstepping, are not aberrations but defining features of the American political system. Importantly, they provide a context for understanding the targets and strategies of social movement mobilization. The American political process facilitates entrepreneurship and, in turn, significant policy leaps, leading economist Tyler Cowen to call the United States a policy "hare" (as opposed to the proverbial tortoise, who makes slow and steady progress).[49] But even as the United States has been a leader in a range of areas from intellectual property rights, the handling of the financial crisis, national defense, environmental policy, and sexual harassment, it has been regarded as a laggard in these very same areas, each sustaining periods of institutional and extra-institutional mobilization.[50]

The longitudinal account of disability politics provided in this book suggests that as readily as political actors and institutions produce important policy innovations, they can just as easily create an environment of backlash and retrenchment. The political evolution of disability exemplifies Cowen's characterization of US policy making as "lunging and lurching forward with big changes, then enduring periods of backlash, consolidation and frustration, . . . often a better description of our political system than is 'gridlock,' which is too one-dimensional a concept to capture reality."[51]

The ADA, which was meant to restore the spirit of Section 504, is a case in point. The law was heralded as the most important civil rights policy since the Civil Rights Act. A product of political compromises, the act became the target of judicial undermining, saw lax enforcement, and struggled to improve the economic well-being of people with disabilities.[52] Amid all the applause, efforts were already under way to undermine the ADA's ability to promote equal rights. In the 1990s, activists inside and outside the government pointed to a series of conservative Supreme Court decisions that watered down Congress's intent in the ADA. As they targeted local and state organizations and institutions, disability rights groups also turned to court-based activism to mobilize the law, which they hoped would settle the issue of enforcement and bring about the structures and provisions needed to actually help people with disabilities by making it harder for detractors to dismantle the law.

In the meantime, members of Congress sought to address the act's failures with the ADA Restoration Act (ADARA) of 2008.[53] But disability activists inside and outside the government struggled to mobilize around a law more than fifteen years old. Recent attempts to undermine this landmark legislation include the Republicans' proposed 2017 ADA Education and Reform Act (H.R. 620) and the Republican replacement of the Affordable Care Act (a.k.a. Obamacare), threatening in-home attendant programs, which allow people with disabilities to live in their communities rather than in institutions. These latest policy developments have evidenced the ongoing attack against disability rights and increased advocacy, public awareness campaigns, and disruptive action by disability groups such as DREDF and ADAPT.[54] In this country, no policy—even one meant to enshrine values seen as fundamental to the spirit of the nation— is ever settled.

The political evolution of disability rights is as much about political institutions and political entrepreneurs as it is about organized citizen participation. A field of motivated political actors, in fact, helped transform members of the disability community into regular participants in the policy-making process. The field of political actors now transcends organizational and institutional boundaries, highlighting the interchangeability of actors' roles and the ease with which they move across the fluid boundary between state and nonstate.[55] For instance, some lawmakers were members of, or had leadership roles in, disability organizations. Disability advocates and activists such as Ed Roberts, the "father" of the independent living movement who would later serve as California's rehabilitation commissioner, went to work as policy makers. Others, such as movement leader Judy Heumann, transitioned from government experience to establishing protest and advocacy groups. In this context, so-called insiders and outsiders relied on each other's long-term efforts to promote the disability rights agenda.

This book discusses how political elites and everyday Americans promoted sociopolitical change and the proximate and broader institutional, organizational, and ideological contexts within which they did so. It is about the nature of change—how incremental efforts pave the way for more significant political transformations to take hold.

As Chapter 2 describes, until the 1960s, a disability policy monopoly promoted a policy image emphasizing ability over disability: rehabilitation was necessary to overcome disability and create "good citizens." This meant making people with disabilities taxpayers rather than tax burdens. Incremental policy changes ultimately fostered a new political and cultural environment that helped frame the plight of a heterogeneous group as a common struggle. It was a small first step in conceptualizing people with disabilities as agentic policy stakeholders and political constituents. Political entrepreneurs championed the removal of architectural barriers, promoting equal access by using existing rhetoric about economic self-sufficiency through rehabilitation and consequently laid the groundwork for rights to flourish.

The political efforts of an activist government, including congressional committees and executive agency jurisdictions, helped expand venues to facilitate a richer, more complex dialogue about disability. Chapter 3 outlines how disability rights entrepreneurs more explicitly carved out a path for civil rights, changing the flow of disability politics.

The book also points to the consequences of legislative change: the way actors went about promoting a new logic around "the problem" of disability shaped policy outcomes, backlash, and most certainly the tools and motivations available to a political constituency to mobilize its rights. And in mobilizing against political, economic, and social institutions, the disability rights movement necessarily challenged cultural understandings and meanings of disability. The political expertise that developed during this period would again be mobilized in fighting ongoing attempts at rolling back disability rights.

As Chapter 4 explains, disability organizations and policy coevolved.[56] Because organizations are shaped by the kinds of frameworks, tools, resources, and political opportunities policies provide, disability groups mobilized around rehabilitative and health services at a time when the interaction between government and voluntary associations revolved around service provision. In the 1970s, the disability organizational sector underwent an "advocacy explosion,"[57] as it adapted to a new rights-focused policy environment. Existing service-provision groups, alongside a proliferation of new advocacy organizations, adopted political advocacy.

Changes in the disability voluntary sector encouraged the expansion of new mobilizing structures that would bring activists together.[58] Chapter 5 looks at the rise of disability protest, particularly in the context of political threats to existing disability rights legislation. Some of the most intense protests took place at the end of the 1970s. In the 1980s and 1990s, demonstrations organized by new and existing disability advocacy groups extended beyond targeting the federal government to include corporate targets (such as public-transit organizations) and state and local governments. Activists demanded the kinds of equal access the federal government had championed more than a decade earlier. In turn, political elites relied on these organization's efforts—from political advocacy to disruptive action—to pressure the government that had jumpstarted a disability rights rebellion.[59] The movement around disability rights in government reflected critical structural and organizational transformations that politicized a constituency.[60] Political entrepreneurs supplied the policy instruments around which disability groups helped mobilize everyday citizens with disabilities to champion their rights.[61]

Chapter 6 returns to the reasons why the United States is both a policy hare and a policy tortoise. The disability rights struggle is, to this day, a story of unresolved policy entrenchment. The same institutional configurations that allowed for policy innovation and political entrepreneurship—the parochial nature of Congress, institutional layering in policy making, porous boundaries between political elites and interest groups, multiple policy veto points, and the compromising process—also led to conflict, obstruction, retrenchment, and undesirable policy consequences. In that vein, Chapter 6 illustrates the institutional and organizational context that generated contentious politics and movement mobilization around disability rights. Indeed, the case of disability rights reveals the ways in which the duality in America's political institutions creates both the resources and the motivations for citizen action.

2 It's Ability, Not Disability, That Counts

SENATOR AIKEN: What is your idea of rehabilitation, Mr. Secretary?

SECRETARY TOBIN: Well, my idea of rehabilitation is, to begin with, to do everything that is possible in a medical and surgical way to restore persons to good, sound health, and in the case of physical impairment, to restore them to a physical condition where they can perform some gainful employment, and then to give them a training in the field of employment for which their physical abilities best adapt them, plus the fact that they have employment opportunity, giving them an opportunity to make good use of their capacities.

SENATOR AIKEN: I think that is a correct definition. I simply thought we ought to get it into the record.

—Senator George Aiken (R-VT) and Secretary of Labor Maurice Tobin, *Vocational Rehabilitation of the Physically Handicapped* hearing, May 1950

FOR MUCH OF THE FIRST HALF of the twentieth century, lawmakers, bureaucrats, social welfare groups, and disability-related voluntary associations believed government's role should be to provide social and rehabilitative programs to better integrate people with disabilities into mainstream society. Their close-knit policy monopoly shaped the development of disability policy by defining the disabled as clients and government as a service provider, offering programs to help the disabled help themselves. After all, as Martin Mahler, president of the New York chapter of the American Federation of the Physically Handicapped reminded Aiken and other members of the Senate Vocational Rehabilitation Subcommittee, "it's ability not disability that counts."[1]

Outdated by today's standards, rehabilitation and the client-service model were at the time seen as modern steps toward a more scientific and practical system for dealing with disabled Americans. For example, this 1918 exchange occurred between Rep. John E. Raker (D-CA) and Rep. William Bankhead (D-AL) in a hearing before the House Committee on Education (chaired by William J. Sears [D-FL], author of the Smith-Sears Act) regarding a bill to create the

Department of the Deaf and Dumb (a response to the large number of soldiers returning from what was then the Great War, deaf from shell shock):

> MR. BANKHEAD: Now, there is a great class of people whom I regard, of course, as more unfortunate than the deaf and dumb, and that is the blind. Why are not they included within the purview of this investigation?
>
> MR. RAKER: The blind can not, I believe, be put on the same plane as the deaf and dumb. The deaf and dumb can do practically everything that you and I can do. The boys play baseball, the girls play basket ball, and the boys are as efficient on the ball field in playing baseball as the boys who can hear.[2]

In the representatives' exchange, we see the benchmark comparison between us and them—that *they* can or cannot do "practically everything that you and I can do," in spite of what Raker called "their defect." It also points to the widespread belief that each disability presented a unique set of considerations that precluded any common struggle or community-wide identity. Even here, the focus was on rendering disabled Americans "proficient" and "self-sufficient" and employment ready without "overeducate[ing] people who are so unfortunate as to be deaf and dumb."[3] Committee members were also aware of discrimination against deaf veterans who were denied factory work. In forming a rudimentary basis for a more systematic rehabilitation program, the client-service model these legislators developed conscientiously and at times unexpectedly shifted how the American public viewed disability.

More than a half century of federal service-provision-oriented policies stand as evidence of the efforts of a policy monopoly and illustrate the endurance of lawmakers' approach to defining and addressing the needs of Americans with disabilities as primarily a problem of adaptation and integration into the social and economic life of the nation rather than any effort to adapt social, political, and economic institutions to be more inclusive of its disabled citizens. To that end, rehabilitationists saw themselves working to facilitate citizens' achieving their full potential, usually in the form of gainful employment. The confluence of institutional, political, and ideological factors that helped support and legitimize this policy network would come to have important consequences for the political evolution of disability rights.

The 1920 Smith-Fess Act was a policy innovation that represented a turning point in the development of the American welfare state: it extended educational and vocational rehabilitation provisions beyond the exclusive purview of veterans.[4] Proponents like Rep. Stuart F. Reid (R-WV) saw this as "salvaging men," taking "helpless human beings from poorhouses and sanitariums and [making] them self-supporting instead of remaining during the rest of their lives a burden to themselves, to society, and to their relatives." That is, passing laws meant doing the *right, noble, and honorable* thing for the disabled.[5] Democrats criticized Republicans like Reid and the act's cosponsor Rep. Simeon Fess (R-OH) for proposing such an "extravagant measure."[6]

Having established vocational rehabilitation policy, the policy monopoly set itself on a course emphasizing the rehabilitation of the disabled. "The experience of persons who have been handicapped in the United States is the most fruitful field on which to construct a proper theory of rehabilitation," testified George B. McGovern, a special agent for the Federal Board of Vocational Rehabilitation, at a 1920 education hearing chaired by Fess.[7] By the 1950s, rehabilitation would grow from theory to industry, the result of concerted efforts undertaken by professionals inside and outside government.

The shift is an example of both successful policy and programmatic entrenchment. Lawmakers established self-reinforcing mechanisms to expand and maintain the goals and objectives of the policies in which they had become invested. In the 1940s, two related processes further cemented the client-service model of disability. The first was a renewed policy concern toward employing and educating disabled veterans after World War II.[8] The second process was more basic: the internal self-aggrandizement of those working in the rehabilitation sector. As an increasing number of health and welfare professionals, nonprofit groups, and policy makers jumped onto the rehabilitation bandwagon, they incrementally expanded services and extended their jurisdiction, with an ever-expanding number of constituents and beneficiaries demanding more funding to ensure programmatic success.

Rehabilitation reached its heyday in the 1950s, as people like Mary Switzer, director of the Rehabilitative Services Administration (RSA), championed bills and amendments to expand and fund programs that would further swell the ranks of "clients" served by government vocational programs:

When I think that this program was perhaps the first program of service that the Federal Government undertook back in 1920 as a part of its responsibility for underpinning of vocational education after World War I; when I think of the limited concept we had then of what we could do for our handicapped citizens, and contrast that with what has happened today, I think it gives us a lift to see what today's possibilities are.[9]

Incremental expansion in rehabilitation begot more jurisdictional expansion through successful institutional work by political elites critical to policy feedback processes. With vocational rehabilitation as their crown jewel, social policies generated new pathways for future expansions, especially by raising the stakes for both program providers and beneficiaries. Rehabilitation, in combining just the right amount of philosophy, core American values, expert science and medicine, and public welfare and service provision, was presented as the perfect solution to the national "problem" of disability. Social scientists like Theda Skocpol and Paul Pierson have noted that it is the ability to mobilize constituencies that helps ward off political efforts to undermine policies that affect them.[10]

Rehabilitation—turning the "hopeless" into clients—informed the interaction between people with disabilities and the state through federal policies, regulated by the Executive Branch through the Office of Vocational Rehabilitation (OVR) in the Federal Services Administration (FSA) and later HEW,[11] implemented by state and local authorities, and mediated by the growing disability service-provision, nonprofit, and interest-group sector. Policy makers and administrators fully realized that expanding the reach of policies—widening the net[12]—would secure a broad base of client-constituents demanding these policies' effectiveness and ensuring their endurance. Part of what Ann Orloff referred to as America's "belated welfare state," rehabilitation survived the Great Depression, war, and attempts by conservatives in both the Republican and Democratic Parties to curtail social spending.[13] Its sustainability can be attributed to the ability of political elites to embed their policies into the political landscape, expanding programs and defending them against potential cutbacks.

Business as Usual for Disability Policy

Beyond the skillful work of policy makers, the relative stability of rehabilitation and the client-service model it represented was a result of the institutional climate of the 1950s. The decade is often characterized as one of closed political opportunity for significant social change, of conformity and policy foot-dragging.[14] With few legislative innovations, the 1950s are largely remembered as what James MacGregor Burns calls a "deadlock of democracy."[15]

It was also a time, as political scientist Morris Fiorina commented,[16] when Republicans and Democrats politically agreed on many issues (like race) or did not think about them at all (like gay and lesbian rights or abortion). In the late 1930s, conservatives from both parties came together in a Conservative Coalition (CC) to fight against Roosevelt's Depression-era policies, which had expanded the size of the federal government. Throughout the 1940s, 1950s, and part of the 1960s, this voting block undermined party unity and proved successful in shaping the policy agenda, especially in regard to curtailing social policy.

Much of the conversation about the government's role related to disability was confined to the House Committee on Education and Labor (where a majority of all congressional hearings were held) and the Senate Committee on Labor and Public Welfare.[17] These committees were embedded in a broader political context that largely prohibited policies (or even discussion of proposed bills) seen as too liberal and, in the case of disability, deviating too far from the dominant client-service framework. This included anything from "reckless" spending bills to new health and educational services and labor laws. In this period, policies targeting people with disabilities would be limited to incremental adjustments and variations on established themes typically involving the expansion of rehabilitation programs and services.

Well into President John F. Kennedy's administration, the House would effectively block liberal presidents' legislative progress. Congress even blocked Republican president Dwight D. Eisenhower's proposals, deeming them too liberal: in 1957, Eisenhower's proposals to help the "mentally retarded" were featured prominently in his legislative requests to Congress, yet even his support could not secure passage by the House Committee on Education and Labor and the Senate.[18]

Partly as the result of political turnover, there were signs by the mid-1950s that both the House as a whole and the House Committee on Education and Labor were liberalizing. Younger, non-Southern Democrats, especially those from eastern and midwestern states, were elected to Congress, though their power was blunted by the seniority system that kept Southern Democrats in leadership positions. As conservative Southern Democrats and Republicans maintained legislative control, liberals in the Democratic Party faced steep opposition to social policy change.[19] Disability-focused policy makers could only stand vigil over the existing system, by then thirty years old.

Institutional Stasis and Incremental Change:
The House, Senate, and Presidency

The House Committee on Education and Labor hosted more than half of all congressional disability-related hearings between the late 1940s and early 1960s. As the committee became more liberal, the House itself shifted (Table 2.1 and Figure 2.1).[20] However, as it did for many committees of the day, it remained controlled by senior conservative Southern Democrats who, Nelson Polsby writes, "liked to dine on liberal legislation."[21] Across party lines, this era's committee members from Kearns to Holt, Landrum, Ayres, Lafore, and Heistand, voted between 80 and 100 percent of the time with the CC (these percentages are called "CC scores" in the *CQ Almanac*).[22] Even as more liberal Democrats were elected at the beginning of the 1950s, the committee remained largely stable and largely conservative; in 1960, 40 percent of the committee's members had served more than seven years. Dramatic turnover came only in 1961, when just about 14 percent of the committee was composed of continuing members (Figure 2.2).

Few actors had the ability to translate conflicting perspectives and dissenting opinions into meaningful discourse, let alone legislation. Members often engaged in partisan debates—their bailiwick included most "social policy" (labor relations, welfare bills, etc.) and all the philosophical questions about government intervention in the provision of public goods that it implies.[23] Nonetheless, with committee chairs like conservative Southern Democrat Graham Barden from North Carolina,[24] new, "liberal" policy ideas about disability

Table 2.1 Average ideological position of select House committees in the 1950s (from most to least liberal)

Committee	Average score
Education and Labor	−0.0632
Financial Services	−0.053
Foreign Affairs	−0.038
Veterans Affairs	−0.0056
Transportation and Infrastructure	0.0062
Ways and Means	0.0124
Energy and Commerce	0.0126
Judiciary	0.013
Appropriations	0.0498
Agriculture	0.0888

Data source: *Voteview* database, at https://voteview.com.

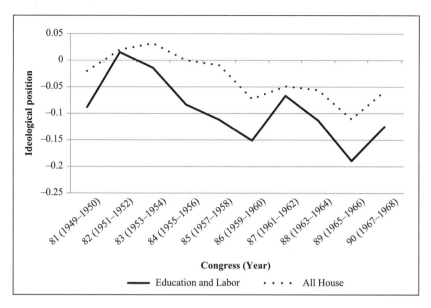

Figure 2.1 Ideological position of the House and House Committee on Education and Labor, 1949–1968. *Source:* Ideological position scores from *Voteview database,* at https://voteview.com. *Note:* Lower numbers indicate more liberal ideology.

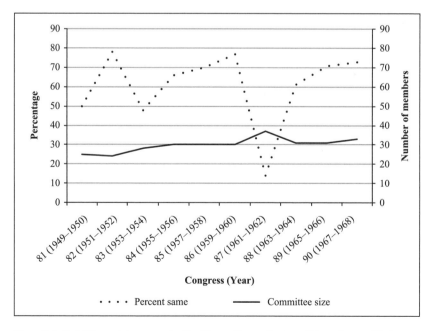

Figure 2.2 Stability and turnover in the House Committee on Education and Labor, 1949–1968. *Source:* Turnover and size data from "Conservative Coalition Tables."

were unlikely to flourish. Rep. Carl Elliot (D-KY), who chaired the Subcommittee on Special Education (1959–1960) and was considered a liberal,[25] claimed that Barden "could effectively choke any legislation that had a liberal smell. . . . If an aid-to-education bill seemed to be gathering some momentum, he would call in a dozen Chamber of Commerce witnesses to kill it with a filibuster."[26] Stewart Udall (D-AZ) (who later served as secretary of the interior under Presidents Kennedy and Lyndon Johnson) said that Barden believed a "good session of Congress" was one in which his committee literally did nothing.[27]

Throughout the period, the government's dealings with the disability community were "business as usual." The committee could boast few proposals that came to fruition. Among them, one law sponsored by Rep. John Phillips (R-CA) incorporated the Columbia Institution for the Instruction of the Deaf and Dumb and Blind into Gallaudet College,[28] and another, sponsored by Rep. Thurston Morton (R-KY) (who would go on to chair the Republican National Committee), amended the 1919 act providing additional aid to the American Printing House for the Blind.[29]

The most significant disability legislation enacted in the 1950s came out of another committee. The amendments to the Smith-Fess Act of 1920—the modern origins of comprehensive disability-service provision—known as the Vocational Rehabilitation Act Amendments,[30] were mostly debated in the Senate Committee on Labor and Public Welfare, particularly the Subcommittee on Health. This committee heard less than a third of the disability-related hearings heard by the House Committee on Education and Labor, but it was considerably more liberal (with an average ideological position score of –0.18 in the 1950s).[31] Rep. H. Alexander Smith, a moderate Republican from New Jersey, was chair when the Vocational Rehabilitation Act Amendments were passed, and his successor, Southern Democrat Lister Hill from Alabama, voted with the CC just 37 percent of the time (and against it 57 percent).[32]

Despite the Senate's more liberal leanings, no policies threatening the rehabilitation monopoly emerged. By the end of the 1950s, important compositional changes in the Senate Committee on Education and Public Welfare—the election of Harrison Williams (D-NJ, who would eventually become the committee chair) and the arrival of Democrat Jennings Randolph and liberal Republican Jacob Javits (NY)[33]—would set the stage for disability rights entrepreneurs in the late 1960s and early 1970s to reshape disability policy. But until then, even newly elected Democrats such as Paul Douglas (IL),[34] who chaired the Subcommittee on Vocational Rehabilitation of the Physically Handicapped, and Herbert Lehman (NY),[35] who served on it would be reluctant to advocate for any major departures from the established system.

With the House and Senate seemingly wedded to the status quo, what motivated the Vocational Rehabilitation Act of 1954? In short, President Eisenhower. In his address to Congress in January 1954, Eisenhower listed the population's growing health problems, highlighting the "two million of our fellow citizens now handicapped by physical disabilities [who] could be, but are not rehabilitated to lead full and productive lives."[36] Eisenhower stressed that the country now had the ability and know-how to increase access to rehabilitation programs, but Congress must mobilize those resources. Otherwise, as Eisenhower put it, in regard to rehabilitating the disabled, the country would continue to lose ground "at a distressing rate."[37]

The Senate took up the president's call, passing the Vocational Rehabilitation Act Amendments six months later in a roll-call vote, 82–0.[38] Two amendments that might have given it more teeth, one authored by Lehman to authorize five million dollars to train specialists in vocational rehabilitation and another by James E. Murray (D-MT), which suggested the establishment of a federal agency for the disabled, were defeated by voice vote. The House passed its version 347–0 but vacated the vote and passed the Senate's version with a few amendments.

For many conservatives, rehabilitation seemed to be the least costly and most palatable approach. The alternative, cash benefits,[39] had none of the strong supporting ideals (or backing from the rehabilitation-dominated policy monopoly) that vocational rehabilitation had in ensuring economic self-reliance among the disabled. Yet ranking Democratic leadership still pushed back on vocational rehabilitation. Barden was apparently "irked" that the committee had not given the measure more consideration and called the Vocational Rehabilitation Act "gobbledygook." He thought what the vocational rehabilitation program needed most was money.[40] Given the defeat of Murray's and Lehman's funding amendments, "more money" seemed unlikely.

Even adding the president's interest in expanding services for the disabled to the liberalization of the committees with jurisdiction over disability, policy makers were limited by the conservative venues in which they operated. Incremental policy changes preserved overall stability, while their proponents laid the groundwork for policy innovation in the coming decades.

The "Record of 84th Congress" best describes the 1950s, including disability policy making: "Professionals were solidly in control. They turned out large quantities of legislation with a minimum of noise and fuss. . . . The session [first session of 1955] was not notable for partisan clashes. . . . Few milestones were erected."[41]

Agenda Stability and the Client-Service Monopoly over Disability

With few outside threats or exogenous shocks, policy monopolies in the mid-twentieth century helped maintain equilibrium in the broader policy agenda.[42] Policy networks were generally confined to a few specific committees. In the case of disability, these included the House Committee on Education and Labor and the Senate Committee on Labor and Public Welfare, embedded in a social policy field encumbered by the weight of the CC. The inertia of conservative venues provides many clues about how political elites influenced the evolution of disability policy: amid stewardship of the status quo, innovative actors sought to move the agenda forward incrementally as they pushed back against political constraints.

First, because these two committees dealt with their fair share of ideological debates, Democratic leadership assigned their members to these committees on the basis of their ideological preferences on specific issues, which allowed junior members to prove party loyalty in these policy areas.[43] Given that labor relations were an especially salient issue, those representing blue-collar districts (mainly Democrats) in eastern and midwestern states saw their appointments as insurance toward reelection.[44] The ways these committees were stacked in this era would have important consequences for how policy makers came to understand the plight of the disabled.

Almost half of the thirty members of Congress working on disability from the late 1940s until the end of the 1950s were assigned to special subcommittees early in their congressional careers. As expected, most were newly elected Democrats from eastern and midwestern states, as were three of the five newly elected Republicans. Carl Perkins was an exception. A Southern Democrat, Perkins would go on to chair the Committee on Education and Labor from 1967 to 1984 and was a key player in Head Start and other Great Society programs of the 1960s. Today, a vocational training center in his home state of Kentucky is named for him; it provides services to individuals with disabilities so they may "achieve sustainable competitive integrated employment, maximize independence, and . . . gain self-respect."[45]

However, any claim that members working on disability-related issues were more liberal than other members should not be overstated. No doubt, more

Table 2.2 Average voting scores with and against the Conservative
Coalition, 1959

Committee	With	Against
House Committee on Education and Labor	29.3	64.3
Subcommittees/Special Committees on Disability	36.3	53.7

Source: CC scores from "Conservative Coalition Tables."

liberal-minded Democrats and Republicans such as Thurston Morton and Peter Frelinghuysen (R-NJ) helped establish bipartisan common ground in approaching rehabilitation program expansion.[46]

At the same time, the disability policy network also included conservative Republicans such as Thomas Werdel (CA, who would go on to run as vice presidential candidate for the States' Rights Party in 1956), Robert Taft (OH, nicknamed "Mr. Republican"), and Harold Velde (IL, who chaired the House Committee on Un-American Activities). The average CC score for those working in these subcommittees was just slightly higher (more conservative) than the House parent committee (Table 2.2). Coupled with the conflict between liberal junior Democrats and conservative leaders like Barden, this ideological environment curtailed the ability of divergent policy preferences (for instance, civil rights) to significantly shape disability agenda setting.

Second, disability (vocational rehabilitation) was a pet project for elites, but in no way did it define their policy agendas. Disability generated relatively little buzz on Capitol Hill,[47] and assignment to the committees in which it was regularly addressed were not as prestigious as Appropriations, Rules, Ways and Means, or Foreign Affairs. Some issues, such as labor, received a lot of attention, but the bulk of the other issues the committee dealt with went unnoticed. This was especially the case when issues, like disability, did not get onto the full committee's agenda. Disability issues were confined to temporary or special subcommittees with a narrow focus rather than the full committees' more central issues of labor and education.[48] As Figure 2.3 shows, the *Congressional Quarterly* (*CQ*) rarely reported on disability-related issues until the beginning of the 1960s. This is another reason that ideological conflict on disability-related issues, according to *CQ* and hearing testimony, was kept to a minimum: disability was seen as a settled nonissue.

Third, because these committees had a relatively large jurisdiction, dealing with a plethora of complex social policy issues—from disability to health, education, and labor—committee members could pick and choose issues to build a positive legislative record that suited their political needs. At the same

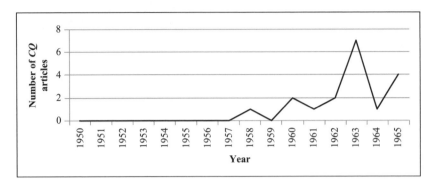

Figure 2.3 Disability issue salience in government, 1950–1965. *Source:* Policy Agendas Project, at https://www.comparativeagendas.net.

time, assignments to these committees (including special subcommittees dealing with disability) were not seen as particularly important or prestigious in Congress,[49] so junior members could work on their chosen issues without much outside pressure. This was especially the case in regard to disability, as they were seen as entering an existing policy monopoly with an established policy preference toward rehabilitation. Coupled with low issue salience and outsiders' deference to the committee's "experts" and jurisdiction, legislators had quite a bit of control over disability. This clear, solid policy area that generated little political vitriol proved enormously helpful to junior members aiming to build a policy record that could get them reelected.[50]

Disability-related issues were part of the legislative portfolios early in the political careers of Democrats like Perkins, Dominick Daniels (NY), Roy W. Wier (MN), Paul Douglas (IL), and Edith Green (OR). Perkins, Douglas, and Wier, in particular, were among nine members of Congress, mostly freshmen, to serve on multiple special subcommittees on disability (the others were Democrats Augustine B. Kelley from Pennsylvania [the only senior member, elected in 1941], Carl Elliot, and Herbert H. Lehman, and Republicans Samuel K. Mc-Connell [PA], Stuyvesant Wainwright [NY], and Wint Smith [KS] [see Table A.1 in the appendix]). Perkins and Wier served on four such special committees throughout the 1950s; Douglas chaired the Subcommittee on Vocational Rehabilitation of the Physically Handicapped in 1950, his first in Congress; and in 1956, Wier chaired the Subcommittee to Promote the Education of the Blind.

Nothing distinguished these nine lawmakers from their peers. Like most in Congress, a majority were lawyers and had served in local and state government and/or in the army or navy. Several of the subcommittee chairs had experience with health and education: McConnell had been on hospital boards, Wier and Kelley had served on boards of education, and Ernest Greenwood (D-NY) had served as director of the Federal Board of Vocational Education (1920–1922).[51] For the most part, however, no one had direct experience with disability programs or even disability itself. Instead, policy makers developed their interests and work on disability-related policy issues through broad, sometimes unrelated, issue experience. For many, disability would become a permanent part of their policy interests. Augustine B. Kelley, who had previously served on the Committee on Invalid Pensions, continued to work on disability issues; while others, like Carl Elliot, would later draw on their experience in other assignments, such as Veterans Affairs. Samuel McConnell would go on to chair the Committee on Education and Labor between 1953 and 1955,[52] and he became the executive director of UCP after resigning from Congress in 1957.

The Rehabilitationists: An "Iron Triangle" of Experts

The early work on disability issues in the 1950s was not undertaken in a framework of "rights." Several proponents would go on to champion civil rights and equal opportunities in the 1960s and 1970s (for instance, Edith Green would advocate for equal rights for women, and Carl Perkins would become one of the few Southern Democrats to vote in favor of the Civil Rights Act), but these legislators began their disability work steeped in the extant logic of rehabilitation.

They were experts in an "iron triangle,"[53] which successfully promoted a defined set of policy solutions meant to address the problem of social and economic exclusion of people with disabilities. Through the use of framing strategies and scientific evidence, disability policy makers encouraged deference to their judgment. The Executive Branch, too, acted as an important advocate for expanding social and rehabilitative services,[54] because administrators and agencies were invested in the solutions they promoted alongside legislators and nonprofit and professional groups; they had a distinct interest in ensuring that programs and policies succeeded. Increasing the number of patrons and clients as well as agencies' jurisdiction and relevance in policy implementation secured the Executive Branch's prominent role in this policy subsystem. The OVR was present in almost half of all disability-related hearings held between 1946 and 1960—perhaps not surprisingly, since its survival rested on these programs' continuation. From the end of the 1940s and into the 1950s, the OVR reified its jurisdictional claims over disability, prompted by the looming reorganization of the Executive Branch and the potential that it might destabilize the policy subsystem.[55]

Elected officials, government bureaucrats, and incumbent interest, disability, and professional groups formed a symbiotic relationship serving their political needs while also doing good. When a bill that, among other things, proposed consolidating services through the Federal Commission for Services for the Physically Handicapped and threatened to reconfigure the existing policy network, organizations and the Executive Branch worked together against the proposed legislation.[56] At a 1949 hearing, the National Rehabilitation Association (NRA) testified that rehabilitation needed more funds, not an administrative reorganization. Oscar R. Ewing of the FSA echoed the argument and emphasized its singular expertise in coordinating rehabilitation services:

> It is impossible to divorce the job of vocational rehabilitation from problems of health, for in 9 cases out of 10, you start with a health problem. . . . It is equally impossible to divorce it from problems of social security. . . . Neither can the function be divorced from problems of education. . . . That is why the Office of Vocational Rehabilitation was placed where it is, in the Federal Security Agency in close touch with services in the fields of health social security, and education. . . . We in the Federal Security Agency have been at work on this problem of aid to the physically handicapped for a long while.[57]

As is so often the case, threats to the status quo led the policy monopoly to shore up its jurisdictional boundaries. In 1950, for instance, the Department of Labor (DOL) opposed reorganization because a new bill added job placement, which DOL argued was under its umbrella, under the proposed new commission's jurisdiction.[58]

When the newly created HEW eventually took over most of the FSA's jurisdiction, including the OVR, the disability policy network remained largely intact. Members of Congress, the Executive Branch, rehabilitation professionals, and disability groups remained unified and served as the stewards of disability policy, securing their place in the government and disability's place on the policy agenda.

The success of this policy subsystem in shaping the political evolution of disability can be attributed to the close working relationship between the government and disability nonprofit and interest groups. Roger W. Jones of the Bureau of Budget aptly summarized these ties:

The greatest impact will grow out of the associations for the physically handicapped . . . things like the Society for Crippled Children, the March of Dimes,
Polio Foundation, things like Good Will Industries and the efforts of the Salva-
tion Army to find employment for persons who cannot maintain their status
in the full competitive swing of our economy, the sort of thing which I believe
you will get ultimately in terms of identification of sheltered activities with the
community rather than with the Federal Government. If everything becomes
a Federal expenditure, it tends to become cold, it tends to become insulated
from those things which we think are of emotional and sentimental value to the
handicapped, those things in which the community interest shares the responsibilities for what they do for themselves.[59]

Political elites shared the view that the federal government must lead the
way in providing social services, and they relied on established voluntary associations for provision of the programs and services to actual clients. Mostly
providing employment and social welfare services (in some cases, charity) to
people with disabilities, these groups had a natural investment in the policy
paradigm—they were as heavily embedded in the client-service paradigm as
the lawmakers with whom they partnered.

Steven Smith and Michael Lipsky once noted that nonprofit voluntary organizations played "a new political role in representing the welfare state to its
citizens, providing a buffer between state policy and service delivery."[60] Disability service organizations enjoyed their (often elite) status because legislators
and bureaucrats relied on them as community representatives, helping both
ensure and entrench rehabilitation policies and programs. Indeed, for liberals
and others working closely in developing social policy including rehabilitation
programs, partnerships with established organizations meant both the provision of social services to those in need and the success of those programs. To
conservatives, government and nonprofit partnerships meant providing services to the "deserving" while keeping government small. Together, government
and nonprofit groups forged a fruitful partnership in providing rehabilitative
and other social services.

Disability organizations' close work with policy makers meant political
access and government resources. Goodwill Industries, for instance, received
grants to "step up" its rehabilitation services.[61] Policies, of course, helped define organizational objectives. The NRA was created through the Smith-Fess
Act, and the American Printing House for the Blind was, in part, overseen by

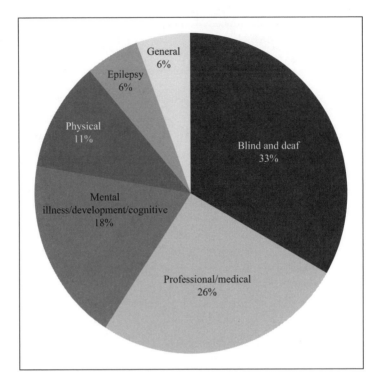

Figure 2.4 Organizations testifying before Congress, 1946–1960.

HEW. As Congressman John Robsion (R-KY) told the Special Subcommittee to Promote the Education of the Blind, "I have never observed an organization that has such a distinguished group of trustees. It has been my privilege to have been on the board of several organizations, and I just wish that I could have any one of those half a dozen fellows on any two of them on the boards that I have been on."[62] Again, many policy makers who worked in disability had already or would later serve on boards as members or directors of these organizations.

Between 1946 and 1960, more than fifty organizations testified across thirty-nine hearings, mostly before the House Committee on Education and Labor and the Senate Committee on Labor and Public Welfare. The three main types of organizations most involved in agenda setting were organizations for people who are deaf or blind, professional associations, and groups related to mental illness and mental/cognitive development (Figure 2.4).

One-third of all organizations represented a single subset of disability constituents—people who were deaf or blind. Many of these groups had been long established, including the Alexander Graham Bell Association for the Deaf and the National Association of the Deaf,[63] and were what William Gamson might call "incumbent," state-legitimated organizations, founded well before the modern rehabilitation paradigm (the average age of the organizations involved in this period of legislation was about thirty-five years).[64] Other established groups included the Association for the Blind (founded in 1903), Conference of Executives of American Schools for the Deaf (1868), Goodwill (1902), National Association for Mental Health (1909), and Easter Seals (1919). A well-established disability nonprofit sector predated and very much predicated the kinds of institutional and sociocultural legacies described in this book.

Professional associations representing experts in numerous areas within the health, education, and public welfare sectors joined disability nonprofit groups in supporting a client-service policy image. In addition to the American Medical Association, American Psychiatric Association, American Nurses Association, and National Association of Social Workers, incumbent disability-related professional groups like the American Instructors of the Deaf (1850), Conference of Executives of American Schools for the Deaf (1868), and the aforementioned NRA (1923) offered expert testimony regarding existing and proposed programs benefiting people with disabilities. These groups maintained close ties to members of Congress and helped define service provision. While many would, to use Debra Minkoff's term, "bend with the wind" later in the century,[65] they nonetheless promoted what by the 1970s would become seen as an outdated and repressive view of disability. Many elites in the disability policy field made "giving" or charity central to their conception of helping the disabled:

> There is nothing about a deaf person that creates within the heart the ability to put your hand in your pocket and to give out. People are not inclined to give to any cause connected with deafness. Blindness is apparent. The spastic is apparent. The crippled person and the heart case, you can see them, because they cannot be active, but deafness does not cause any concern in the heart of the human breast. You see, it is a very difficult thing to get foundations and individuals to become concerned about deafness, and that is why such institutions seem to have had a very difficult time in getting grants.

This statement, made by Ralph Gwinn (R-NY), member of the House Committee on Education and Labor in 1954,[66] reveals two traditional points of view from the disability nonprofit sector: people with different types of disabilities confront specific problems and did not constitute a broad group, and getting involved in disability must be motivated by an emotional, pity-driven response.

Figure 2.5 Norman Rockwell's *The Paycheck*, 1958. *Source:* Goodwill Industries International.

These groups worked to promote rehabilitation, including the provision of employment services to rehabilitated individuals. For example, the 1958 Norman Rockwell painting commemorating Goodwill's fiftieth anniversary depicted a disabled laborer speedily heading out from a hard day's work with a paycheck in one hand as the other pushes his wheelchair (Figure 2.5). The painting embodies the underlying values supporting rehabilitation policies.

The 1940s and 1950s also saw the creation of new groups such as the National Association of Retarded Children (NARC), National Epilepsy League, National Federation of the Blind (NFB, 1940), National Paraplegia Foundation (1948), UCP (1949), and the National Association of the Physically Handicapped (1958). These groups became important templates for future organizing efforts discussed in greater detail in Chapter 4. For example, the American Federation of the Physically Handicapped, founded in 1940, is considered one of the first disability groups to cut across different types of disabilities, and NARC, founded ten years later, became an important advocacy group for people with developmental and cognitive disabilities. Its founder, Elizabeth Boggs, served on John F. Kennedy's Panel on Mental Retardation in the early 1960s and directly incorporated NARC's legislative goals in that position.

Access to the political process meant promoting the existing policy agenda, not challenging it. Thus, the structure and strategy of nascent disability groups largely reflected the existing organizational field and its main patron, the federal government. This process is often described as "institutional isomorphism."[67] Newer groups had every incentive to model themselves around incumbent organizations to gain access to the disability policy network. For example, throughout the 1960s, about two-thirds of the organizational field was dedicated to service provision. By the early part of that decade, more than one-third of all active disability groups had a federated structure (emulating the structure of American government) with diffuse power to local, state, and regional subunits. About one-fifth of the disability organizational sector was made up of groups with more than ten thousand members. Average membership in the early 1960s was about ten thousand, with a median of about eighteen hundred. Disability groups had a relatively large membership base, and a significant number of organizations had exceptionally high membership.[68]

In the early 1960s, among the largest groups were Disabled American Veterans, the National Multiple Sclerosis Society, the NRA, the National Epilepsy League, and NARC, which had been operating for only a decade yet already counted hundreds of local chapters and thousands of members. Other recently founded groups such as the National Association of the Physically Handicapped, National Tay-Sachs Association, National Parkinson Foundation, National Foundation for Neuromuscular Disease, and the Muscular Dystrophy Association would have robust memberships and numerous local, state, and regional chapters by the 1960s.

Ironically, these organizations' participation in the disability policy subsystem may have helped stymie policy alternatives. Their paternalistic approach often excluded people with disabilities from the political process. As the rallying cry "not about us without us" suggests, the disability rights movement would later target the role of nondisabled "experts," politicians, and organizational leaders setting the policy agenda.[69] But it is important to situate these disability groups in the institutional and cultural reality of the time: they may not yet have been championing rights, but they were shaping the agenda within the confines set by the policy monopoly.

Organizational leaders saw their role as central to the policy-making process, and policy makers sought their involvement. When the Senate considered ways to improve employment opportunities through rehabilitation,[70] it consulted the American Federation of the Physically Handicapped. According to its New York Chapter director, Martin Mahler, the bill was "written by the handicapped for the handicapped" and "for the first time, provides practical, economical, and efficient services for all handicapped, including the severely disabled."[71] The demand for disability groups' participation was about ensuring that services, outlined in government policy and administered by the OVR, were provided efficiently and expansively. Mahler's emphasis on maximum employment and independence echoed the framing that had been established around disability policy that made ability, not disability, count. No one actively challenged these understandings.

Many political elites were conscientious about paternalism and made concerted efforts to include disability groups within the policy process. They even held hearings regarding the importance of these organizations in creating spaces for people with disabilities and highlighted their important work in providing services. For instance, in 1959, the Committee on Education and Labor considered proposed legislation to protect the right of the blind to self-expression through organizations for the blind. At a hearing chaired by Carl Elliot, Kennedy confederate Walter Baring (D-NV) recommended the bill's passage,[72]

> not only because of my own close association with the courageous struggle for independence and self-expression on the part of the blind of my State, and of the Nation, but because of my deep conviction of the simple justice and imperative necessity of this legislation. . . . Their organizations, both on the State and National level, have often been refused the right of consultation and advice in the administration of programs directly affecting their welfare which is recognized everywhere as the established right of clientele and beneficiary groups with respect to public programs.[73]

Though the bill ultimately failed, the arguments around it reveal at least some policy maker sensitivity to the inclusion of beneficiaries in policy design.

In their public dealings with policy makers, disability organizations provided the kinds of information legislators could use as evidence to promote their policy objectives. This often meant presenting information about the specific needs of their constituents and undertaking studies about the current status of programs.[74] The National Paraplegia Foundation, in a 1953 hearing, listed the key points of its legislative objectives, including medical care, the training of personnel, and research and development,[75] and the National Organization for Mentally Ill Children presented reports and studies summarizing the problems associated with childhood mental illness.[76] "It is not my purpose here in any way," Beatrice Hill, director of the National Recreation Association, told one committee, "to quarrel with the concept of the rehabilitation of the chronically ill and handicapped. We are all gathered here precisely because of one thing, our belief in this, the third phase of medicine, rehabilitation, and because all of us wish to contribute whatever we can toward expanding and improving this service, rehabilitation, to the severely ill and handicapped citizens of the United States."[77] None of the organizations sought an alternative policy trajectory; they worked only to fit the needs of the communities they represented to the rehabilitative framework that had become successfully entrenched in policy circles.

Because lawmakers and bureaucrats sought out these groups when they required technical/scientific knowledge or information about their efforts in service delivery, they were conferred legitimacy as important structures in that successful entrenchment. Recall that the OVR, FSA, and HEW benefited from the work of disability groups that ensured government-mandated services were reaching as many people as possible, gaining friendly constituencies, and demonstrating policy successes that scored elites political points. Organizations also supported the efforts of administrative agencies. For instance, at a 1960 hearing, a representative of NARC expressed its confidence that HEW could provide the consultation and services necessary for states to address the needs of individuals with cognitive disabilities.[78] "I have served as an officer on three national organizations that are directly related to the kind of legislation you are considering," testified Vivian Shepherd of the National Rehabilitation Institute. "You as Members of the Congress have been a tremendous force in providing for and stimulating growth in rehabilitation services on a national scale and at a local level. This has caused interest in the rehabilitation of the disabled to develop with a rapidity and to an extent never seen before."[79]

Considerations of Both "Humanity and Self-Interest"
Shepherd had recently become disabled. She told the Subcommittee on Special Education that "the humanitarian aspect of rehabilitation is easily understood, but as private citizens and as a nation we probably have not fully

grasped the impact of disability on our economy and the worth and necessity of providing dynamic programs of rehabilitation to lessen the strain."[80] This kind of testimony was quite common in constructing the "problem" of disability; the humanitarian *and* economic aspects of rehabilitation resonated with political elites on both sides of the aisle. HEW secretary Oveta Culp Hobby echoed Eisenhower's mandate that "considerations of both humanity and self-interest demand immediate measures for the expansion of our rehabilitation programs."[81] Helping the disabled was the morally right thing to do, but it was also in the nation's self-interest to employ people with disabilities. These were powerful supporting ideas on which elite efforts and policy outputs rested.

Values—equality and fairness, economic opportunity, and self-reliance—motivating policy elites to mobilize legislation drew on deeply American ideals.[82] The moral or humanistic justification for government involvement, on the one hand, and the economic self-interest, on the other, characterized the general understanding of the government's role in disability from the 1920s onward.[83] It was the federal government's job to put these moral values into action. Throughout this period, on the few occasions when political elites talked about justice for the disabled, they intended not for minority or civil rights but for the right to be independent of the state.

Rehabilitationists thus inscribed one notion of the model citizen: someone "who takes care of himself in every way. He supports his family. He supports himself and he is thoroughly independent of any help in order to take care of his personal affairs."[84] It was therefore the government's role to provide opportunities to "the unfortunate people who have been handicapped" to make them so-called useful citizens. This typically meant finding employment, the last stage in the rehabilitation program. Rep. Leroy Johnson (R-CA) warned that the government should not "stand by idly and lose the services of the millions of disabled."[85]

Disability policy experts skillfully tapped into both practical and moral sensibilities. Seeking to build the most convincing case for their policy approach,[86] professionals would, as proxies, present technical and scientific evidence to support policy makers' claims. For example, Dr. John J. Lee, graduate dean at Wayne State University and one-time supervisor of Michigan's special education programs, framed rehabilitation in a 1950 hearing as part of health and educational services because the former can help "remove or minimize handicap or an illness" and the latter helps "rehabilitate persons into lives of independence and pride and self-support."[87] A disability expert, Lee held positions in government and was past president of Easter Seals.

Practitioner experts also provided facts demonstrating the effectiveness of rehabilitation programs in making the disabled independent and self-sufficient to emphasize appropriation needs. They focused hearings on the rehabilitation of formerly "lost causes" and, in so doing, made it clear that widening the net meant transforming ever-greater swaths of the disabled into both clients and success stories.

Typical evidence included statements like those provided by Mary Switzer, head of the RSA. Testifying before the House Committee on Education and Labor, she provided data (see Figure A.1 in the appendix) on the total amount of federal spending on rehabilitation programs and the total number of program beneficiaries.[88] In 1943, the federal government was spending about the same amount on vocational rehabilitation as state and local governments combined. By the beginning of the 1950s, it was spending about twice as much. Total federal funds spent on rehabilitation (in 1952 dollars) increased by about 423 percent in the 1940s. Switzer also reported that the number of people who benefited from rehabilitation services more than doubled in the second half of the 1940s and argued that two million *more* Americans with physical handicaps could be helped with appropriate increases in funds and support for federal rehabilitation programs. Again, this was a testament to successful policy entrenchment by this network of lawmakers, bureaucrats, and nonprofit organizations.

Experts frequently used anecdotes as rhetorical tools to showcase the successes of rehabilitation.[89] These stories illustrated the intersection of evidence, pragmatism, and the core values of self-reliance and independence. For instance, Hill of the National Recreation Association told the story of eighteen-year-old Jimmy Seaborn, whose entire spine was afflicted with rheumatoid arthritis. In 1949, Hill said, the possibility for Jimmy to receive

vocational rehabilitation rating is zero. Rehabilitation teams say, "Sorry, kid, we can't do a darn thing for you." . . . Today, 10 years later, Jimmy . . . is a full time recreation leader in Peoria, Ill., 1,000 miles from Goldwater Memorial Hospital in New York City, for so many years his permanent home. . . . The answer to Jimmy Seaborn and his triumph over his crippling handicap was motivation through social rehabilitation.[90]

This was not just a story about a disabled boy's triumph, but the triumph of rehabilitation—of the policy subgovernment that worked to provide federal aid and programs. Dr. Edward E. Rosenbaum, chief of the Rheumatology Clinic at the Oregon School of Medicine, told a similar story in his testimony to the Subcommittee on Special Education in 1960:

> Six years ago, I had a 35-year old girl who was totally disabled. . . . The thinking at that time was that a chronically disabled person would be disabled for life and it would be a waste of State funds to spend money on this type of person. We would not have undertaken any help on this girl except she was able to put some pressure on us politically and so we began the project of rehabilitation. Today this girl is gainfully employed, is self-supporting, and is taking care of herself. This is six years later. As a matter of fact, she is working more than I would like to see her.[91]

Again, we see the rehabilitationist's dream, that ever-more individuals once thought "uneducable" and "untrainable" might be transformed into self-sufficient individuals who do not require institutionalization (and thus would not be expensive burdens on the state). The expert testimony simultaneously applauded rehabilitation's success and urged Congress to extend rehabilitation programs because they had not yet reached their full potential. Disability experts and elites created a growing client base in a self-reinforcing, positive feedback loop;[92] more clients made for more successes and more people with a stake in maintaining the policy paradigm. Challengers would be hard-pressed to argue against helping Jimmy Seaborn, putting a paycheck in the hand of Norman Rockwell's paraplegic, or recommending that Rosenbaum's forty-one-year-old disabled "girl" might be working too much.

The Legacy of Disability Policy Making

America's odd welfare state, the "welfare state nobody knows,"[93] saw dramatic expansion in rehabilitation services in the mid-twentieth century, with strong consensus that these policies were *the* solution to the "social problem" of handicap. So entrenched were these perspectives and programs that alternative policy frameworks—anything, including equal access and discrimination, that would too seriously clash with a client-service model of disability—were effectively stalled.

Midcentury policies did not evolve from an institutional and cognitive space that conceived of people with disabilities as a collective minority group—quite the contrary. Single-issue-focused policies divided the community along impairment lines, often creating competing subgroups demanding government attention. Nine of the nineteen federal laws passed between 1948 and 1960 dealt specifically with deaf/blind constituents, and five, with mental health. Even though incremental efforts on the part of rehabilitationists were normatively constrained, they would come to have profound impacts on the way the American public and political elites framed disability.

Both the 1954 Vocational Rehabilitation Act and 1956 amendments to the Social Security's Old-Age and Survivors Insurance (OASDI) are examples of the kinds of incremental changes that would backdrop more significant political developments over the next two decades. Disability insurance was the result of decades-long efforts by those working in social security to expand the system. Opposition to any form of "unearned" cashed benefits was pervasive, but as Daniel Reed (R-NY), who chaired a 1954 hearing about disability insurance, and Secretary Hobby agreed, disability insurance would complement the efforts of vocational rehabilitation to provide both an economic and social gain.[94] Assistant HEW secretary Roswell D. Perkins adamantly testified that disability insurance would not undermine rehabilitation in favor of cash benefits. That is, in a point that is still argued today, logic would dictate that no one would leave a well-paying job to collect insurance unless the individual was "truly disabled."

Like OASDI, the Vocational Rehabilitation Act reflected policies of the time—amending existing legislation, reauthorization, and extensions. At the same time, the act was an important political step toward thinking about disability as a cohesive community (albeit a community of *clients*, not *citizens*). Importantly, rehabilitation programs provided an actual alternative policy pathway to institutionalization and warehousing and became key to the deinstitutionalization movement, which would move away from custodial care to nonresidential treatment involving social, health, and educational service provision for the disabled within the community.[95] Rehabilitationist and deinstitutionalizationist values, philosophy, and goals were congruent in that rehabilitation was about breaking "with a good many of the old traditions of sending a patient into a mental hospital";[96] and they were also about removing the intolerable "burden on the taxpayer who must pay to support the deaf and those with impaired speech in institutions."[97]

Thus, rehabilitationists generated an institutional basis for the independent living movement of the 1960s and 1970s.[98] Freedom from institutionalization is, of course, a perennial issue in the politics of disability. In the mid-1990s, health-care reform and the funding bias favoring nursing homes over in-home care significantly revitalized the issue. Even today, recent political efforts such as the Republican Repeal and Replace of Obamacare threaten independent living (discussed in Chapter 5).

Additionally, with an expanding client base in the 1950s and 1960s came a broadening definition of who is "deserving" of federal government intervention. Given that concerns and (sometimes conflicting) interests around different types of disabilities evolved at varying speeds and around distinct—sometimes competing—approaches, that broadening was slow. Politicians, government officials, and disability groups continued to discriminate between people who were deaf, blind, or developmentally disabled, and policies unevenly targeted people with different disabilities. Consequently, the structure of the disability organizational sector developed as clusters around specific clients (for instance, even in the 1950s, the most established and legitimate disability groups were associations for people who were blind or deaf). And organizations most identified with disability well into the 1960s continued to perpetuate a certain image of disability policy and of being disabled.

A 1965 Easter Seals magazine ad epitomized the strategy, tactics, and underlying ideology of contemporaries: rehabilitation was beneficial not only for individuals but also for American society (Figure 2.6). As the ad claims, any resources expended on these efforts would be more than paid back. Of course, the appeal also relied on emotions including pity, gratitude, fellow-feeling, and hope. As Joseph Shapiro wrote, "The poster child is a sure-fire tug at our hearts."[99] Thus, organizations told the public that helping will "make you feel good all day."

But experts increasingly came to view people with disabilities less in terms of individuals with specific medical conditions and more like a group of client-constituents who could collectively benefit from government-led programs aimed at social reintegration. Rehabilitation politics brought together disparate groups of people with disabilities and helped lay a base for the rights frameworks of the ensuing decades.

The policy image underlying rehabilitation was that all people with disabilities, regardless of their disability, could be rehabilitated. Distinctions became less about disability type and more about who is educable/trainable. Actors within the policy monopoly worked to convince political elites and social welfare professionals that individuals who in the past were deemed lost causes could, in fact, be turned into productive citizens. Federal agencies and non-

Hey, Mister!

Lend me a dollar to help me walk and I'll make you feel good all day (P.S. I'll pay you back when I'm rich)

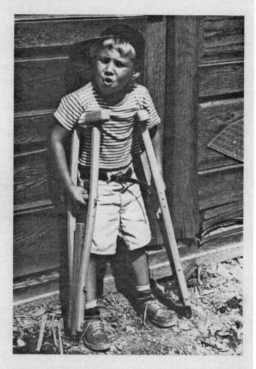

Giving to the Easter Seal Kid, here, besides making you feel good in the mysterious way that giving does, enables him and 250,000 others all over the U.S.A. to keep coming to us for help in overcoming these crippling disorders—accidents, poliomyelitis, cerebral palsy, multiple sclerosis, muscular dystrophy, arthritis, birth deformities, speech defects, and many others.

Easter Seal Fund Appeal

National Society for Crippled Children and Adults • 2023 West Ogden Avenue, Chicago, Illinois 60612

71

Figure 2.6 Easter Seals fund-raising campaign magazine advertisement. *Source: Life Magazine*, April 1965. Reprinted with permission.

profit organizations bridged policy makers and the beneficiaries of proposed policies and were critical in interacting with "the disabled" as a constituency rather than just "the blind," "the deaf," or "the retarded."

Political discourse in the 1950s revealed a growing tension between the association of pity with doing the morally right thing and promoting independence—

a key characteristic of good citizenship. In his testimony to the Special Subcommittee for Establishing a Federal Commission for Physically Handicapped in 1949, Colonel Robert S. Allen argued:

> This is not a plea for charity. It is not a plea for sympathy. It is basically a plea for just simple, plain justice. Go down to the Goodwill Industries here, one of the greatest institutions, in my mind, in the country. They get down to the lowest denominator in the social structure. . . . Go down there; it is heart-breaking but at the same time a very exhilarating, thrilling experience, to see the deaf and the blind and the halt doing things for themselves. These disabled, the handicapped—whatever you want to call them—the impaired, are a fabulous social resource, an economic resource, a human resource. They are not just discards.[100]

Rehabilitation not only changed the institutional context around what to do about disability; it also created new cognitive opportunities that shifted the focus away from pity and, to a lesser extent, charity, toward a more scientific, rational, and comprehensive approach in generating productive, independent citizens. The disability rights movement would eventually fight hard against these oppressive symbols of charity and pity; from March of Dimes and Easter Seals fund-raising campaigns to Jerry Lewis Telethons,[101] rooted in the institutional and cultural paradigm of disability as a negative condition to be overcome.

Among the lessons we see in what appeared, in the 1950s, to be a settled policy field is that actors need not overtly challenge norms and values to creatively combine and shape policy agendas.[102] Jacobus TenBroek, a lawyer, early human rights advocate, and founder of the NFB, wrote that the blind are caught between social and physical disadvantage.[103] Effective policies should assume that the blind are *regular citizens* confronted with the same needs as other Americans. In keeping, policies should encourage self-reliance and self-sufficiency within which the right to be economically independent is incongruent with discriminatory practices. Lawmakers working in disability largely agreed that the right to opportunities to participate in social and economic arenas should be encouraged, not denied.[104]

For instance, a law enacted in 1948 amended the Civil Services Act to outlaw discrimination based on physical disability in the civil service.[105] This law did not emerge from the traditional venues within which disability policy was discussed, and no hearings were held on the proposal. It was a response to efforts in the 1940s, such as National Employ the Physically Handicapped Week (which began in 1945), seeking to forge ties with employers so that they would hire rehabilitated people with disabilities. The government did not want to appear hypocritical in promoting vocational rehabilitation and mounting public awareness campaigns about the merits of hiring people with disabilities in the private sector while limiting employment opportunities in the civil service. Howard Rusk, a physician who frequently wrote for the *New York Times* on disability-related issues, suggested in his articles that discrimination was pitched as an economic inefficiency incongruent with a good business model. Thus, while the language of the amendment included antidiscrimination, legislators were not thinking of antidiscrimination within a framework of civil rights but in terms of rehabilitation and economic self-sufficiency.[106] It was the federal government's responsibility to increase the rights to employment and productivity among people with disabilities. Government would lead the way.

Lawmakers and organizations set the policy agenda around helping the disabled help themselves—a powerful ideal that brought together individuals with different policy interests and ideological backgrounds.[107] As Dr. R. M. Little, former chair of the Federal Compensation Committee, testified regarding the problem of unemployment and economic independence, "We are never going to make any appreciable advance until we set the hands of the Federal Government and State Governments to solve it."[108] Kenneth Griffith, the thirty-second judicial circuit judge, best summarized government involvement to Carl Elliot:

> I know that the thing that brings this committee here today is a labor of love, because a nation that can produce Representatives that have the humanitarian touch in their heart . . . as evidenced by their taking time out to go all over this Nation to inquire into the needs of the unfortunate people whom nature has marked, and try to help them help themselves, it must be a source of satisfaction to you in this kind of work. Knowing you, Congressman Elliot, as I do, I know it must be a source of satisfaction to you to help these people help themselves.[109]

Members of Congress, professional and disability associations, and the Executive Branch all had mutual interests in maintaining the status quo. Conformity, deference, minimal conflict, and low issue salience allowed for largely uninterrupted policy entrenchment. But another amendment to this decades-old policy by disability rights entrepreneurs would jump-start a movement inside the government to reshape the policy image around disability. The 1973 Rehabilitation Act would have far-reaching consequences in politicizing a constituency and redefining how the state interacts with citizens rather than clients.

3 Reshaping the Policy Agenda

Abraham Lincoln once characterized America as "a nation conceived in liberty and dedicated to the proposition that all men are created equal." Those words were spoken in the aftermath of a battle which had been fought to end discrimination against racial minorities and to make good on the promise of freedom guaranteed by the Constitution. Three years ago the Congress acted to protect the rights of yet another minority group in our society—the disabled.

—Senator Harrison Williams, *Rehabilitation of the Handicapped Programs, 1976, Part 3* hearing, 1976

THE 1960S OPENED WITH MEMBERS of the Subcommittee on Special Education considering how best to serve people who were moderately or mildly retarded, thought "educable" and "trainable."[1] Intellectual and developmental disability resonated with President John F. Kennedy. The issue was personal for him, "influenced by the fact that his sister, Rosemary, was mentally retarded."[2] The Kennedy family established the Joseph P. Kennedy Jr. Foundation in 1946, and throughout the 1940s and 1950s as a member of Congress, Kennedy established a liberal voting record in housing, welfare programs, and education bills (many rejected by the conservative Congress of the time).[3]

As president, Kennedy bolstered the legitimacy of rehabilitation. His legislative requests to Congress focused mainly on the so-called twin problems of mental retardation and mental illness.[4] In this way, Kennedy's narrower platform on disability was less comprehensive and less ambitious than that of his predecessors. In his request for a broad health program emphasizing the creation of a National Health Program and National Program to Combat Mental Retardation, Kennedy underlined "the urgency of the Nation's need for long-postponed solutions to a long-neglected problem, and to urge once more their prompt enactment by the Congress."[5] In 1961, he created the President's Panel on Mental Retardation. Kennedy's message about mental retardation tied what was traditionally seen as a public health problem to socioeconomic disadvantage. It also reflected the ongoing mandate to "cure" and prevent disability and to expand mental retardation facilities.[6]

The early 1960s looked a lot like the 1950s in regard to policy makers' attitudes and practices concerning the disabled. The network of political elites that governed disability politics was still in place, and both Republicans and Democrats, along with the American public, bought into rehabilitation's lofty goals. Despite general support for policies meant to help "deserving" disadvantaged groups such as the disabled, enduring criticisms of federal government expansions blocked more significant legislative outputs. Even following the 1964 Economic Opportunity Act (the War on Poverty), for example, "the main argument Republicans used with Southern Democrats was the charge that the anti-poverty bill ignored 'states' rights.'"[7] People with disabilities were seen as one of "the toughest welfare problems of our country," because policies geared toward them were a "potential source of danger to the domestic tranquility and harmony of which the Constitution speaks."[8]

By the mid- to late 1960s, a new institutional environment facilitated the introduction of new ideas and allowed the disability policy agenda to loosen rehabilitation's hold. Some of these changes were exogenous to the disability policy network: the rise of younger, non-Southern Democrats; the dramatic turnover in the House Committee on Education and Labor in 1961; and new political opportunities brought by growing interest in urban decay, discrimination, and poverty.

Interest in the Great Society created a legislative context from which disability entrepreneurs more readily drew. Influenced by this new social policy agenda, elites reconceptualized disability, which ultimately had a profound impact on the lives of everyday citizens. By the 1970s, political elites came to see Congress and federal agencies as vehicles for embedding disability rights into American social policy. Disability rights entrepreneurs in Congress, such as Sen. Bob Bartlett (D-AK), Rep. John Brademas (D-IN), Rep. Kenneth Gray (D-IL), Sen. Hubert Humphrey, Sen. Charles Vanik (D-OH), and Sen. Harrison Williams, framed the government's role in ending discrimination as a moral imperative, much in the same way they and their predecessors had championed rehabilitation.

Williams drew from the legacy of President Lincoln to argue that the federal government must finally make good on its promise to end discrimination against people with disabilities. Williams and Brademas were joined by freshman, non-southern Democratic members of Congress, such as Mario Biaggi

(NY), Bella Abzug (NY), and Alan Cranston (CA), as well as northern liberal Republicans—the so-called Rockefeller Republicans—such as Jacob Javits (who succeeded Democrat Herbert Lehman) and Robert Stafford (VT). Together, they formed a civil rights–oriented policy community seeking to carve out a new trajectory for disability policy.

Arguably, these policy makers' true innovation was how they shifted disability away from patient/client policy models without abandoning social-service provision. They built on the extant disability policy subsystem, which incorporated vocational rehabilitation and deinstitutionalization and would later involve architectural barriers and antidiscrimination. These incremental changes, punctuated by more explicit civil rights language available in the early 1970s, made the merging of a rights and client-service paradigm seem organic, and they were manifested in policies such as the 1973 Rehabilitation Act (particularly Section 504).

As Chapter 2 describes, the political evolution of disability reflects innovations within the constraints of institutional, ideological, and cognitive frameworks. Lawmakers in the 1960s and 1970s came to see civil rights as a logical next step rather than a rupture in the rehabilitation paradigm. At the same time, they knew that their legislative actions were extending challenges to the social norms and beliefs about disability far beyond the policies of their predecessors.

The Great Society "Cannot Fail the Handicapped"

Kennedy created momentum around comprehensive mental health and mental retardation policy that would carry into Lyndon Johnson's first year as president. In his February congressional address, Johnson explicitly cited Kennedy's policy preferences when he proclaimed, "The mentally ill and the mentally retarded have a right to a decent, dignified place in society. I intend to assure them of that place. The Congress has demonstrated its awareness of the need for action by approving my request for supplemental appropriations for mental retardation programs in the current fiscal year."[9]

The success of rehabilitation policy served as a model for Johnson's other social policy interventions. By the mid-1960s, the disability policy network—legislators, administrators, and disability organizations alike—was increasingly tied to the politics of social welfare. In the spring of 1964, the Subcommittee on War on Poverty Programs held hearings regarding bills that "sought to mobilize the human and financial resources of the Nation to combat poverty in the United States."[10] Charles Goodel (R-NY) asked about the "mental retardation group as to whether they are rehabilitatible in any sense at all ... to make themselves self-supporting."[11] This emphasis on rehabilitation as a means to self-reliance would shape discourse surrounding the Economic Opportunity Act.

Disability policy makers were increasingly subsumed by the institutional logic of the Great Society programs that dominated social policy making. Under these new mandates, the jurisdictions of the two committees that traditionally governed disability in Congress—the House Committee on Education and Labor and the Senate Committee on Labor and Public Welfare—expanded significantly. Figures 3.1 and 3.2 illustrate the increasing breadth of topics they engaged with as their focus became less concentrated on a limited set of issues.[12] Their complex jurisdictions (entropy) touched on ever-more-intersecting policy domains, from health to transportation to civil rights (see Figures A.4 and A.5 in the appendix). As the federal government sought comprehensive solutions to persistent socioeconomic and political disadvantage while embracing the logic of civil rights, all of these issues, including disability, appeared more and more multifaceted.

Sar Levitan and Robert Taggart have appropriately characterized the federal government in the 1960s as "a lever of institutional change."[13] The early part of the decade saw several "major investigations,"[14] especially in the areas of labor and public welfare. These included Lister Hill's Special Subcommittee on Employment and Manpower, Jennings Randolph's investigation of manpower problems, and Pat McNamara's (D-MI) Special Subcommittee on Problems of

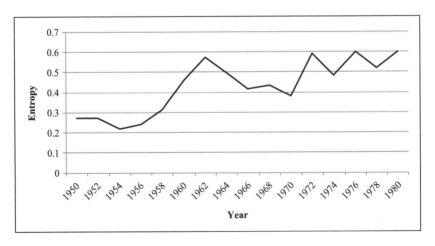

Figure 3.1 Expansion of House Committee on Education and Labor's informal issue jurisdiction, 1950–1980.

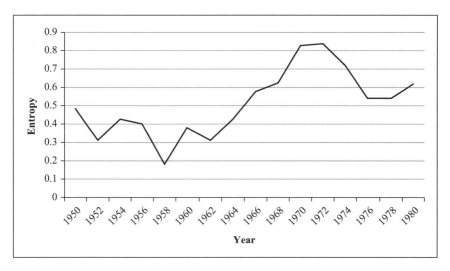

Figure 3.2 Expansion of Senate Committee on Labor and Public Welfare's informal issue jurisdiction, 1950–1980.

the Aged and Aging. As more attention was paid to disability, an increasing number of bills and laws pushed welfare spending as well as public spending specifically on the elderly, blind, and disabled (Figure 3.3). By the mid-1970s, nearly all low-income Americans with disabilities were receiving some form of federal assistance.

It certainly helped that the ideals and objectives of the rehabilitation-focused disability policy network fit nicely with Congress and the administration's intent to expand the federal government's role in social welfare. Making disabled people independent and self-sufficient through educational and economic interventions dovetailed with growing policy interests in alleviating material need and lifting people out of poverty.

In 1966, the Ad Hoc Subcommittee on the Handicapped was established to "study in depth the problems facing the handicapped and their families," according to committee chair, Hugh L. Carey (D-NY).[15] The subcommittee held numerous hearings, notably in regard to a law establishing a model secondary school for the deaf operated by Gallaudet University.[16] Carey believed this law was "an opportunity for the Federal government to exercise leadership."[17] He had experience working on deaf education, having served on the National Advisory Committee on Education of the Deaf and championing the National Technical Institute for the Deaf Act.[18] At a June 1966 hearing, committee chair Carey announced:

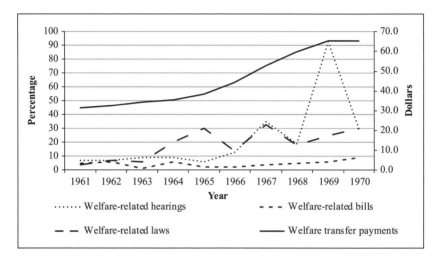

Figure 3.3 Growth of the welfare state in the 1960s. *Source:* Data on welfare-related hearings, laws, and bills from the Policy Agendas Project, at https://www.comparativeagendas.net; data on federal welfare transfer payments from *Economic Report of the President*, 1961–1970.

At this time in history when our Government is showing its concern for every citizen, so that opportunity for every man exists, we must call on the total resources available in our Government, in all of the governments, State and local, to meet the needs of the handicapped persons since we cannot in this day and age say that we did everything possible for everyone but the handicapped. In other words, we cannot fail the handicapped.[19]

Helping people with disabilities rise to their full potential encompassed the "nexus of variables" that informed social policy in the 1960s: addressing the links between adequate education, job training, and discrimination that affected citizens' economic and social well-being were firmly within the purview of the federal government.[20]

The spotlight would again shine on rehabilitation programs, which had been permanently authorized until 1965 and were now up for reauthorization.[21] Even as Congress worked to increase the total number of people rehabilitated, it reauthorized funding only until 1967–1968. In his January 1965 special message to Congress, "Advancing the Nation's Health," President Johnson included a section titled "A New Life for the Disabled" in which he promised to cut waste and increase the yearly number of rehabilitated persons from 120,000 to 200,000. To that end, he recommended legislation that would help states expand their services, add special federal matching funds to raise the number of severely disabled people receiving services, and construct and modernize workshops and rehabilitation centers.

By spring, congressional discussion of disability revolved around the Vocational Rehabilitation Act Amendments of 1965.[22] In the following years, Congress would add proposals regarding the Vocational Rehabilitation Act Amendments of 1967 and 1968,[23] as discussions continued to promote the client-service model so firmly embedded in America's policy approach to disability. Mary Switzer, the Vocational Rehabilitation commissioner, now under HEW, testified in most of these hearings, reifying the disability policy network's influence by situating it within the broader objectives of the Great Society. When questioned by Edith Green, who chaired the Special Subcommittee on Education in 1965, about the status of the rehabilitation program, Switzer replied:

> I do believe firmly in the kind of work that has been done by the rehabilitation agencies through the years, in their approach to this through a client-oriented goal for each individual. I do not think you can solve the personal problems of poverty another way. I am absolutely convinced that the rehabilitation philosophy, and the way we have built the atmosphere that you create when you work with people in our centers and in our facilities, is really the most effective way that I have seen to make a dent in this poverty problem.[24]

When Green asked Switzer about being receptive to new ideas, Switzer said that members of the administration "try to keep an open mind. Of course, I suppose 10 years is not very long in the life of a public agency, but I can see even in the 10 years since our 1954 amendments, the tendency to become bureaucratized and get things institutionalized."[25] Switzer's testimony points to the continued success of the rehabilitation policy image—an industry with vested interests among both government and nongovernment actors—that successfully, in Switzer's terms, became entrenched, protecting, as it were, client-service policies from serious political deviations.

The Special Subcommittee on Education held hearings in the spring of 1965 to consider numerous rehabilitation amendment bills. In addition to Green as chair, the subcommittee included key figures such as Carey and John Brademas. Brademas, who would become Williams's House counterpart, was a disability rights entrepreneur with close ties to the disability policy community, from Williams and his staff in the Senate to the Executive Branch. Also involved in rehabilitation policy in the mid-1960s were the incumbent nonprofit organizations, including the American Federation for the Blind, NARC, and the NRA. That year, they worked to increase federal funding for training workshops and programs enabling physically and mentally handicapped people to hold jobs.[26] Likewise, Williams and Jacob Javits in the Senate Subcommittee on Health worked to authorize grants for training programs and the construction of rehabilitation facilities, hoping to encourage increased program participation by "mentally retarded" and other handicapped individuals.[27]

There had always been opposition, especially regarding appropriation of funds to what detractors characterized as "catch-all" policies relating to disability.[28] Earlier in the decade, mental illness and retardation policies strongly backed by Kennedy and his HEW secretary, Anthony Celebrezze,[29] ran into budget problems. Among Kennedy's broad new mental health/retardation programs, the only funds approved for the 1964 fiscal year were in the Labor-HEW appropriations bill,[30] which provided $1.5 million to train teachers for the deaf and $1 million for training teachers for the handicapped. These were not new programs but were set to expand with the Kennedy-backed legislation.

All this was indicative of broader hurdles in US social policy making: Even where there was bipartisan support to provide for the disadvantaged and vulnerable, the parties would argue over the appropriation of funding for this legislative agenda.[31] Liberal Democrats saw that they still faced obstacles in Congress—and some came from within their own party. Attempts to enact liberal policies usually meant amending existing legislation; anything more would come under fire, especially in terms of spending.[32]

By the end of the 1960s, funding for the War on Poverty was becoming uncertain. The congressional climate was one of fiscal austerity (especially in the House) that emphasized spending cuts. Many in Congress saw the War on Poverty as expensive and ineffective, and the administration feared Republicans would succeed in dismantling the Office of Economic Opportunity. Nevertheless, funding for the War on Poverty received authorization up to the 1969 fiscal year. Similarly, despite heated debates regarding Social Security amendments, the eventual 1967 Social Security Act Amendments increased OASDI benefits by 13 percent, liberalized the definition of blindness for the purposes of program coverage, and provided cash benefits to young workers disabled before age thirty-one (Figure 3.4).[33]

The 1967 Vocational Rehabilitation Act Amendments promised an expansion to increase the number of individuals rehabilitated.[34] The bill coming out

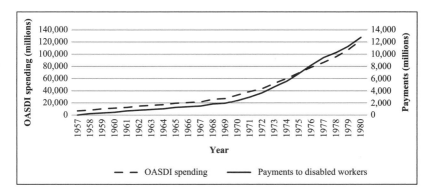

Figure 3.4 OASDI spending and disability insurance benefit payments, 1957–1980. *Source:* Data from Social Security Administration statistical tables, at http://www .ssa.gov/oact/STATS/index.html.

of the House Committee on Education and Labor with strong backing from the Johnson administration passed the House 340–0 on a roll-call vote. The Senate passed the House bill by voice with no debate.[35] Rehabilitation again expanded dramatically with the 1968 amendments (sponsored by Democrat Dominick Daniels),[36] extending vocational rehabilitation to include all disadvantaged groups, broadly defined.[37] This meant an attendant shift in the understanding around who is "deserving" of government assistance, as the program gained funding until the 1972 fiscal year. Congressional staff referred to the amendments as both a "major expansion" and a "major breakthrough in working with the disadvantaged," but not necessarily as a "new undertaking," given that the law, again, only extended existing programs.[38]

Conservatives, in a now-established pattern, questioned the cost. Carl Perkins responded that the increase in authorizations "will assure an orderly development of the program and a steady increase in the number of individuals served and rehabilitated" and that "we are presently not spending enough in the field."[39] The bill passed the House, but the Senate's Committee on Labor and Public Welfare (chaired by Southern Democrat Lister Hill) amended the bill by deleting the 1972 authorizations (replacing them with grants for special projects). The House accepted the amendments with little discussion.

An important force protecting social welfare, including disability policies, from retrenchment was the self-reinforcing positive feedback afforded by both an expanding number of disabled clients and the government bureaucracy invested in protecting its programs. As James Patterson put it, "HEW . . . was a liberal bureaucracy with every reason to aggrandize itself."[40] The agency actively joined liberal Democrats in Congress to politicize social issues, in-cluding disability and old age.[41] HEW created the Special Staff on Aging, and HEW undersecretary Wilber Cohen led a 1960 task force that proposed ex-tending Aid to Families with Dependent Children (AFDC) later approved by Congress.[42]

Cohen is today most remembered as a pioneer in the 1935 Social Security Act. He later defended the program against proposed limits by the Carter ad-ministration and also oversaw implementation of programs for people with cognitive disabilities outlined in policies of the early 1960s.[43] When Cohen be-came secretary of HEW in 1968, he and allies like Mary Switzer were aware that the kind of support for the social welfare programs in which HEW was heav-ily invested, including vocational rehabilitation, faced uncertainty under the Nixon administration. As Jonathan Hughes writes, "Time was running out for people who thought like they did."[44] Nevertheless, even in the early 1970s, HEW sought to expand its jurisdiction. New policy subareas such as the removal of architectural barriers and, eventually, the rise of both disability rights and anti-discrimination legislation would offer ample opportunity.

Building Momentum: The Movement
to Remove Physical Barriers

The emergence of architectural barriers as a disability policy agenda item re-veals an important policy link between the rehabilitation and civil rights para-digms. As a part of the political evolution of disability, the turn toward physical spaces resulted from more than a decade of incremental policy actions.

Discussion of architectural barriers first surfaced in 1957, when Harold Russell, chair of the President's Committee on Employment of the Physically Handicapped (later renamed the President's Committee on Employment of the Handicapped [PCEH])[45] and himself a wounded veteran and chairman of American Veterans (AMVETS), created an ad hoc group to investigate the issue.[46] Russell's interest in architectural barriers was motivated by an incident in which a man who worked locally to promote wheelchair accessibility had to be carried by two marines to receive the 1957 "Handicapped American of the Year" award because the venue hosting the celebration was not wheelchair accessible. But in the late 1950s, proposed legislation meant to provide equal access to public spaces would have been too far removed from the concerns of legislators inside and outside the disability policy monopoly. Promoting acces-sible spaces was not in the PCEH's mandate. Even if it had been, the PCEH did not typically take sides on proposed legislation; members testified only when invited. Russell reiterated that the committee's mandate was to promote employment of the disabled, mainly through information dissemination and coordination between state and nonstate actors.[47]

The efforts of Russell's ad hoc group investigating architectural inaccessibility made little legislative impact. Although policy makers were not yet drawing direct comparisons between equal access and civil rights, many working directly on disability-related issues in the 1960s supported civil rights for African Americans and other groups. The "second session of [the] 86th Congress convene[d], with politics and civil rights on most minds."[48]

In hearings related to the 1965 Vocational Rehabilitation Act Amendments, members of the disability policy monopoly talked, for the first time, about removing architectural barriers. Howard Rusk testified before the Senate Subcommittee on Health regarding the recently constructed Lincoln Center, pointing out that "Lincoln Center has found many people who were interested in giving funds . . . so that disabled people could be cared for. So this has been bread cast on the water that has come back, not only with a little butter but maybe a little jam, too, for the Center itself."[49]

Accessibility generated little publicity, as it was framed as widely appealing, uncontroversial, necessary, and doable—a benign extension of the accepted understanding that rehabilitation is of little use to a person who cannot access buildings and places of employment. Those heavily invested in rehabilitation policies saw the removal of physical barriers as an auxiliary to their primary objectives. Consequently, efforts to remove architectural barriers were included in the 1965 Vocational Rehabilitation Act Amendments, which also established the National Commission on Architectural Barriers.[50] Endorsed by Mary Switzer and her assistant, Kathleen Arneson, who lobbied heavily for an architectural barriers law, as well as established groups like PVA, the special committee lent "much weight in opening more doors for the disabled."[51]

Harold Russell would have to wait, however, until 1967 to testify about architectural barriers at a hearing convened by B. Everett Jordan (D-NC), chair of the Senate Subcommittee on Public Buildings and Grounds.[52] The hearing was about Sen. Bob Bartlett's bill to ensure that public buildings financed with federal funds were so "designed and constructed as to be accessible to the physically handicapped."[53] This would become the Architectural Barriers Act (ABA) of 1968,[54] a law that "was not the initiative of an interest group, technical experts, or government agencies" but the pet project of Bartlett, motivated by a personal experience in which his aide had been unable to access the National Gallery.[55]

Apparently, the proposed legislation purposely emphasized "public buildings" to ensure that it was sent to the Committee on Public Works (within which Jordan's Subcommittee on Public Buildings and Grounds operated), chaired by Jennings Randolph, a key disability rights entrepreneur. As they would so many other times, policy makers strategically used cues to signal assignments of legislative proposals to favorable venues.

In his testimony, Russell acknowledged that "the movement to alter the physical environment for the benefit of the handicapped owes its beginning and present-day momentum to the Federal Government."[56] Twelve Democrats and six Republicans cosponsored the bill in a display of bipartisanship Bartlett said was evidence of the "righteousness of this cause." The legislation sought an immediate remedy, compromising on the potential scope of its impact. It required only that newly constructed public buildings financed by the federal government be made accessible. Bartlett testified that he would be "opposed to amendment to this bill requiring alteration of *existing* public buildings" because that would be too expensive.[57] The attention to budget obviously facilitated bipartisan support for the law. Almost all who testified before the committee emphasized that the ABA reflected no extra costs in design and, according to Rep. Charles Bennett (D-FL), that "it is not a controversial matter, but it is vitally needed."[58] Indeed, no one voted against the ABA.

As chair of the PCEH, Russell testified about architectural barriers again before the 1968 House Select Subcommittee on Education in hearings regarding the Vocational Rehabilitation Act Amendments. It was originally assumed that the General Services Administration (GSA) would administer the law,[59] but Switzer and Arneson worked to include architectural barriers within the Vocational Rehabilitation Administration (VRA) under HEW's jurisdiction.[60] Arneson served as executive director of the newly created National Commission on Architectural Barriers, and Congress instructed the PCEH to promote awareness of the commission's efforts in making spaces accessible.[61] The disability policy network maintained control over all aspects of disability policy making.

The ABA was the first stand-alone federal legislation to emphasize reforming the environment rather than reshaping the person to fit the environment. It added an additional layer to the existing client-service policy model and opened a new door for a reconfigured policy paradigm. But it was an incremental step toward rights endogenous to the burgeoning disability policy community. The law was conceived in a fairly limited fashion and was not framed to be a matter of civil rights but "to ensure successful vocational rehabilitation," as Jordan testified, helping "the handicapped in their efforts to carry on a normal life."[62] The law made certain concessions—a strategy in getting legislation passed characteristic of disability policy making—and disability rights entrepreneurs would work for years to broaden the law's scope. The ABA was a modern piece of legislation because of what it sought to do and how it came about—a process that would inform policy making from Section 504 to IDEA to the ADA to ADARA.

Throughout the 1960s, the federal government "encroached" on issues previously left to states, such as education, health, and transportation,[63] and it promoted new policy areas, such as civil rights. Emerging disability rights entrepreneurs sought to move the political discourse on disability around questions that went beyond rehabilitation and architectural barriers. The elite-driven movement to extend their policy domain, however slowly, set the stage for a more explicit minority-rights language to punctuate disability policy making.

The Expanding Policy Community of Disability Rights Entrepreneurs

Congress in the 1960s was a place of upheaval. It saw significant turnover, new electoral and party realignments, Democratic presidents with a strong social policy agenda, and the collapse of a seniority system that had kept conservatives in charge of committees—venues where new social policy ideas could flourish. The obstacles that prevented liberals from pursuing social policy were largely giving way.[64] Still, as Nelson Polsby described, packing the committees was a "slow and difficult process," and liberalizing Congress was done "inch-by-inch over hostile terrain, a matter of two steps forward and one step back."[65]

Though social welfare dramatically expanded on the policy agenda,[66] not all policy networks felt the effects of these exogenous forces simultaneously. Disability was increasingly tied to the welfare politics of the 1960s, even though it was also a long-established policy area that held its ground throughout the decade. As this network grew into a broader community of actors who moved in and out of disability as it touched on other policy areas (including civil rights), policy elites adapted or filtered exogenous influences making them particular to their own political activities in the area. Both the ABA and Section 504 of the Rehabilitation Act were the result of elites acting as intermediaries between incremental shifts endogenous to their policy network and broader institutional

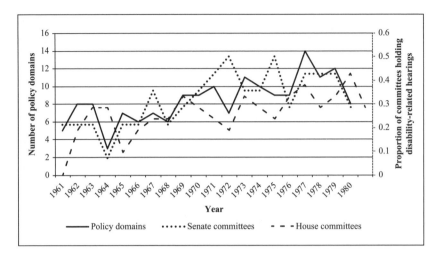

Figure 3.5 Expanding venues and issue diversity in disability, 1961–1980.

changes gripping the world outside. New ideas flourished through a creative combination of the existing client-service model and the emerging minority rights concept of disability.

In addition to the expanding jurisdictions *within* the House Committee on Education and Labor and Senate Committee on Labor and Public Welfare (see Figures 3.1 and 3.2), important macrolevel changes *between* venues also helped reshape the disability policy network. The late 1960s marked the beginning of a steady expansion in the number of venues holding hearings on disability-related issues (Figure 3.5). As a result, disability came into contact with an increased number of policy domains: from expected policy areas such as labor, education, health, and social welfare to transportation, public lands, law and crime, defense, and the nascent policy area of civil rights.[67]

New venues, actors, and overlapping issue domains helped topple institutional and cognitive constraints and expand the disability conversation beyond rehabilitation. Throughout the 1960s and 1970s, the number of hearings and overall hearing-days Congress spent on disability—a reflection of the institutional resources expended on the issue—rose substantially (Figures 3.6 and 3.7).[68] By the late 1970s, the number of disability-related hearings held by Congress had increased more than twofold.

Two additional trends point to the increasingly looser, more porous boundaries around disability policy making in this period (see Figures 3.6 and 3.7). First, hearings, while more frequent, became shorter. Where past hearings often

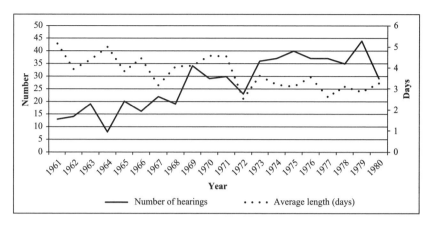

Figure 3.6 Disability-related congressional hearings, 1961–1980.

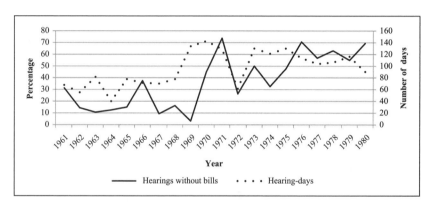

Figure 3.7 Hearing-days and nonbill referral hearings, 1961–1980.

lasted a week or more, now they might only take a day. Second, fewer hearings were held regarding actual policy proposals (i.e., bills). Instead, short hearings, unaffiliated with specific legislation, were used for pre-policy-making information gathering, precedence setting (so that future bills can strategically be referred to certain committees), turf building (such as expanding a policy area jurisdiction), and claims making (i.e., controlling how to define problems and legislative solutions).[69]

These trends were associated with the expansion of venues involved in disability; committees holding disability-related hearings even when they had few formal ties to the issue became part of the expanding disability policy network.[70] Increasingly overlapping jurisdictions resulted in more intense claims making by political elites seeking to secure their turf. Disability jurisdictional boundaries were increasingly shaped according to where discussions were held and by whom; thus, expanding committee interests helped sympathetic elites get disability rights onto the policy agenda (see Table A.3 in the appendix).

Soon there were competing policy frameworks. For the first time in forty years, conflict about the federal government's role in disability had set the stage for prolonged contention between disability advocates and detractors. That is, with more and more stakeholders attending to disability in more and more venues, a once-bipartisan issue was becoming truly contentious.

Conflicting Policy Images: Challenging the Status Quo

A relatively straightforward approach to disability became "messy" in the 1960s and 1970s. As political entrepreneurs expanded their focus by incorporating civil rights into existing service-provision paradigms, intense disagreements arose around the needs of the disabled. There is no better example than the policy battles fought over transportation, battles that, by the 1980s, moved outside government when disability organizations began to protest against what they viewed as the government's broken promises about ensuring equal access to transportation (the focus of Chapter 5).

Because Congress had an interest in urban renewal, both the House and Senate Committees on Banking and Currency held a series of hearings regarding urban mass transportation (an issue traditionally in their jurisdictions).[71] The hearings resulted in the Urban Mass Transportation Act of 1964.[72] The discussions had begun with 1960 efforts to amend the 1954 Housing Act, and disability factored into these discussions only because transit policy experts saw the elderly and disabled as new customers who would help reinvigorate mass transit. In 1961, various city mayors, as well as the US Conference of Mayors, testified about possible ways to better serve the young, the elderly, and the disabled— those thought least likely to have drivers' licenses and personal transportation.[73]

The following year, the committee heard testimony regarding Kennedy's mandate on housing and transportation, framing the needs of the disabled as "special problems."[74] Special problems required special solutions, and, for the most part, transportation for the disabled was defined as a matter of separate, cost-effective "paratransit" systems (such as Dial-a-Ride). In the wake of the Supreme Court case *Brown v. Board of Education of Topeka*,[75] which deemed segregation illegal, and with legislative momentum building around black civil rights, disability rights entrepreneurs would eventually seize on the "separate but (un)equal" transit solutions as the wrong policy approach for disabled

Americans. In the early 1960s, no one argued against what were thought of as pragmatic, effective, and efficient solutions to transportation for people with disabilities; the idea of anyone's *equal right* to mainstream public transit had not yet been recognized.

So disability was rather tangential in early discussions of urban mass transit. The House and Senate Committees on Banking and Currency, as well as the Department of Transportation (DOT), were largely outside the disability policy network, and none of their members were "experts" on disability (see Table A.2 in the appendix). Even within the disability policy network, as political elites in the late 1960s kick-started the architectural barriers–free movement, the issue of access to public transportation was barely raised.[76] When it was mentioned, it was within the dominant rehabilitation framework.[77] Timothy Nugent of the University of Illinois testified that "physical architectural barriers, or the inaccessibility of buildings and facilities and public transport, stand in the way of total rehabilitation."[78] As institutional and cognitive linkages between accessible buildings and transit began to emerge, no one at this hearing—not Katherine S. Fossett, who represented the National Association of the Physically Handicapped, or the director of the American Institute of Architects, despite the organization's support for making transit stations accessible—advocated for the accessibility of the actual buses and train cars.[79]

By March 1968, however, it was becoming clearer that some in the House Committee on Public Works, such as disability rights entrepreneur Kenneth Gray (who also chaired the Subcommittee on Public Buildings and Grounds), intended that the federal government would be picking up the tab if local transit authorities made their systems accessible. That year, Housing and Urban Development (HUD) contracted the National Academy of Sciences to investigate ways in which to make public transit systems accessible to the disabled, signaling a new government willingness to broaden the scope of the ABA to include equal access to public transportation. Entrepreneurs like Gray saw the government's role in disability policy as extending beyond rehabilitation to include equal rights and implementation of these objectives. Referring to HUD's regional offices, Gray insisted, "One thing I do know is that people in these regional offices have great authority in telling local housing authorities ... whether it is going to be designed this way or that. ... And if they can do that, they can insist in providing something to protect the handicapped."[80]

Just a few months later, Gray submitted a report regarding the ABA to the Committee of Conference.[81] Through that report, he ensured that all government agencies (e.g., HUD, DOT, and the Department of Defense) would have to consult with HEW in writing ABA regulations. Gray even dropped "reasonably" from "reasonably accessible" in the original language of the legislation, helping widen the definition of accessibility. This marked a deviation from the original intent of the law, as envisioned by its chief sponsor, Bob Bartlett. It also created a legislative precedent casting *reasonable* accessibility at odds with equal access and rights. This critical maneuver, which transpired *after* public debate over the proposed legislation had taken place, was just the tip of the brinksmanship that disability entrepreneurs would undertake.

By 1969, the movement around accessible spaces extended beyond public transit stations to include public-transit vehicles. An amendment to the recent ABA, which Gray cosponsored, struck out the term "personnel" and added "bus, subway car or train, or similar type of rolling stock."[82] The venue was crucial: This was done in the Subcommittee on Public Buildings and Grounds, which had jurisdiction over buildings but not transit vehicles. Transit systems were under the jurisdiction of Banking and Currency, whose membership was generally uninterested in disability as a policy area. As rights entrepreneurs worked to link architectural barriers to broader issues of equality (for a list of key entrepreneurs, see the Chapter 3 section in the appendix),[83] the barrier-free movement upset existing policy networks, creating "turf wars" between policy subsystems.[84]

"Special Efforts" in the Right to Equal Access

In 1970, newly elected representative Mario Biaggi from New York sought to amend Section 8 of the Urban Mass Transportation Act so that "elderly and handicapped persons have *the same right* as other persons to utilize mass transportation facilities and services."[85] This was among the first explicit uses of disability rights language in a policy proposal predating attempts by existing rights entrepreneurs to amend the 1964 Civil Rights Act in 1971. The language was neither envisioned nor sought by the authors of the Urban Mass Transportation Act or ABA.

How, then, did an "outsider" come to propose this important amendment? Biaggi, with no preexisting policy record, and certainly with no ties to disability or the transportation committee, was, according to Robert Katzmann's interview with Biaggi's assistant, looking for a cause to champion.[86] He framed his involvement as a logical extension of momentum in the disability policy community around equal access, especially the 1968 Vocational Rehabilitation Act

Amendments. He formed ties with Charles Bennett,[87] himself disabled and a strong supporter of the ABA (he would go on to champion the ADA in 1988), although not at the time working within the disability policy area. Biaggi's self-interested appearance in disability policy ended up having important consequences for a large group of Americans who had not yet in any appreciable way demanded their civil rights.

Biaggi's actions were significant in setting a precedent for disability rights for two related reasons. First, he clearly stated that rights for the disabled would not cost the government any extra money. Second, even if costs were a consideration, framing the issue as a matter of civil rights would mean that costs, whatever they might be, could not override fundamental rights. He testified, "We are not talking about specialized programs or adding to the Federal bureaucracy. We are simply talking about granting equal rights to a large segment of the population to use public facilities with the same ease as everyone else."[88]

No one appeared to object to the principles Biaggi laid out beyond considering the overall cost of the urban mass transit program. It helped that John Wright Patman,[89] chair of the House Committee on Banking and Currency, immediately censured dissent. He claimed that the committee had already determined costs and, if brought to conference, the House and Senate would still approve this amount. He continued that this is "the regular way to legislate" and that amending the original amount would be a slap in the committee's face.[90] Although Patman's position on the legislation had to do with procedure—preventing deliberations on a bill's content already agreed on by the committee—quashed potential opposition.

The end of the 1960s marked a growing schism between disability rights entrepreneurs calling for equal access, on the one hand, and public-transit policy networks that simply did not share in those norms, values, or policy experiences, on the other. Legislators promoting disability rights would testify in venues that were unreceptive to and inexperienced about their agenda; for instance, at hearings about the 1970 Federal-Aid Highway Act held by the House Subcommittee on Roads (a committee with no prior history in dealing with the right of disabled people to access public transit), William F. Ryan (D-NY), an advocate for civil rights, testified that "highways are useless to those who cannot or do not own a car. The poor, the elderly, and the handicapped cannot travel around if they do not drive, cannot afford taxis, and have no access to transportation systems."[91] His point, however, was tangential to the main objectives of these hearings and this committee's traditional jurisdiction. It would take a lot more creative entrepreneurship to make headway in this area.

The term "special efforts" began to appear across bills and legislation around 1970. It was often employed by Biaggi to refer to government efforts aimed at ensuring the right to equal access, for example, but there was no real definition for "special efforts" operating in policy circles. The term appeared in Section 16 of the 1970 Urban Mass Transportation Assistance Act,[92] which used the language of rights but also used the term "effectively utilize," which suggested effective mobility (including separate-but-equal measures) rather than equal access. Subsequent legislation, like the 1973 Federal-Aid Highway Act, used the phrase "adequate and reasonable access," and the conference report from the Senate Committee on Public Works that same year, which framed accessible transit as crucial in allowing people with disabilities to get to their jobs, called for "adequate transportation."

The intersection of two policy areas and the insertion of rights into legislation that otherwise had little to do with civil rights generated confusion about congressional intent—a criticism later lodged by opponents to disability rights legislation, including federal courts. Writing and implementing regulations became exceedingly problematic and conflict ridden. DOT interpreted "special efforts" as meaning any effective system that would provide transportation to the handicapped, not the equal right to mainstream transit.

Disability rights entrepreneurs like Gray, Biaggi, and Williams continued to fight for a definition of special efforts that included equal access and rights. In a protracted back and forth between a seemingly frustrated Gray and members of the Washington, D.C., transit authority, Gray publicly criticized the transit industry for failing to accommodate all handicapped people in the design of their systems.[93] A representative from the Washington Metropolitan Area Transit Authority, Warren Quenstedt, noted, "Over a long period of time there have been what I would call healthy disagreements between the persons representing the handicapped and all persons in the transit industry."[94] Ultimately, as Chapter 5 describes, these disagreements would become an outright battle between disability protesters and the transit industry.

When they were met with obstacles in specific policy jurisdictions, disability rights entrepreneurs used the appropriations process to pressure agencies to implement rights. In 1974, to pressure DOT, Biaggi proposed withholding funds for transit projects that did not guarantee equal access. The move was echoed in subsequent legislation, such as the Federal-Aid Highway Act Amendments of 1974,[95] the National Mass Transportation Assistance Act of 1974, and the National Mass Transportation Assistance Act Amendments of 1975.[96] The latter was authored by Williams and stated that all transit vehicles must be made accessible. Robert Stafford strongly supported the measure.

In the early 1970s many disability policy makers came to see that while the Committee on Public Works served as a highly favorable institutional context for promoting disability rights in transportation, the Committee on Banking and Currency (which maintained jurisdiction over transit systems) did not. As Banking and Currency blocked a rights-based policy approach to transportation, rights entrepreneurs found ways around this closure. Equal rights in transportation was a "big idea"—a policy innovation fraught with backtracking and retrenchment. As opposition to equal access became more organized in the late 1970s, costs, despite the insistence from rights entrepreneurs that they would not be a factor, became an important tool in justifying lax enforcement of accessibility policies.

Getting Civil Rights for the Disabled onto the Policy Agenda

In the early 1970s, attention to the issue of civil rights for minorities reached its peak;[97] America's minority rights revolution was in full swing. In 1971, disability rights entrepreneurs took a more comprehensive approach in establishing disability rights. Charles Vanik introduced a brief two-page amendment to Sections 601 and 605 of the 1964 Civil Rights Act that banned discrimination based on disability.[98] He worked closely with his aide (who was disabled) on issues facing people with disabilities in his district. Because Vanik's bill involved the Civil Rights Act, it was sent to the Judiciary Committee (which had a history of addressing civil rights issues for African Americans and, more recently, women).[99] However, the committee expressed little interest in holding hearings on the issue of disability.

In 1972, Hubert Humphrey, whose granddaughter had Down syndrome and was denied entry to kindergarten, and Chuck Percy (R-IL), a Rockefeller Republican elected four years earlier,[100] cosponsored Vanik's bill in the Senate.[101] Humphrey referred to "the hypocrisy of America" and having tolerated the "invisibility of the handicapped." Revealing his personal experience with disability, Humphrey stated that "too often we keep children, whom we regard as 'different' or as a 'disturbing influence,' out of our schools and community activities altogether, rather than help them develop their abilities in special classes and programs."[102]

Despite their efforts, the amendment failed. Political entrepreneurs found workarounds: chair of the Senate Labor and Public Welfare Committee, Harrison Williams, created the Subcommittee on the Handicapped in 1972—a committee that, according to Cranston, served "as a viable and dynamic forum in which the problems of handicapped Americans can be freely discussed and dealt with."[103] In this new favorable venue, political elites could ensure that rights became part of the Vocational Rehabilitation Act Amendments of 1972.

The subcommittee was composed of mostly liberal members and, in the early part of the decade, had an average CC score of only 24, compared to more than 50 in the overall Senate (see Figure A.3). The committee was stacked in a way to guarantee that rights would be the prevailing policy image of legislation coming before it, not just because it had a liberal disposition but also because it included members that were committed to civil rights for the disabled. Williams was the creator (and a member) of the committee, which also included Jennings Randolph as its chair, Robert Stafford, Jacob Javits, Edward (Ted) Kennedy (D-MA), Alan Cranston, Adlai Stevenson (D-IL), Walter Mondale (D-MN), and Claiborne Pell (D-RI).

In May 1972, the subcommittee held its first hearing to discuss numerous Senate bills related to the Vocational Rehabilitation Act Amendments.[104] Cranston believed the "consumers" of vocational rehabilitation programs must have a voice in the hearings to amend the legislation (he attributed this to knowledge gleaned during his time as chair of the Veterans' Affairs Subcommittee of the Labor and Public Welfare Committee), and the committee would subsequently become an important venue for disability organizations to express their views and become involved in the policy process.

Section 2 of the 1972 Vocational Rehabilitation Act Amendments outlined four main objectives: to continue to provide services, ensure that rehabilitation leads to gainful employment, develop new innovations in rehabilitation, and expand existing and initiate new services. Nowhere in the policy's objectives does rights or antidiscrimination language appear, though it had briefly featured in the discussions when committee members agreed that discrimination was wrong in education and employment and that Vanik's original civil rights amendment would have helped in that regard.

Disability rights evolved, instead, as the Subcommittee on the Handicapped held more hearings. The National Association of the Physically Handicapped and the Center for Concerned Engineering linked the success of rehabilitation to outlawing discrimination.[105] Unlike the first hearing, a new set of amendments introduced later in 1972 included a Section 604: "No otherwise qualified handicapped or severely handicapped individual in the United States, as defined in section 6 of this Act, shall, solely by reason of his handicap, be excluded from the participation in, be denied the benefits of, or be subjected to discrimination under any program actively receiving Federal financial assistance."[106] The bill was written and sponsored by Randolph, Williams, Cranston, Stafford, Javits, Robert Taft Jr. (R-OH), John Glenn Beall Jr. (R-MD), Thomas F. Eagleton (D-MI), Ted Kennedy, Mondale, Pell, and Stevenson.

Thus, the spirit of Vanik's bill found its way into legislation that had no original mandate to extend rights to people with disabilities. Its primary goal was to reauthorize rehabilitation programs. Nonetheless, the bill sailed through the Senate with little controversy. A veto by President Nixon, not because it contained a civil rights mandate but because it was "a waste of taxpayer dollars,"[107] raised some outside interest around the Rehabilitation Act.

In early 1973, by Cranston's own account,[108] Randolph had resubmitted virtually the same bill.[109] Section 600, which proposed the creation of the Office of the Handicapped under HEW, and Section 705 would now contain the antidiscrimination provision without the term "severely handicapped." Of significance is that the antidiscrimination and rights language included in the legislation was purely the design of political entrepreneurs in the Senate, not the House. In fact, the Committee on Conference noted this discrepancy. Ultimately, the House ceded the point.[110]

At hearings about Randolph's 1973 bill, Gloria Wright of NARC urged that vocational rehabilitation must not discriminate against people with severe mental impairment, especially those who would be released from institutions under Nixon's support for continued deinstitutionalization. Among the disability policy community, only John F. Nagel of the NFB testified specifically about the antidiscrimination provision. Nagel stated that it would bring "the disabled within the law when they have been so long outside of the law."[111] Not surprisingly, the organization TenBroek founded had a long history of advocating for nondiscrimination in employment as part of the right to independence. The group was then more than thirty years old, but it was still evolving along with the normative and cultural shifts brought about by federal disability policy and responding to emerging political opportunities to expand the concept of rights and nondiscrimination.

Nixon again vetoed the bill, citing costs, and the Senate failed to override his veto. Again, detractors never mentioned the antidiscrimination provision. According to a *New York Times* article in July 1973, the Senate Committee on Labor and Public Works promised to work with the White House in lowering proposed costs, already ninety-two million dollars over the administration's budget requests.[112] Randolph reintroduced a scaled-down version of the amendment in the Senate, and John Brademas did the same in the House.[113] The new version retained the antidiscrimination language and became Section 504 of the 1973 Rehabilitation Act.

Section 504 was the behind-the-scenes work of political entrepreneurs. Those outside the disability policy network saw this wrangling as just another reauthorization of the Vocational Rehabilitation Act. Inasmuch as those outside the disability policy area were paying attention to disability politics, the law was generally regarded as "designed to help the handicapped prepare themselves for employment," not to establish a civil rights act for the disabled.[114] When Nixon finally signed the Rehabilitation Act into law in September 1973, he referred to it as an example of executive-legislative leadership in which he had been forced into the "painful" position of vetoing the law to protect fiscal responsibility. By the mid-1970s, however, the rights language would become a much more significant part of the political discourse surrounding the federal government's role in disability policy.

Entrenching Disability Rights

Entrepreneurs used their resources to champion, wherever possible, a rights-based approach. When the environment was nonresponsive, they sought to change or reconfigure venues to their advantage. Their objective was to ensure the longevity of disability rights through the legislation's incumbency, structure, and implementation,[115] all of which would be contested in the years to come. In the meantime, now that civil rights for people with disabilities was codified in legislation, the disability rights policy network governed over a growing political interest in disability. Policy begot more attention and more legislative proposals (see the Chapter 3 section in the appendix).[116]

The Subcommittee on Urban Mass Transportation, considerably more conservative than the Subcommittee on the Handicapped,[117] wanted to maintain jurisdiction over transportation. Despite its preexisting claims on transportation, the committee quickly encountered competition from the House Committee on Public Works. But in 1975, Public Works won jurisdiction over public transportation. The committee was not any more liberal and did not have any more formal claims over disability than the Committee on Banking and Currency (in fact, it had a narrower issue focus than Banking and Currency; see the Chapter 3 section in the appendix).[118] Yet it was more sympathetic to the rights-based approach championed by disability rights entrepreneurs; after all, Kenneth Gray was the chair.

Williams was also a key figure in the Senate Committee on Banking, Housing, and Urban Affairs (formerly the Senate Banking and Currency Committee). This committee had no formal jurisdiction over disability, but it did have a relatively large and heterogeneous jurisdiction that included transportation (see the Chapter 3 section in the appendix). In his capacity as a member, Williams promoted the Biaggi Amendment. To compel DOT to pursue HEW's Section 504 regulations, Williams held 1975 hearings regarding the Urban Mass Transportation Act before the Subcommittee on Housing and Urban Affairs.[119] He made it clear that all aspects of public transit, including vehicles, must be made equally accessible to all people with disabilities and that the secretary of DOT "shall not approve any program or project unless he finds that such requirements have been complied with."[120]

Although Housing and Urban Affairs was chaired by a Southern conservative Democrat (John Sparkman of Alabama), it had an average CC score of 36; that is, in comparison to the other committees involved in the issue as well as the Senate as a body, it was quite liberal. The subcommittee included Williams, Cranston, Joseph Biden (D-DE), and Edward Brooke, a liberal Republican from Massachusetts and the first African American elected to the Senate. Together, they invited testimony from established groups like PVA that pushed for a rights approach. The committee's hearings served to undermine the effective mobility paradigm (such as paratransit) that had been promoted by the transit policy subgovernment for the last decade.

With competing policy images around equal access, disability was becoming a disorganized policy subarea. Conflict intensified. The field included disability rights entrepreneurs like Williams who clearly supported equal rights; the PCEH, which argued that a separate transportation system would still be needed;[121] and public transit authorities and bureaucrats in DOT who championed effective mobility, not equal rights. There was also growing debate between HEW, DOT, PCEH, and Williams about whether equal rights should be sent back to Congress for further legislative clarity or be pursued through the regulatory process. Williams argued that for the last five years, Congress had made its intentions about equal access known, alluding to a frustration with some in the Executive Branch (e.g., DOT), whom he saw as reluctant in promoting congressional intent.

Adding to these voices, the Subcommittee on Housing and Urban Affairs heard from APTA, the interest group representing public transit authorities. APTA would, especially in the 1980s, become a main target for disability protesters (discussed in Chapter 5), and it favored dealing with regulations rather than revisiting legislation in Congress. APTA likely thought it had more clout with regulatory bodies, especially with DOT (with which it had an established rapport), and hoped that by keeping the conversation in the Executive Branch and bypassing Congress, it could prevent "special efforts" from being interpreted as equal access. APTA vehemently objected to lawmakers' use of the phrase "the same rights as everyone else."

No clear idea yet existed in the late 1970s about how disability rights would be implemented, regulated, and enforced. Political entrepreneurs in Congress relied heavily on their staff as well as members of the Executive Branch to promote a rights-based policy image following the passage of the Rehabilitation Act. Staffers, particularly William's aide, Lisa Walker, and Randolph's aide, Bob Humphreys, worked intimately on the Rehabilitation Act and continued to influence the course of subsequent legislation.[122] They worked on the 1974 Rehabilitation Act Amendments,[123] sponsored by Brademas, which were once again vetoed, this time by President Gerald Ford (the Senate overrode the veto).[124] Walker and other staffers like Patricia Forsythe (also one of Randolph's aides) and Nik Edes (another of Williams's staffers) were involved in the Education for All Handicapped Children Act, in which they proposed providing funds to states to improve mainstream education for disabled children,[125] and the Education Amendments of 1974.[126] In this way, rights language made it into legislation. For instance, in 1975, Edes, Walker, and Walker's intern, Judy Heumann, worked on the Developmental Disabilities Services and Facilities Construction Act. Although the law dealt mainly with the construction of institutions, a section was included "ensuring that the human and civil rights of these persons are not violated."[127]

Staffers were repeatedly recognized by lawmakers such as Williams and Cranston, as well as Randolph, who thanked them for their "hours of study and research."[128] Referring to their work on a bill targeting developmental disability, Randolph claimed that the "intensive" efforts of people like Walker, Forsythe, and Humphreys "are the basis of this vitally needed bill."[129] Walker and other staff were also critical in liaising with members of Congress and the White House. They were central players in the disability rights network linking members of HEW, the Committee on Labor and Public Welfare, the Subcommittee on the Handicapped, the House Select Subcommittee on Education chaired by Brademas, and the House Committee on Education and Labor chaired by Carl Perkins. They were also instrumental in coordinating with disability organizations, including the newer advocacy groups that had emerged in the early 1970s, such as DIA, the advocacy group founded by Judy Heumann. In fact, staffers' efforts in bringing disability groups into the legislative process was encouraged by rights entrepreneurs.

Williams, along with Cranston and Randolph, worked hard to ensure that HEW, particularly the OCR, won jurisdiction over developing and implementing disability rights regulations. Walker, Heumann, Humphreys, Edes, and Forsythe were instrumental in those efforts. At the same time, the OCR was particularly entrepreneurial in expanding its role in civil rights matters; it saw Section 504 as an important part of that project. The OCR, often operating independently of HEW, made every effort possible to secure jurisdiction. In 1976, pressured by rights entrepreneurs like Vanik as well as incumbent and newer disability political advocacy groups, President Ford's Executive Order 11914 made HEW *the* agency tasked with writing Section 504 regulations. The executive order compelled all other agencies, including DOT, to subscribe to HEW's regulations and gave HEW responsibility for defining the terms "handicapped" and "discrimination." Members of the OCR, in consultation with legislative staffers, actually drafted Ford's executive order.

Martin Gerry, director of the OCR, and John Wodatch, acting director of new projects in the OCR, oversaw Section 504 regulations. Neither had prior experience with disability policy, but both had experience with civil rights enforcement concerning gender and race in health and education. They expected that they should treat Section 504 similarly, given Gerry's testimony that "the pattern set up for civil rights enforcement . . . is clearly appropriate for the section 504 responsibilities."[130] Wodatch saw this as a way to grow professionally, and staffers told Richard Scotch that "Wodatch felt that the job provided him with a good opportunity to be in charge of a big project from start to finish and to gain experience with policy development."[131]

Now that the administration formally recognized HEW's role in implementing disability rights law, the agency expanded. It brought in new staff, such as Raymond Keith and Ed Lynch, who fit well with the entrepreneurial spirit of the

office. Both men saw Section 504 broadly, testifying before a 1976 Subcommittee on the Handicapped hearing that it should extend to those being discriminated against because of cancer, epilepsy, and heart problems.[132] Gerry assured
Randolph that despite proposals to decentralize HEW,[133] he would ensure that
the focus remained on keeping "a centralized administration of the section 504
program. . . . We would propose to have a centrally-directed, specially policy-
development-oriented 504 operation." Randolph replied, "That is realistic."[134]

Although Section 504 was a product of entrepreneurship and received little
outside attention, HEW and the OCR became key players in disseminating information about it to the disability community. They consulted a wide range
of organizations, from incumbent groups such as Easter Seals, Goodwill, and
the NRA, to newer political advocacy groups such as the ACCD and DIA. Gerry
claimed, "We have developed and maintained personal contacts with many of
these individuals and groups."[135]

It seemed at first that political entrepreneurs were succeeding in establishing self-reinforcing mechanisms for disability rights policy through activist
public agencies and the growing involvement of disability groups with a stake
in policy success. Gerry was eager to begin enforcing these rights. The problem
was that it was 1976—three years since Section 504 and the Rehabilitation Act
has been passed—and no compliance regulations had been issued. Williams
questioned Gerry about the delay. He was growing concerned that they had
missed the opportunity to entrench disability rights policies and that their future was in jeopardy. As policy makers noticed the reluctance in implementing
legislation, disability groups and activists began to mobilize against the government that had promised but failed to deliver their civil rights.

"So Far So Fast"

The disability rehabilitation–focused policy subsystem that flourished under
the Great Society shared a core philosophy with the objectives of the War on
Poverty.[136] By the latter half of the decade, the largest plurality in history would
oversee the culmination of the incremental work of actors in the 1950s and
early 1960s seeking to increase the government's role in disability. A changing
institutional context allowed the release of pent-up frustration between those
seeking significant social change and an old guard blocking their efforts. Complex and overlapping areas within social policy expanded,[137] and inequalities
based in disability status were increasingly seen by both elites and everyday

Americans as a "social problem" rather than just a medical or service-provision problem.

A generation after the passage of the 1954 Vocational Rehabilitation Act, disability rights were part of the national conversation about civil rights and minorities. This would not have happened without the institutional work of political entrepreneurs.[138] They considered themselves "the Martin Luther Kings of the disability movement on Capitol Hill and in the government.... The movement [of disabled people] was stimulated by the acts of a very few individuals who were in the legislative branch."[139] They made it acceptable that the government should protect this group from discrimination and promote their civil rights. Larry Malloy, director of the National Art and Handicapped Information Service, told a *New York Times* reporter in June 1978:

> It would hardly be socially acceptable to make negative remarks about the handicapped. There are stronger taboos against that than against, say, making a racist or chauvinistic remark. That's why the drive for civil rights for the handicapped has gotten so far so fast. There's really no organized opposition.[140]

Disability rights got so far so fast because skilled entrepreneurs made it part of the policy agenda. They creatively combined new and old ideas about disability, bypassing obstacles inherent in amending the Civil Rights Act while, unfortunately, bypassing the Civil Rights Act itself. As activists inside and outside the government were learning, disability rights would not benefit from the kinds of implementation and enforcement mechanisms associated with the Civil Rights Act (including the 1972 Equal Employment Opportunity Act that allowed the Equal Employment Opportunity Commission to define discrimination and to initiate its own enforcement proceedings of the Civil Rights Act).[141]

Crucial to political elites' vigilance and activism in seeking to entrench rights were the important relationships they forged with a variety of disability groups that would become critical in championing rights, especially when the government began to back-step on disability rights. Malloy's comments reflected a widespread belief among disability rights entrepreneurs that no one would think to oppose rights for the disabled—that was uncontroversial and bipartisan.[142] Yet pushback would eventually develop into full-on backlash against disability rights in the 1980s.

The government's retreat from disability rights had important consequences for the relationship between institutional activists and the advocacy groups and grassroots activists of the late 1970s and 1980s. Political entrepreneurs relied on nonstate actors to fight for the cause, since institutional obstacles tied their hands. This catapulted the growing number of disability advocacy organizations into sustained conflict with the federal government and necessitated extra-institutional pressure tactics if the government was to make good on disability rights.

4 How Disability Advocacy Made Citizens out of Clients

What began as an effort to remove architectural barriers has broadened and developed over the years into an advocacy effort that encompasses programmatic access and employment discrimination as well. This involvement, in a very real sense, parallels the gradual change in the societal view toward disabled persons. We are coming to realize that while physical barriers are still a critical, urgent problem, the more insidious and often more formidable barriers to a rewarding life are those caused by stereotypical attitudes and prejudices.
—B. Richmond Dudley Jr. (Paralyzed Veterans of America), *Equal Employment Opportunity for the Handicapped Act of 1979* hearing, 1979

THE GOVERNMENT WAS AHEAD of the public on disability rights. But to secure significant and long-lasting social change, the message would need to be disseminated broadly across segments of the American population. By the end of the 1970s, as B. Richmond Dudley Jr. notes in the epigraph, advocacy groups would shape disability culture and collective identity. These, in turn, would become the basis for the contemporary disability rights movement.

It is important, however, to situate these organizational vehicles of change—these mobilizing structures[1]—in the preexisting organizational field that is among the oldest and largest in the United States. Many of these groups grew alongside America's "belated" welfare state, empowering policy makers to pursue service-oriented policies that brought more clients into contact with rehabilitation programs. They legitimized the efforts of this policy monopoly of which many elite groups were a part.

As Figure 4.1 illustrates, the disability sector increased steadily throughout the 1960s and 1970s.[2] Throughout the 1970s, disability organizational density outpaced racial and ethnic organizations and, in the early 1980s, women's groups too. The expansion was, in part, a response to growing issue attention and expanding political opportunities; new venues were becoming available for claims-making activity (see Table A.4 in the appendix). As Theda Skocpol has

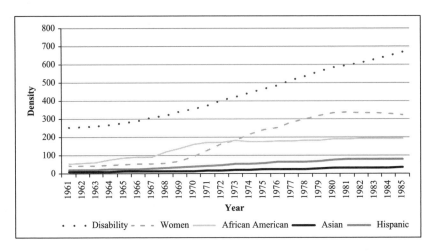

Figure 4.1 Nonprofit organizational density by constituency, 1961–1985. *Source:* Data on women, African American, Asian, and Hispanic organizations provided courtesy of Debra Minkoff; disability organization data from analysis of *Encyclopedia of Associations,* 1961–1985. *Note:* Density is the number of existing active organizations at the end of the year plus the number of new organizations minus those that became inactive or defunct.

described, "New modes of ongoing access to government favored the proliferation of professionally run advocacy groups and nonprofit institutions."[3]

Between 1961 and passage of the Rehabilitation Act in 1973, the disability organizational sector grew by 67 percent. At the same time, many existing, already-large federated organizations saw dramatic increases in their membership, including Disabled American Veterans, National Multiple Sclerosis Society, NFB, NRA, and NARC. As newer, smaller organizations joined the fold, finding their footholds in the late 1960s and early 1970s, median membership declined somewhat, as the largest groups' memberships were balanced by that of their much smaller counterparts.

For the most part, even within the movement decade of the 1960s when so many constituencies were working toward minority rights expansion,[4] disability groups were not mobilizing around civil rights. But when Dudley described how movement in the government evolved into broader political advocacy that would come to include well-established organizations like his, he was describing a fundamental shift in the goals, strategies, and tactics of disability organizations.

These profound changes to disability groups partially grew out of those broader shifts in the American nonprofit and social movement sectors: the minority rights revolution and the advocacy explosion of the 1970s, including feminist, LGBTQ, and environmental groups. Groups in related sectors, such as those representing senior citizens, were moving away from service provision and toward political activism in the 1970s and 1980s.[5] Organizers responded to changes in political opportunities and resource flows through a process Debra Minkoff defined as the "institutional ecology of organizational development."[6]

In much the same way the Civil Rights Act and Economic Opportunity Act created opportunities for institutional advocacy across the nonprofit sector in the 1960s, the policy focus on equal access and rights exemplified by the Architectural Barriers Act, Rehabilitation Act, and the Education for All Handicapped Children Act created new political opportunities for both long-established groups and new upstarts to get involved in disability advocacy.

"The Edge of Change"

Taking their lead from policy makers, venerable organizations such as Easter Seals became involved in the fight to remove architectural barriers by framing the problem as a matter of national economic interest.[7] Following the ABA, disability groups expanded their efforts, beginning to champion the full removal of all kinds of barriers to participation, especially in education and labor markets. Rather than challenge existing policy, these efforts were made to fit national policy objectives. As a representative of the NFB put it in 1968, "It has long been the established policy of the U.S. Government to encourage and enable physically disabled persons to participate fully in the social and economic life of the Nation, and to engage in remunerative and constructive employment."[8]

In light of policies such as the ABA and the Biaggi Amendment, organizations worked with policy elites to prepare the ground for a more vigorous pursuit of disability rights. In 1969, the President's Committee on Mental Retardation introduced a 1968 document titled "The Edge of Change" into the record.[9] It featured Lyndon Johnson on the cover with a quote, "We cannot rest as long as there is one child who becomes retarded through our neglect, one individual who lacks the care he needs because of our indifference, one person who fails to reach his potential . . . no matter how limited."[10] While it served mainly to outline disabled citizens' service needs, the committee's document notably included a declaration of general and special rights for people with cognitive disabilities, using UN language as a model.

That year, the Senate Subcommittee on Health held hearings about the Developmental Disabilities Services and Facilities Construction Act introduced by Ted Kennedy and cosponsored by many rights entrepreneurs.[11] The sub-committee was known as one that paid heed to civil rights, though the legislation at hand was mainly a service provision and program expansion bill meant to help states deal with people who, twenty years earlier, would have been institutionalized. Nevertheless, the bill gained strong support from UCP and NARC and contained signals of a more comprehensive understanding of the plight of Americans with disabilities as both a minority group and as a civil rights–bearing constituency.

Disability organizations evolved and adapted alongside these institutional and ideological changes. Sherwood Messner of UCP described the evolution of his organization's efforts and focus: "In the beginning, UCP affiliates stressed treating what was physically correctable. . . . The knowledge that cerebral palsied children lag in development behind normal youngsters has more recently stimulated the establishment of nursery, preschool and developmental centers, special 'head start' programs for children with multiple handicaps." In his testimony, Messner assured the committee that, in addition to services, training, and rural and urban outreach, the bill could help UCP with its new goals and efforts aiding in protecting disabled Americans' "civil and human rights."[12]

Like so many other organizations, UCP was embedded in a policy network. It was working within its boundaries, seeking to incrementally expand the conversation without challenging policy objectives. Rarely, in this period, did leaders of the disability community outright reject the social service–oriented objectives of the federal government meant to improve the lives of disabled Americans. Even the newer advocacy organizations, such as DIA, framed their calls for rights and antidiscrimination legislation around the inclusion of the disabled as productive, employable citizens rather than tax burdens. If the goal was civil rights for the disabled, the language of economic and social integration would be the Trojan Horse smuggling those rights into policy.

Members of the disability policy network often commented on the mutually beneficial relationship between lawmakers and disability groups, which was long-standing. Messner concluded his testimony before the Senate Subcommittee on Health by stating, "The voluntary sector and the state and federal governments can provide a comprehensive program to maximize the potential of all of the developmentally disabled."[13] The very next day, NARC's Boggs told Chairman Yarborough, "When NARC was organized, there had been little Federal activity in behalf of the retarded. Thanks to our friends in Congress, support was slowly built up during the 1950's and it has been only in this present decade that concerted Federal support for a range of necessary programs for the handicapped has become evident."[14]

Disability rights entrepreneurs were similarly quick to point to their allies in the voluntary sector. The Developmental Disabilities Assistance and Bill of Rights Act's chief supporter, Jennings Randolph, made it clear that any program coming from this policy would involve disability groups who had been advocating for improved services.[15] In his discussion of the groundwork already laid toward guaranteeing that institutionalized individuals' civil rights were not violated, Randolph said that such efforts "are the fruition of a partnership of governmental agencies, of professional organizations of practitioners in the field, and of consumer representatives, working together in the interest of improving services to mentally retarded and other developmentally disabled persons."[16] Many of these organizations relied on funding built into these policies.

And in his opening remarks, House Select Subcommittee on Education chair John Brademas attributed the success of rehabilitation to "the working relationship between the Federal agency and its partner, the State rehabilitation agencies, and, third, the unique involvement of voluntary agencies as major suppliers of services for a publicly supported program."[17] Brademas acknowledged the traditional role of incumbent disability organizations in promoting the social welfare of their constituents and providing the services the government funded.

In the early 1970s, disability groups saw themselves as preservationists: they guarded against cutbacks to the policies they had worked so hard to establish. As the executive director of the NRA told Brademas, these organizations ensured that programs were not completely incapacitated from lack of funding.[18] They also worked with disability rights entrepreneurs to broaden the conversation about the role of rehabilitation in a context of growing economic inequality and pervasive labor-market discrimination. A panel of leaders representing numerous organizations for the blind, including the American Foundation for the Blind, NFB, and Catholic Guild for All the Blind, testified about their role in ensuring program expansion, coverage, and improving delivery and services in the face of continual social and economic obstacles. One leader testified, "Too many of the severely handicapped who have a potential for normal, ordinary employment are in workshops at substandard wages without ordinary fringe benefits."[19] In the face of persistent discrimination, disability groups would have to simultaneously protect the funding and government support they had and work to advance policies to protect their constituents' rights.

Since much of the rights focus occurred outside the hearings process and without the express involvement of disability groups, what little public conversation there was revolved mainly around the Nixon administration's cuts to rehabilitation programs. Little did disability organizations know that disability rights entrepreneurs would turn the renewal of policies governing vocational rehabilitation into the linchpin of the disability rights project.

The Demand for Political Advocacy

Congressional intent on civil rights for people with disabilities came by way of the 1973 Rehabilitation Act, a law that otherwise had little to do with rights. Thus, the demand for political advocacy around civil rights cannot be entirely divorced from a demand for advocacy to promote, protect, and expand social services. Disability organizations, however, would be forever changed by the new politics of disability brought about by policy innovations such as Section 504, which undoubtedly rendered certain organizational modes outdated. Referring to HEW secretary F. David Mathews, Martin Gerry of the OCR claimed, "He really just didn't get the idea that these were rights and that you really weren't talking about nice things to do for Easter Seal Children. . . . These were obviously derelicts and they were so far from Easter Seal Children, things had truly run amok."[20]

Service organizations continued to be a dominant strategic organizational form (today they still represent the majority of all active disability organizations); the 1970s saw a leveling off and then a decline in the formation of new service groups (Figure 4.2). At the same time, political advocacy became an increasingly more salient and legitimate way for organizers to mobilize the disability constituency.

The "new face" of disability groups was the result of two related process: the adoption of advocacy by long-established service-provision groups and the proliferation of newly created advocacy organizations. Between 1971 and 1982, fifty-one disability organizations moved away from service provision in favor of some form of political advocacy (there had been no such recorded shifts in the 1960s).[21] Much of the change to either advocacy or to a service-advocacy hybrid (about 70 percent of all recorded change) occurred between 1975 (the year with the most change) and 1978.

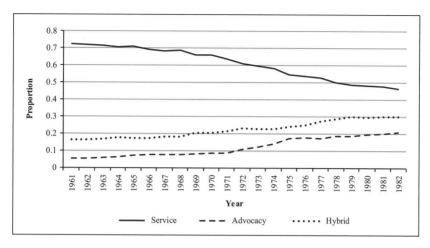

Figure 4.2 The rise of advocacy in the disability nonprofit sector, 1961–1982. *Source:* Data from analysis of *Encyclopedia of Associations*, 1961–1982.

During this period, for example, organizers in the deaf and blind communities, many representing groups that had flourished under the client-service rehabilitation policy regime, responded to policy shifts spearheaded by political entrepreneurs. Newer service groups founded in the 1960s, such as the National Society for Autistic Children and Mothers of Young Mongoloids (a.k.a. Parents of Down Syndrome Children), appeared to easily transition to political advocacy as part of their central strategy. And many well-established organizations (such as Easter Seals, which Gerry referred to as a "derelict") adopted advocacy as part of their core strategy in efforts to modernize.

Organizers in the 1970s were inclined to adopt institutional advocacy as a viable and legitimate strategy to foster a more politically oriented identity, increase political participation, and work with political elites on (among other things) rights-oriented policy, which included mounting pressure on the government to commit to newly enshrined disability rights laws. The 1970s saw a host of new advocacy groups providing the necessary organizational basis to sustain prolonged political challenges against the growing belief that disability rights policy was untenable (by the 1980s, this view was quite pervasive in government). As the next chapter illustrates, advocacy groups did this by providing important material and psychological resources needed to coordinate and sustain disruptive protest throughout the 1980s and 1990s.

Deaf and blind organizations, which were among the most established in the nonprofit sector in America, experienced a particularly significant move toward political advocacy. Deafpride, founded in 1972, directed its efforts at policy-oriented and consciousness-raising activities. It worked to fight against shame and stigma associated with deafness, promoting a stronger, more politicized deaf culture. The National Alliance of Blind Students, created in 1974, emerged as young blind Americans sought to expand political and legislative advocacy and consciousness-raising campaigns among existing groups like the American Council of the Blind. And in 1977, the Rainbow Alliance of the Deaf sought to improve the social welfare of gay and lesbian deaf people while also mobilizing new disability rights laws.

A related trend in the voluntary sector was a move toward increased representation of people with disabilities within the leadership of existing groups. Even though most groups encouraged a diverse membership that included nondisabled allies, people with disabilities wanted to be instrumental in mobilizing people with disabilities. This fundamentally changed the image of service provision. As Frank Bowe of ACCD testified in 1978 before the House Subcommittee on Select Education, these organizations "share the conviction that disabled people deserve and reserve the right to speak for themselves in the determination of needs and priorities in the provision of services."[22]

All this new attention focused on disability rights within the halls of government empowered advocates, activists, and organizers to leverage their political opportunities. Three notable rights groups emerged in 1976: The Disability Rights Center, a group influenced in part by Ralph Nader's consumer rights movement; the National Legislative Council for the Handicapped; and the Mental Disability Legal Resource Center, which, along with the National Center for Law and the Handicapped founded five years earlier, monitored policy developments and framed their efforts in improving economic opportunities through civil rights legislation.

"A Backlash Reverse": How Much Will It Cost to Be Fair?

> There is no great enthusiasm for attending to the will of Congress in these matters on the part of the administration.
> —John Brademas, *Vocational Rehabilitation Services to the Handicapped* hearing, 1972

Section 504 of the Rehabilitation Act would become symbolic of a growing movement's efforts to change the way Americans thought about and treated people with disabilities. "Section 504 regulations are not just another series of dull, impersonal bureaucratic regulations; they represent fresh civil rights legislation affecting the lives of over 25 percent of our country's population. They are the logical follow up to the civil rights legislation of 1964 which concerned itself with racial discrimination," testified Thomas P. Carroll of the National Center for Law and the Handicapped.[23] Although policies provided important language and frames to the disability community, activists and organizational leaders' motivation to mobilize against the state is more accurately understood as a drive to protect against threats to newly enshrined rights.

By the end of Johnson's presidency, political opportunities for the expansion of civil rights in general were contracting. It was a period of rising anti–Great Society sentiment in which welfare provision programs were framed as costly social failures.[24] Nixon's assault meant cutting social programs, refusing to appropriate new funds, letting programs expire, and undermining program efficacy to justify terminations (closure via neglect).[25] Nixon eliminated the RSA's Division for the Blind and Visually Handicapped, which had been operating since 1936. Irvin P. Schloss, a legislative analyst for the American Foundation for the Blind, testified that the move "was done without any kind of public hearings or any consultation with the concerned public."[26]

Nixon became the first president in decades to make no comprehensive legislative requests regarding disability policy.[27] He gained a reputation for vetoing legislation (including the Rehabilitation Act), proclaiming, as he did in his 1970 message to Congress, that this was the "new realism to the management of our economic policies."[28] His actions and inactions would set the tone for at least the next three administrations. Trying to make sense of the administration's position regarding the Rehabilitation Act, Alan Cranston referred to Nixon's veto as "incomprehensible as the act of disapproval itself,"[29] and a frustrated Brademas saw the administration's position on disability as navigating a "jungle of its convoluted process."[30]

Disability groups reminded policy makers of the promises the federal government had made around rights and antidiscrimination. For the first time, the disability policy network faced a significant uphill battle in mobilizing the policies they enacted. Despite the "policy victory" of Section 504 and IDEA, for example, proponents and activists charged that the policies had not reached their full potential in improving educational and employment outcomes. Discriminatory attitudes and practices had not significantly changed, and the government seemed unwilling to give their policies teeth.

On the future of disability policy, Brademas clearly felt that lawmakers were being kept in the dark. He sarcastically asked whether someone might "be kind enough to send a postcard to the administration asking them if they will tell the members of Congress what they have in mind."[31] Congress and the administration were becoming outright adversarial regarding Section 504 enforcement.

Thus, dissatisfied with the OCR and HEW's inaction on Section 504, disability rights entrepreneurs in Congress grilled members of the Ford administration in public hearings before the Subcommittee on the Handicapped.[32] In asking Gerry what he and his agency, the OCR, was doing to implement disability rights policy, both committee chair Randolph and Harrison Williams emphasized the importance of including disability groups in the process. Gerry testified that his department had in fact, consulted a wide range of at least sixty disability groups from ACCD to Goodwill.[33] Yet Williams appeared suspicious that Gerry and the Ford administration were finally moving forward with Section 504 regulations. Williams first asked about Gerry's background, pointedly stating that, because his appointment had not required Senate confirmation, legislators knew little about him. Williams then questioned Gerry about the administration's delay in drafting and signing regulations. Gerry argued that Congress had moved ahead with no public hearings on the matter of rights and that HEW was now in the process of holding such public consultations with disability groups. Although Williams and other disability rights entrepreneurs commended the active participation of disability groups in the process, he nonetheless implied that Gerry's argument was only a stalling tactic:

WILLIAMS: There seems like an awfully inordinate period of time for the agencies here charged with the responsibility to insure opportunity for handicapped individuals; an inordinate period of time to find out who the individuals who are protected under this act. It is a long, long time, and I gather it is still being formulated, who your constituency is.

GERRY: Well, I indicated in my testimony, Mr. Chairman, that we will publish a draft of the proposed regulation by the end of this month. So that brings us close to the period of time.

WILLIAMS: Now all right. Now we have got something specific, hard and fast. By the end of the month of May, there will be submitted, there will be promulgated, just exactly what?

GERRY: There will be a draft of the—

WILLIAMS: That is not a promulgation; that is a draft.

GERRY: That is right.

WILLIAMS: A suggestion for a later—

GERRY: No. What I am suggesting is that the Department will publish a draft of the regulations which have been prepared, which we have been working on, as part of the official publication in the Federal Register, with the goal to, obviously, issuing—through the proposal-making process subsequently and thereafter—in final form the regulations. We believe that it is extremely important to have lengthy and, I think, detailed public involvement, but we don't believe that public involvement can occur meaningfully without a publication of the draft of the proposed regulations.

WILLIAMS: Well, now, you certainly have had considerable public involvement for quite a period of time; am I right? You have not operated in a vacuum; you have had a substantial amount of public suggestion to date.[34]

Organizations demanded that congressional subcommittees and disability rights entrepreneurs carefully monitor the administration's plans regarding disability rights, especially the OCR—once a much more reliably active and supportive environment for rights. But their mood was somber. As Bowe put it in his opening remarks, "We meet today, however, not to celebrate but to reflect and to plan. Grave questions demand our attention, the answers to which will determine in large part how much of the promise of section 504 reaches full realization."[35]

Anticipating backlash from policy stakeholders, agencies under both Ford and Carter were seriously concerned about implementing Section 504. Even HEW, the agency charged with enforcing disability rights, noted in a DOT appropriations hearing that it anticipated difficulty in enforcement and implementation, given how many different areas of government and policy disability rights touched on (transit, education, etc.).[36] Finally, in 1977, following pressure from Congress and protests organized by disability organizations and encouraged by disability rights entrepreneurs, Carter's HEW secretary, Joseph Califano, signed the regulations. In his letter to Congress, Califano recognized the strong civil rights regulations, in accordance with congressional intent, and wrote that the legislation "opens a new era of civil rights in America" (Figure 4.3). Yet, as noted the Chapter 1, Califano was privately reluctant to move forward and saw the demands of Congress as unrealistic.

The political dynamics emerging in this early part of the 1970s would become the "new normal" in legislating disability rights. Now more than ever, disability rights entrepreneurs relied on the efforts of nascent advocacy

/0

THE SECRETARY OF HEALTH, EDUCATION, AND WELFARE
WASHINGTON, D.C. 20201

April 28, 1977

TO THE MEMBERS OF CONGRESS

SUBJECT: Regulation Prohibiting Discrimination Against
           Handicapped Americans

Enclosed is a regulation that I have issued today implementing Section 504 of the Rehabilitation Act of
1973. That Section provides:

      "No otherwise qualified handicapped individual
      shall, solely by reason of his handicap, be
      excluded from participation in, be denied
      the benefits of, or be subjected to dis-
      crimination under any program or activity
      receiving federal financial assistance."

As you will note, the regulation issued pursuant to
Section 504's broad mandate works fundamental changes
in many facets of American life.

A number of you have urged me to sign a strong regulation.
This regulation is strong. In many cases it calls for
dramatic changes in the actions and attitudes of
institutions and individuals who are recipients of HEW
funds. In implementing the unequivocal Congressional
statute, this regulation opens a new era of civil
rights in America.

In light of the limited legislative history, I think it
especially important that Congress evaluate the regulation,
and the implementation process, to ensure that they conform
to the will of Congress.

I am also enclosing a statement I issued in conjunction
with promulgation of the regulation.

Joseph A. Califano, Jr.

Enclosures

Figure 4.3 Joseph Califano's letter to Congress, introduced into testimony at a September 1977 hearing. *Source: Implementation of Section 504, Rehabilitation Act of 1973*, 95th Cong. 76 (1977) (statement of Jim Jeffords).

organizations to promote and protect social welfare and civil rights policies alike. Early on, Sen. Bob Dole and others applauded the efforts of a variety of organizations, such as the Epilepsy Foundation of America, National Association of the Deaf, and Association for Children with Learning Disabilities, for holding a vigil at the Lincoln Memorial, a space inaccessible to people in wheelchairs. Dole specifically commended the work of two diverse groups coming together for a common cause: "the work of both the United Cerebral Palsy Associations and Disabled in Action, although separate organizations, for helping the developmentally disabled find a measure of their potential." And the groups recognized Dole for "his active voice on behalf of the developmentally disabled." They needed each other in this tumultuous period for civil rights.[37]

Advocacy groups were increasingly dismayed at the limits of disability rights policies' largesse,[38] especially in regard to enforcement. In fact, Dudley of PVA was testifying at a hearing called in direct response to failed policy implementation— a theme continuing to define disability politics and mobilization today.

This political back-stepping invited a "disability rebellion."[39] Advocacy coalitions like the ACCD—the so-called handicapped lobby—brought together advocacy and service organizations into what Sharon Barnartt and Richard Scotch have called a "politically sophisticated" network.[40] Organizations disseminated information about new rights to the American public, aiming to gain buy-in from an ever-broader base of supporters by alerting them to their rights and to the threats against those rights. For instance, DREDF, a hybrid service-advocacy group providing important educational and legal resources to disabled Americans, became heavily involved in policy development and eventually targeted the Department of Justice (DOJ) when the Reagan administration sought to narrow Section 504 in the early 1980s. Collectively, these advocacy groups mobilized support beyond the immediate policy network, hoping to find new allies and sources of political pressure.

By the end of the 1970s, organizations young and old representing professionals, parents, and disabled citizens, included a range of groups such as the National Association of the Deaf, National Council of the Blind, Easter Seals, NARC, UCP, Council of State Administrators of Vocational Rehabilitation, NRA, Goodwill, National Center for Law and the Handicapped, and DIA. These provided a broad organizational basis for mobilizing citizens into a social movement that would target the federal government and later expand to other targets on a variety of disability-related cultural and political issues. The profusion of flexible, hybrid service-advocacy organizations would become an institutional fixture in the disability rights struggle, even when the disability rights movement showed signs of demobilization (see discussion in Chapter 6).

These groups echoed the sentiments of members of Congress that the disability rights struggle was being erroneously characterized as practical administrators rejecting the idealistic vision of institutional activists in Congress. Just five months after the regulations were signed, Sen. Jim Jeffords (R-VT), a strong supporter of disability rights, criticized "passing the buck" between Congress, the numerous administrative agencies now involved in rights implementation (like HEW and DOT), and the courts. "I am concerned," Jeffords explained to Brademas, Perkins, and Biaggi, "because, as you know, both recent Secretaries have cried to Congress to provide guidance in these areas and now they are putting regulating out, and you have the courts getting into this."[41]

Rather than bring diverse policy stakeholders together, the rule-making process around Section 504 seemed to push actors with conflicting interests farther apart. The Carter administration was facing pressure from people such as Randolph, Williams, and Brademas, as well as newly established advocacy groups like ACCD and DIA, to implement Section 504 and from powerful critics such as educational institutions and public transit authorities (and their interest groups, including the National Association of College and University Business Officers and APTA) seeking to undermine the application of Section 504.

Indeed, detractors were making inroads with policy makers in preventing vigorous enforcement of Section 504. At a hearing on equal access to public transit, APTA pointed to a 1977 letter issued by David O'Neil of the OCR in which he agreed with APTA's much narrower interpretation of rights to equal access and rejected the claims disability entrepreneurs and leaders in the disability community were championing.[42] In another case, an attorney representing the Lebanon School Board sent a letter to Congressman John Myers (R-IN) charging that there were "many more implications" to Section 504 than just compliance and lodging concern that the regulations might expand at the discretion of the HEW secretary (Figure 4.4).

Representing the nonprofit group Council of Chief State School Officers, John Adams not only cited costs as a factor preventing school officials from signing any compliance document but also warned that school officials were unlikely to comply because they viewed OCR involvement as increasing future disability rights litigation (an argument employed against the ADA in future fights).[43] These detractors shared in the overarching concern that, under the OCR and HEW, the definition of "handicapped" would continue to expand, bringing more qualifying individuals demanding accommodations within the laws' purview, preemptively weaponizing complaints. The Lebanon School Board attorney concluded that the regulations "will completely destroy all local control of our schools."[44]

Well before Reagan-era rollbacks, the growing number of detractors in government and relevant policy stakeholders in the late 1970s established a path

$\mathcal{W}endell\ \mathcal{B}.\ \mathcal{I}ddings$ **OCT 7 1977**

ATTORNEY
815 WEST NORTH STREET
LEBANON, INDIANA 46052

MAIL ADDRESS
P. O. BOX 366

October 3, 1977

Congressman John Myers
House of Representatives
Washington, D.C. 20515

            Re: Regulations issued by the
                  Department of Health, Education
                  and Welfare requiring compliance
                  with Section 504 of the Rehabili-
                  tation Act of 1973.

Dear Congressman:

In June of 1977, the School Boards of this country were
notified that they would be required to sign an insurance
of compliance of Section 504 of the Rehabilitation Act of
1973, as amended. As a member of the Lebanon Community
School Board, I examined this and find that this simple
paper has many more implications than mere compliance with
the Section of said Act. It also requires compliance with
any and all regulations which the Secretary of HEW might
see fit to adopt in the past, now, or in the future. Our
School Board has refused to sign this compliance until some
changes are made in the regulations and in the definition
of "handicapped". I submitted a position paper to my School
Board, outlining my reservations on this act. A copy of
this position paper is enclosed for your information. I
strongly urge you to re-define those persons who are considered as "handicapped" under this Act. To proceed with
the Act with compliance under the present regulations, will
completely destroy all local control of our schools.

                       Sincerely yours,

                       WENDELL B. IDDINGS
                       Lebanon School Board

WBI/kjv
Encl.
c.c.:   Lebanon School Board Members
        Superintendent Robert McFrye
        Dave Hutton
        Steve Kain

Figure 4.4 Letter from attorney Wendell B. Iddings, representing the Lebanon School Board, to Congressman John Myers. *Source: Implementation of Section 504, Rehabilitation Act of 1973, 95th Cong. 597 (1977).*

for more outright attempts at policy retrenchment in the 1980s. They used arguments and language that served as a precursor for organized opposition against disability rights in the 1990s and 2000s, placing members of the disability policy network in an awkward and complicated position. To them, the government's intentions on disability rights were clear: Section 504 was analogous to the 1964 Civil Rights Act and should be enforced accordingly. Carroll referred to Cranston and Stafford's position that Sections 503 and 504 be enforced just as Section 601 of the Civil Rights Act and Title IX of the Education Amendments of 1972 had been. He also pointed to the administration's official stated position on the matter, in which Califano himself equated Section 504 to Title VI of the Civil Rights Act and Title IX of the Education Amendments.

Opponents of enforcing disability rights measures framed the ongoing political conflict in terms of the rights of a few placing undue burdens on public institutions, thus undermining the quality of services for the many. Even sympathetic allies began to worry about costs and inefficiencies that might be leveraged as pushback against the implementation of disability rights. In a fall 1977 exchange with Brademas, Adams, and Carroll, just after the Section 504 regulations were published, Senator Jeffords wondered:

> If we require, as this law does, states to push on to those educational systems additional costs relative to 504, what is going to happen? We don't know whether or not the taxpayers, who feel they are overburdened with property taxes already, will not only rebel against taxes but also against the handicapped. . . . We are going to lose that general feeling of support we have for the handicapped now and turn people who generally support the handicapped against the handicapped . . . if it requires taking money away from day care centers or other great needs which people perceive, and forcing them to use it for the handicapped, I am afraid that without any Federal help we are going to have a backlash reverse.[45]

Carroll responded, astutely, that costs would be a perennial argument and argued that there was no time to lose in resolving the issue: "My feeling is the fiscal argument will always be brought up and it will be three more years and three more years; and we are dealing with the civil rights of people. I don't know if it is exactly fair to talk about people's civil rights in terms of how much it will cost to be fair."[46]

By the end of the decade, a full-fledged, programmatic opposition to disability rights had created seemingly insurmountable institutional obstacles to implementation. Disability rights entrepreneurs were exasperated. They still fundamentally believed that without active, federal oversight, no barriers, whether institutional, physical, or cognitive, would ever be eradicated. At one hearing, seemingly questioning their entire decade-long effort, Brademas asked representatives from NARC, Council for the Retarded, and National Center for Law and the Handicapped whether there was "a responsibility on the part of the National Government to provide money to institutions to encourage them to obey the law? I don't think that we have, with one exception perhaps, similar statutes with respect to the Civil Rights Acts' requirements that there be compliance with non-discriminatory requirements in respect of women, people of religious minorities, or race or age."[47] Those sympathetic to disability rights recognized costs as a barrier to rights, but all agreed that the federal government had to keep its "house clean" and lead by example.[48]

Carroll, however, seemed to have raised a more fundamental question underlying the conflict over disability rights: Was securing the rights for disabled citizens different from efforts to secure the rights of other disadvantaged groups?

Rising Expectations in the Disability Rights Community

Along with the ACCD in 1978 and 1979, PVA, the Epilepsy Foundation of America, and Mainstream, Inc. testified in hearings about the effectiveness of Section 504. As Mainstream's Leslie Milk insisted, employers would never comply with rights legislation if the law were not properly enforced:

> We believe that legislative action is needed to do what legislative intent failed to do, to clarify the employment protections of handicapped people guaranteed by the Rehabilitation Act of 1973. . . . Without clarifying amendments, the movement toward equal protection in the workplace will have taken a giant step backward.[49]

Leaders like Milk turned to disability rights entrepreneurs to promote the disability civil rights agenda within government. He promised legislators that their "continued attention to the agenda of handicapped rights, and [your] periodic action *when that agenda does not move forward*, will, I believe, make a classic difference."[50]

Activists pointed to a recent study by the DOL showing that a majority of employers who received federal contracts were not yet complying with the rights provision in the Rehabilitation Act.[51] Similarly, according to the OCR itself, school administrators were pushing back against signing the Section 504 compliance document.[52] The law was struggling to change structural and attitudinal barriers. With the uncertainty about the validity of disability rights and the extent to which these were equivalent to rights afforded to other minority groups, Section 504 no longer looked like a clear-cut political victory.

For institutional activists like Cranston, Al Quie, Stafford, and staffers like Lisa Walker, blame for these failures rested with administrative agencies. They charged that the agencies had perverted congressional intent and given the White House bad counsel. James Gashel of the NFB wrote that the Rehabilitation Act had been hailed as "the 'new beginning' in our nation's efforts to provide rights and opportunities for handicapped citizens," yet "many hopes have not to this date been realized because of the bureaucratic inertia which always seems to pull against the tide of change and innovation."[53]

Within the administration, of course, the inability to entrench Section 504 was laid at the feet of Congress and its "act now think later" approach to civil rights. In regard to putting policy into practice, administrators thought Congress was cavalierly injecting civil rights into existing policy areas, ignoring the repercussions.[54] White House wavering on the rights issue and the congressional stalemates over what to do with Section 504 evolved into a Reagan-era rights rollback.

Frustrated with the regulatory process, rights entrepreneurs at the end of 1970s were calling for an amendment to the Civil Rights Act to prohibit discrimination. Effectively, they wanted to return to the original, but failed, 1971 Vanik and Humphrey proposal.[55] Williams, who sponsored the bill, the Equal Employment Opportunity for the Handicapped Act (S. 446), with twenty-eight other legislators, including eleven Republicans, referred to it as having "a broad spectrum of support including the Leadership Conference on Civil Rights, the ACCD, and groups representing disabled American veterans."[56] A liberal Republican from Connecticut, Lowell Weicker, commented, "People say this is not the right time. Well, whenever was it the right time in the history of this country to go ahead and act in behalf of its minorities? I think this is a darned good time, and I hope that you are successful in your efforts."[57]

The ACCD, American Council of the Blind, and NARC were now systematically monitoring incidents of employment discrimination and other policy developments. They brought what Bowe called a "special vigor" as they drew from an oft-used rehabilitationist frame to turn the costs argument on its head and claim that the costs of not hiring people with disabilities was far higher than any potential costs in accommodating disabled employees. Bowe urged the committee

> to act with all deliberate speed on S. 446, I do so in full cognizance of the costs we might expect—and, even more, of the costs we must expect if we do not move firmly and promptly to eliminate unfair discrimination in employment. The answers to massive joblessness among disabled Americans will be found in

measures such as those proposed in S. 446. We must prohibit employment bias on the basis of an individual's disability. Some will ask whether existing law is adequate in this respect. And the answer is that it manifestly is not.[58]

Williams asked the ACCD for its opinion in amending the Rehabilitation Act to include protections from discrimination in the private sector,[59] but Bowe favored an amendment to the Civil Rights Act. A year earlier, in 1978, the EEOC—the agency responsible for enforcing the Civil Rights Act—had taken over enforcement of Section 501 from the DOL by executive order. Section 501 prohibits discrimination based on disability for federal employment, and the thinking was that enforcement would be more vigorous if led by the EEOC. Disability advocacy groups now saw enforcement agencies and the courts as an important target of action if the law was to be upheld. Between April 1978 and June 1979, Disabled American Veterans (DAV) filed more than 150 complaints, anticipating that many would receive final resolution with the EEOC. Ronald Drach of DAV told Williams, "I think we will have somewhat of a barometer as to EEOC's commitment and effectiveness."[60]

In the meantime, federal courts made their position known regarding disability rights. The year Milk testified before Congress, two court cases—*Trageser v. Libbie Rehabilitation Center*,[61] which limited disability-based discrimination victims' ability to sue, and, more infamously, *Southeastern Community College v. Davis*—seriously curtailed the efficacy of Section 504 to end discrimination. Initially, the courts seemed convinced by the administration's charge that Congress simply had not thought through the implications of its legislation. One representative of the American Council of the Blind interpreted the situation as courts being convinced that legislators did not really mean what they said about rights.[62] Political entrepreneurs and leaders of disability advocacy groups feared the potential impact of these cases and referenced them often in congressional hearings.

Bowe reminded Williams that the courts already criticized Congress for being too ambiguous in legislation and leaving interpretation to the Executive Branch (which, in the court's opinion, had overreached its authority). The *Davis* ruling had come down against Davis a week before these Senate hearings, and Bowe was forceful in calling for precise definitions, terminology, and objectives. He believed including disability in the 1964 Civil Rights Act would mediate some of the conflict between policy and rule making. Even the EEOC, new to the disability rights debate, complained that enforcement would be problematic given the broad language used by rights entrepreneurs in Congress. Williams, who stood at the center of these fights, was sympathetic to the demands of advocacy groups and sanguine about policy making: "Legislation, of course, cannot be that detailed, to meet the possibilities of every situation, so what we have to do is to do better than we have in other legislation without having some kind of a civil code which would incorporate every possibility."[63]

With looming uncertainty about the future of disability rights, the push to amend Title VIII of the Civil Rights Act gained some traction outside the disability policy network. Support came from the labor movement, the American Federation of Labor–Congress of Industrial Organizations (AFL-CIO), and the Leadership Conference on Civil Rights. However, when S. 446 was reported by the committee to the Senate in September 1979 and cosponsored by Javits, Randolph, and Pell, among others, the bill ultimately died on a technicality. According to the Committee on the Budget, S. 446 authorized the enactment of a new budget authority for 1980, but the authorization was not reported in the Senate by the May 15, 1979, deadline.[64] After outlining its major concerns about excessive costs, the committee's official response was that it "supports the principles represented by S. 446. However, the committee believes that it is inappropriate for the Senate to consider a bill of potentially major cost impact, without an adequate analysis of inflationary impact as well as a clear definition of the benefits of employment opportunities for the handicapped."[65] It appeared that alleged costs and inefficiencies once again impeded the entrenchment of disability rights into the American institutional and cultural landscape.

As they railed against costs, detractors also now framed advocacy groups' efforts as impractical. Stanley Bristol, director of special education in Chicago, testified, "The advocacy movement rooted in lofty purposes has too often had the effect of generating unrealistic demands on the schools. The focusing on rights tends to obliterate any discussion of practical limits." Theorizing about revolt in a climate of unfulfilled expectations, Bristol claimed, "The linking of the advocacy system with the due process structures has sharpened the angle of takeoff of rising expectations."[66] Indeed, broken promises and dashed expectations would bring the disability rights movement out into the streets.

"Going Wrong with Handicapped Rights": From Innovation to Retrenchment

Williams said, of the political approach in pursuit of disability rights and the fights over Sections 503 and 504, "There are problems, problems, problems;

sure there are technical problems, and we know there will be enforcement problems." Yet to Williams these technical problems should not be able to obscure the bigger picture—they "should not deter us, right?"[67] Frustrated that disabled Americans still faced gross injustice, six years following the Rehabilitation Act, Williams was searching for policy solutions well beyond Section 504. He thought that the real conflict pitted "big ideas" against immediate programmatic fixes, with the latter only postponing more robust interventions.

Rights entrepreneurs, then, were not naïve. Biaggi observed, "We find ourselves still groping to achieve the lofty mandates of the act. . . . We approach this hearing as advocates of Public Law 94-142. Yet, we do not pledge blind allegiance. We are aware of present day realities."[68] Attitudes, particularly among Democrats, were shifting amid the rise of the conservative movement. Reagan's election looked like a reflection of changing public sentiments about the role of government in solving social problems. Reagan's famous inaugural address line that "government is not the solution to our problem; government is the problem" perfectly encapsulated the moment. Elites both in and out of government bought into this perspective; coupled with tremendous pushback from policy stakeholders, it led many legislators sympathetic to disability rights to soften their position.

When the House Committee on Education and Labor held oversight hearings regarding the Education for All Handicapped Children Act in 1979 and 1980, Brademas, Perkins, and Biaggi reiterated that Section 504 should be leveraged as a way to undermine persistent discrimination in education. They paralleled discussions in the Senate Subcommittee on the Handicapped chaired by Jennings Randolph and, later, Lowell Weicker. Consensus remained: without the federal government taking the lead, history dictated that cities and states would not endeavor to integrate children with disabilities into mainstream educational programs. Disability policy actors like Russell of the PCEH and New York Democrat Ted Weiss knew all too well that this was not about the federal government imposing a burden by ensuring rights and equal access to mainstream education; it was about federal government changing policy that could lead to widespread attitudinal change too.[69]

Opposition to mainstreaming grew more vocal and more organized. School administrators cautioned that legislation would increase the number of students (and parents) seeking special education in regular schools. Teachers and teachers' unions claimed that accommodating children with disabilities would take away from educating nondisabled students. The *New York Times* published an editorial along these lines, "Going Wrong with Handicapped Rights," in which the author conceded, "It is only right to remedy a pattern of neglect," before insisting, "but it is perverse for Congress and the courts to define an 'appropriate' education only for the handicapped and to write rules that result in the deprivation of other children."[70] Albert Shanker, president of the American Federation of Teachers, pointed to the piece when he testified, "If the *New York Times* is prepared to take this stance, consider the emotions and frustrations fermenting throughout the country."[71]

On the other side, groups such as National Society for Autistic Children and UCP criticized school administrators' reluctance to mainstream children with disabilities. A representative from UCP sarcastically told the committee: "I am sure that school administrators are leery of educating some of these parents too fully, probably figuring that there is going to be a marching band walking into their offices, demanding more than what they feel they can accomplish."[72] Disability rights policies lacked legitimacy from these policy stakeholders who saw policies as external, foreign impositions—burdens—on the institutions they governed, in turn posing a major obstacle to the entrenchment of disability rights legislation.

Several disability groups focused their efforts on inadequate enforcement of the Education for All Handicapped Children Act. The Association for Children with Learning Disabilities (ACLD, a.k.a. Association for Children and Adults with Learning Disabilities), founded in 1964, had transitioned into a service-advocacy hybrid organization in the early 1970s. By 1980, it was a pure advocacy group with eight hundred chapters and sixty thousand members focused on policy monitoring and development. Concerned with lack of compliance, the ACLD called for the establishment of Special Education Advisory Councils (mainly composed of parents) to independently assess compliance.

In his opening remarks before the Subcommittee on the Handicapped, which he now chaired, Weicker summarized the political context:[73] "At no time in the brief history of Federal support for education and training programs for handicapped children and adults has there been as strong a challenge as there is today to substantially reduce Federal funding and monitoring of such programs."[74]

As Ronald Reagan took office, the UN designated 1981 the International Year of Disabled Persons. The United States had once been regarded as a leader in disability rights, but now, as the world celebrated such advances, its activists and policy makers were fighting off attempted rights rollbacks.

NARC already expressed concerns about Reagan, particularly his proposed block grants, which would reduce federal involvement in implementing disability rights policy through a sort of outsourcing. Weicker agreed. Recently elected Orrin Hatch now chaired the Senate Committee on Labor (parent committee of the Subcommittee on the Handicapped), and the self-proclaimed fiscal conservative eventually sponsored seventeen balanced-budget amendments and supported rollbacks to the Fair Housing Act. Hatch, however, had personal experience with disability and often told the story of his brother-in-law who, as a result of polio, was in an iron lung and had to be carried, by Hatch, up the steps of the Mormon temple in California.[75] Hatch, who would support the ADA (along with Harkin, Kennedy, Jeffords, Pell, and Dole) and cosponsor the 1994 Developmental Disabilities Assistance and Bill of Rights Act Amendments (among other things, these proposed creating state developmental disabilities advocacy councils), looked like a bright spot for those hoping to stave off Reagan's program cutting.[76] Perhaps Tom Nerney of NARC was right: "Senator Hatch, taking Senator Williams' place as chairman, has been our new ally in the recent budget considerations for programs with persons with handicaps."[77]

Teresa Hawkes of Health and Human Services (HHS; formerly combined with the Department of Education as HEW) was defensive of the hostile administration: "The most important thing that we can do, not only for the groups we are concerned about in the social service programs, but for all citizens, is to put the Nation's economy on a sound-footing and reduce the inflation that makes economic self-sufficiency so difficult for so many people."[78] All the while, interactions between rights entrepreneurs and the administration were growing even more acrimonious.

An exchange between Weicker and Hawkes provides a case in point. Weicker tried to get the administration to state, on the record, what it thought would happen when states did not fulfill a commitment to their disabled citizens, given that the block grants facilitated *but did not require* addressing the needs of the disabled. Unhappy with the response, Weicker poignantly described to representatives of the administration what he believed would be the outcome of the new administration's position:

> You see, my problem is that, as you know, even now, to remove this from the Federal side, even now as the battle for the dollars—as the dollars diminish and the battle grows at the local level, the minorities of our society—in this sense, now, I am talking about the disabled, the retarded, etcetera; I am not using it in an ethnic concept—are the ones that are left at the starting gate. And everybody knows it, but then everybody realizes also that their decision will be ratified by the majority at the polls. And unfortunately, we know all along what we are dealing with here is a minority in a political sense.[79]

Not only did Weicker emphasize the politicization of the disability constituency—that Americans with disabilities were citizens entitled to minority
rights protections and not just clients deserving of services—he also reminded
Hawkes that the disability community would protest the denial of their rights.
As hostilities intensified, Weicker's 1982 opening statement to the Subcommittee on the Handicapped pointed to the institutional arrangements that
allow for policy retrenchment in US policy making:

> We have been asked to repeal Public Law 94-142. We have been asked to cut its
> funding by 25 percent, then another 8 percent, and, failing, an even 30 percent.
> We have been promised legislation repealing portions of the act, and we have
> rejected every single one of these proposals. Now, we are being told that the
> same people who asked us to decimate the law and to slash funding are selling
> a regulatory rewrite as an improvement for the disabled. We shall see today
> whether that is the case or whether the administration is attempting to do by
> regulation what it has been unable to do in the Congress: to eliminate our Na-
> tion's system of special education.[80]

Weicker described the ways legislators fought against "death by a thousand
cuts," highlighting a perennial concern: the rule-making process was able to
function as a veto point for detractors seeking to weaken legislative provisions.

As disability groups coordinated their testimony and policy-monitoring
efforts with policy entrepreneurs' work, they also increasingly came together
to form advocacy coalitions. The Consortium Concerned with the Developmentally Disabled (CCDD) consisted, in 1982, of nineteen disability organizations.[81] It had originated in the years following the Developmental Disabilities
Services and Facilities Construction Amendments of 1970 (Pub. L. 91–517),[82]
and it became more formalized as it worked with legislators on the 1975 Education for All Handicapped Children Act. Paul Marchand, chairman of the
CCDD, told members of the Subcommittee on the Handicapped in 1982 that
the administration's efforts reflect "a fundamental erosion of the rights and
protections of handicapped children and their parents,"[83] words echoed almost
exactly by Vermont senator Robert Stafford.

In the meantime, Reagan broke the policy stalemate that had developed
in public-transit accessibility.[84] Urban Mass Transportation Administration
(UMTA) administrators who felt pressured to adopt Carter-era rules, including the production of accessible "Transbuses," soon found themselves in a more
favorable environment. The 1981 Transit Assistance Act would reduce "the reg-

ulatory burden the Federal Government places upon mass transit operators."[85] The administration clearly sided with public-transit authorities and APTA, which had worked hard to undermine Section 504 regulations.

Republican Dick Lugar of Indiana chaired the Subcommittee on Housing and Urban Affairs on which rights entrepreneurs Williams and Cranston both served. By today's standards, he would be considered a moderate Republican, but in 1980, Lugar had a CC score of 85.[86] He had little experience with the disability rights transit debate and praised the Reagan administration's Proposed 1981 Mass Transit Amendments, referring to UMTA as "one of the most burdensome of Federal agencies."[87] DOT secretary Drew Lewis agreed wholeheartedly and proposed that volunteerism—not the federal government—should and would help provide transportation for low-income, elderly, and disabled people.[88] Disability groups were quick to remind detractors that even under prior administrations, federal law had allowed transit authorities to exercise local options to provide transit services to the disabled, but almost none exercised that option. As Reese Robrahn, executive director of the ACCD, put it, "The advent of the publication of the Department of Transportation's 504 regulations brought forth the hue and cry for 'local option.' The big stick so handy and available was and is cost, cost that is outrageously exaggerated and shamefully misrepresented."[89]

Representatives from ACCD, UCP, and the National Spinal Cord Injury Foundation did not mince words. They told the committee that the government in the early 1970s raised and then crushed the aspirations and expectations of people with disabilities. Vincent Macaluso of ACCD said, with disappointment, "We never thought we would have to come back here and ask you the same thing we asked you in 1970."[90]

From Elite to Mass Politics

PCEH's Harold Russell argued that policy changes and the rise of the handicapped consumer movement were "deeply connected" and "not at all coincidental."[91] Rights policies made citizens out of clients with a stake in ensuring that their rights are upheld; advocacy groups served as important intermediaries in the development of that political constituency.

The institutionalization of advocacy dramatically increased information dissemination and public awareness campaigns as well as the ability of citizens to monitor policy developments. As director of Programs in Special Education and Rehabilitation Services, Lisa Walker noted that the disability rights cause would "not get much further without dogged persistence and commitment from top level policymakers and outside political forces."[92] And Russell believed that "the evolution of organized groups of handicapped persons, as articulate and activist consumers, has characterized this past decade. They have turned to the courts and to the law to back up their efforts."[93] Policy makers now recognized that disability groups were translating the demands of a politicized constituency questioning traditional models of service provision while advocating for their civil rights. Using institutional advocacy as well as more disruptive tactics, organizations pressured political elites and raised public awareness of the government's failures to implement the policies they enacted.

Organizational coalitions displayed considerable flexibility in how they used tactics to challenge various targets. Building from the protest momentum initiated after Nixon vetoed the Rehabilitation Act, groups organized sit-ins at HEW offices while their leadership lobbied Congress. Leaders and attorneys representing DIA, ACCD, National Paraplegia Foundation, PVA, and UCP made sure members of the House Subcommittee on DOT Appropriations were aware that some disability representatives could not attend the 1977 hearings because they were protesting at HEW secretary Califano's office.[94]

These were no longer the organizations of a bygone era. As Dudley of PVA testified, past groups had been limited to promoting "an image of hopelessness and pathos in an effort to raise funds."[95] Political advocacy, stimulated by a new rights focus and policy retrenchment, also transformed the long-established service sector, including rehabilitation. Surinder Dhillon of Rehabilitation, Inc. proclaimed, "Advocacy is very necessary to change discrimination. . . . Rehabilitation counselors should be (and have been) the chief advocates for the disabled."[96] Their efforts were directly influenced by the institutionalization of political advocacy and the rise of hybrid advocacy-service organizations.

Activists, organizational leaders, and policy entrepreneurs agreed that policies were "a necessary catalyst to initiate an admittedly long-term process."[97] Attitudes, values, and beliefs were slowly catching up to the institutional and organizational transformations that led the way in the struggle for disability rights. Bearing out Dudley's comments quoted earlier, the rise of institutional advocacy had helped create a social movement that went a long way in changing hearts and minds both inside and outside the government.[98] The disability rights movement came into its own when activists realized they could no longer rely on their routine access to policy-making institutions to effect social change.

5 Politics Is Pressure

If we can't ride, nobody rides. At least Rosa Parks could get on a bus.
—Chant by disability protesters at a Greyhound bus terminal in 1997[1]

FOR DISENFRANCHISED DISABLED AMERICANS, the 1970s ended in frustration. They acknowledged that social change was under way—reaching a point of "symbolic acceptance of the rights of disabled people to live and work in the mainstream"—but believed it would be a long fight before they could, as Mainstream, Inc.'s Leslie Milk testified, "reach real acceptance."[2]

At a protest against the 1979 *Davis* decision, Ed Roberts, founder of the independent living movement, bitterly told the *Los Angeles Times* that the Carter administration had "made tremendous commitments. Not only have they not delivered but they actually have hindered us and made it very difficult to get new legislation to help us take our place in the mainstream." Activists accused Carter of "betraying the trust the handicapped had bestowed upon him."[3]

Of disability activism, Roberts forecasted, "Politics is pressure in this country and the more pressure we can exert, the more quickly we can move toward equality."[4] Protests led by DIA, NARC, National Federation for the Blind, and ACCD targeting the federal government were only the leading front in a storm of disability activism. Activists expanded their targets to include local and state governments as well as public and private corporations (and their lobby groups). Even the issue focuses were widening, from accessibility to welfare and Medicaid cutbacks, community-based care, pity-driven fund-raising like the Jerry Lewis Telethon, and to AIDS, right-to-life, and assisted suicide. Activism on all these fronts went a long way in changing the image of disability and the disabled. As rights-based language eclipsed pity and charity-based arguments for social-service provision, antidiscrimination, and accessibility efforts, one DIA protester told reporters, "How are you going to employ somebody if you have just cried about them? . . . Exploitation is not entertaining."[5]

The ability of the nascent disability rights movement to sustain mobilizing efforts using a range of tactics—from lobbying to disruptive demonstrations and sit-ins against a range of targets—was largely the result of changes within the disability organizational sector. Threat is a powerful motivator,[6] and activists and advocacy groups coalesced around rising political threats. Rather than instill a sense of defeat, retrenchment efforts emboldened the rising disability rights movement, demonstrating how political threats raise the cost of inaction.[7] When political backlash threatened disability rights, a community now equipped with legal tools and "collective vehicles" such as advocacy organizations and activist networks, mobilized to protect its policy interests.[8] Disruption was not really about gaining access to the policy-making process; after all, the disability community historically already had routine access to political elites through voluntary organizations. Activists were fighting instead for reinstatement among policy entrepreneurs as citizens protecting their legislated rights.

In 1981, activists mobilized against Reagan's conversion of federal programs into block grants. One disability activist told a *Washington Post* reporter that the federal government was trying to "wipe its hands of its responsibilities" to implement "settled" rights policies.[9] Within the year, they would also fight proposed cuts to federal funding for a black lung disease disability program, joining more than one hundred organizations representing the poor and the elderly in Nationwide Action for a Fair Budget demonstrations. Rallying against Reagan's social program cuts, some activists carried signs echoing a popular antiwar slogan and mocking the president's well known sweet tooth: "Jellybeans are unhealthy for children and other living things."[10]

The following year, more than one hundred individuals using crutches, canes, and wheelchairs "walked out or crawled out or rolled out" at a demonstration to protest Reagan's "new federalism."[11] Reagan ordered the DOJ to review all federal agency regulations, including Section 504. One protester told reporters, "Our rights, our dignity, our quality of life is being sacrificed here."[12]

The administration attacked IDEA early, first replacing the policy with block grants and then trying to cut its budget by more than 25 percent (Congress fought off this effort). When Education Secretary T. H. Bell, who had been appointed by Reagan to oversee the dismantling of the Education Department, published revisions to the regulations, parents with school-age children with disabilities were particularly incensed. Weicker, now chair of the Senate Subcommittee on the Handicapped (later, a key proponent of the ADA), held an

August 1982 hearing. In his opening remarks, he outlined the achievements of Congress in passing and supporting the IDEA since 1975 and alleged, "To date, the only proposals we have seen from this administration have sought to gut special education."[13] Paul Marchand and the CCDD agreed.

While groups such as the Association for Children and Adults with Learning Disabilities and International Association of Parents of the Deaf joined in the protests around cuts to IDEA, Bell called for October hearings. Weicker feared the administration would change the rules while Congress was out of session. One parent-protester captured the fear in this moment: "The way these regulations are designed, the message is loud and clear. It puts these freaks away where we don't have to look at them."[14]

To civil rights leaders such as Vernon E. Jordan, former president of the National Urban League, and Joseph Rauh of the Leadership Conference on Civil Rights, Reaganism looked like a civil rights counterrevolution.[15] Disability advocacy groups thus joined a broader coalition working to protect civil rights. Groups such as DREDF testified along with the National Association for the Advancement of Colored People (NAACP), Leadership Conference on Civil Rights, and the National Women's Law Center at a 1982 Judiciary Committee hearing about the Reagan administration's unwillingness to enforce civil rights laws.

The Subcommittee on Civil and Constitutional Rights was chaired by Don Edwards (D-CA). Edwards was considered one of the most liberal Democrats and a strong champion of civil rights.[16] After commending the subcommittee for its role in the Voting Rights Act amendments, Rauh made his pitch: "The civil rights community desperately needs the help of this committee in its struggle to resist the administration's counter-revolution against civil rights and its efforts to lay bare the current hostile attitudes of the administration toward the enforcement of the civil rights laws of the Nation."[17]

The backlash around civil rights revealed a conflicted education secretary. On the one hand, Rauh pointed to a letter from Secretary Bell to Sen. Paul Laxalt (R-VA), Reagan's so-called first friend,[18] that had apparently spelled out an anti–civil rights view: "The Federal courts may soon be after us for not enforcing civil rights laws and regulations. Your support for my efforts to decrease the undue harassment of schools and colleges would be appreciated. It seems that we have some laws that we should not have and my obligation to enforce them is against my own philosophy." Later, however, Bell defended the federal government's role in protecting civil rights in education and declined to serve as secretary in Reagan's second term.

Advocacy organizations appealed to sympathetic elites and monitored the administration's actions, especially efforts to curtail enforcement by revising regulations without any public consultation. Nancy Mattox of DREDF cited a DOJ letter to Clarence Thomas, then assistant secretary of education for the OCR, agreeing that the department's practices have stopped the complaint process and "stifled morale in the OCR."[19]

DREDF became central in the fight. For example, DREDF's Patricia Wright organized a lobbying campaign to protect IDEA by urging the enforcement and administration of existing disability rights legislation. In 1984, the Supreme Court ruled in *Smith v. Robinson* that a plaintiff who exhausted the administrative process could not then circumvent IDEA's administrative rules by way of Section 504.[20] In response, institutional activist efforts joined with advocacy groups in forcing Congress to address the decision by amending the law to allow plaintiffs to bring suit under Section 504.

Nonetheless, disability rights entrepreneurs remained concerned that the court for the first time directly cast doubt on available remedies set out in two separate pieces of legislation.[21] Weicker, who sponsored the original amendment in 1984, argued that the court misinterpreted and frustrated Congress's intent (a perennial congressional accusation). In direct response to the court, disability rights entrepreneurs amended the Educational for All Handicapped Children Act (which became IDEA in 1990) in 1986 by passing the Handicapped Children's Protection Act.

Throughout the early 1980s, no policy area would generate more conflict than equal access to transportation. Transit accessibility came to neatly encapsulate the fits and starts and back-stepping characteristic of the political evolution of disability; the innovation, threat, retrenchment, and citizen mobilization. In the 1960s, rights entrepreneurs guaranteed equal access to transportation, but they would spend ten years fighting backlash and taking to the streets alongside advocacy groups defending their rights. In the 1980s, only a few months after Reagan's swearing in, Lugar's Transit Assistance Act heralded the new administration's policy philosophy and reduced the federal government's "regulatory burden" by cutting the funds dedicated to statutory enforcement.[22] Under explicit political threat, protests related to equal right to transit lasted well into the 1990s.

Even years after the ADA supposedly ended any doubt about the government's commitment to equal access, DIA organized protests in San Diego, Los Angeles, and San Francisco. When activists chanted, "If we can't ride, nobody rides. At least Rosa Parks could get on a bus," at a Manhattan Greyhound bus terminal in 1997, it was only a hint of the pent-up frustration of people disappointed by the federal government's follow-through and commitment to civil rights.[23]

Taking the Fight for Equal Access to the American Public

> This is a symbolic protest, just like the civil rights protests of the '60s.
> —Wade Blank (ADAPT member and protest organizer), quoted in Cooley,
> "Disabled People Block Bus at Terminal"

A decade following the Biaggi Amendment proposing that special efforts be made to make mainstream public transportation accessible to the disabled, the Carter administration's promise about accessible buses was unfulfilled. A decade after the Architectural Barriers Act was passed, the ACCD protested the persistence of barriers, including those in transportation.

Local transit authorities saw the early transit protests as a few people "causing problems throughout the city."[24] A *Los Angeles Times* reporter captured the frustration at a 1981 protest in Tarzana:

Jynny Retzinger positioned her chair in line with the rear doors, in front of the blue decal indicating access for the handicapped. The doors slid open.

"Can I get on?" she asked.

The doors slid shut.

Despite the symbol on the door and the specially designed lift built into the two-week old General Motors Corp. bus, it was apparent that no wheelchair rider would be able to board.

An annoyed driver stepped to the sidewalk. Retzinger repeated, "Can I get on the bus?"

With reporters watching, the driver testily replied, "No you can't." He had little more to say.[25]

Dozens of disruptive protests in Washington, D.C., Los Angeles, San Francisco, Cincinnati, Dallas, Denver, and Atlanta, now mainly organized by the nascent ADAPT, helped "dramatize the fact that we are being left out" of equality. Protesters echoed the tactics of the early black civil rights movement when they "captured" buses, shutting down routes as they demanded accessibility. Animosity festered between activists and APTA for years as ADAPT protests expanded to target private bus operators such as Greyhound. Disability demonstrations went beyond symbolic borrowing to make the issue of equal transit salient outside policy circles.

The introduction of the ADA in 1988 was meant as a new federal pledge to, finally and definitively, address inequalities, accessibility barriers, and discrimination. The legislation sought primarily to rectify discrimination in employment, while disability rights entrepreneurs linked transportation barriers to high unemployment (much like their predecessors did with Section 504 in the 1970s). The majority whip, Tony Coelho, testified that some 28 percent of Americans with disabilities attributed their unemployment to transportation barriers, and legislators intended that the ADA would cover, among other entities, transit companies.[26] ADAPT continued its protest activities, which typically did not directly invoke federal legislation. Protests targeted immediate local- and state-level conditions, generating parallel, loosely connected, mobilizing efforts at the federal and local levels in the 1980s and 1990s.

In March 1988, twenty-three wheelchair users and one blind protester were arrested after chaining themselves to shuttle buses at an all-night sit-in at DOT offices. The following year, protesters occupied an Atlanta federal building for two days. They won a pledge of government support (but not an actual order requiring an increase in wheelchair lifts). In the meantime, counsel for UMTA, which was monitoring ADA-related developments in Congress, agreed with the principle of accessibility, assuming the ADA would pass eventually. A month later, Sen. John McCain, who supported the law, raised concerns about what the policy would mean for retrofitting transportation services.[27] Costs were the enduring sticking point in any equal access debate. But optimistically, Democratic Iowa senator Tom Harkin proclaimed, "If we stay together as a community and we work with the groups representing employers and the hotel, restaurant, communications and transportation industries, I believe we can succeed."[28]

By the end of the decade, the ADA fostered a renewed dialogue about equal rights among protesters, government officials, and the public-transit industry by refocusing (in part) the policy agenda and increasing issue salience. In the months before the ADA was signed, disruptive protests against companies like Greyhound would bring enormous public attention to the equal rights fight. Even disgruntled officials and exasperated public transit riders came to reflect the more and more empathetic American citizenry: one Metro bus driver in Washington, D.C., said, "I sympathize with these people. Probably they have some legitimate beefs";[29] and a passenger who had been caught in a two-hour ADAPT bus blockade nonetheless told reporters, "I see where they are coming from. I hope something is done about it."[30]

Early commitments to disability civil rights raised the expectations of a community, and the contentious politics that subsequently emerged were the result of broken legislative promises. As activists took their fight to the streets, they brought their case to the American public, raising awareness about inequality and discrimination.

The Disability Protest Cycle

Like the "cycles of protest" Sydney Tarrow used to depict the movement era of the 1960s and 1970s,[31] the disability rights struggle encompasses specific institutional, organizational, and ideological shifts coupled with the timing of contentious disability politics. A political constituency increasingly seen as a minority group entitled to civil rights had found and mobilized activists where none were thought to exist.

Jocey French, an ADAPT member, said at a protest in 2000, "We're just trying to boldly go where everyone else has already been."[32] The protest was spurred by frustration with government gridlock over in-home care (as the Senate considered a bill aiding community-based services). Her words are revealing: she wanted the right to live like everyone else, freely in the community; she alluded to disability activists' finding inspiration in earlier civil rights demands; and she expressed a sullen disappointment with rights delayed and denied.

The disability protest cycle reflected the ongoing change in the interaction between political elites and advocacy organizations fighting retrenchment efforts through institutional and extra-institutional means. Organizations—many no stranger to the political process, having worked closely with legislators—more readily turned to disruptive collective action. Disability-related protest events were directly associated with an organization about half the time, usually with a single organization coordinating a demonstration.[33]

As Figure 5.1 illustrates, the initial rise of protest—what made disruptive action a legitimate tactic in the disability rights movement—began in the early 1970s with mobilization around lax enforcement of Section 504. This "first wave" of disability protests targeting the federal government peaked in the late 1970s and early 1980s, leveling off and declining before the introduction of the ADA. Here, prominent groups like DIA, NARC, and the ACCD—all of which worked with disability rights entrepreneurs on various legislation—would be crucial to coordinating disruptive action (Figure 5.2). These more prominent groups were occasionally joined in solidarity efforts by, for instance, the NFB and American Servicemen's Union.

To build on the early demonstrations organized by DIA against the federal government, local Centers for Independent Living helped foster a mobilizable base of activists—for instance, San Diego's Community Service Center for the

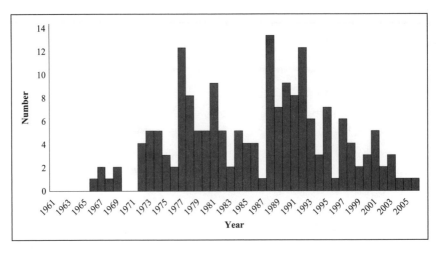

Figure 5.1 Disability protest events, 1961–2006 (*N* = 179).

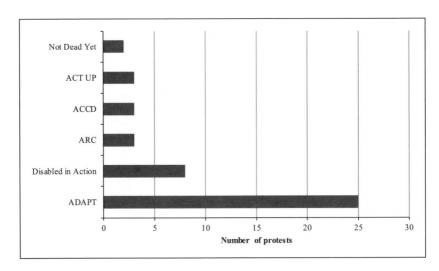

Figure 5.2 Most active protest groups.

Disabled, founded in 1976—and local groups such as Barrier Free Anaheim, which protested the inaccessibility of city hall in 1976.

Parents of children with disabilities also took to the streets, though more frequently in one-time protest demonstrations ranging from dozens to hundreds of participants and rarely organized by a specific local or national organization. These discrete events generally protested the closure of schools and other facilities or funding cuts to social and educational services.

They were reminiscent of the handful of protest events that occurred in the late 1960s around social welfare cuts, yet the availability of rights language encoded in Section 504 now equipped parents with a more effective toolkit for framing their activism. Local coalitions and activist networks in the 1970s rarely mobilized directly against the federal government, focusing their efforts instead on local issues. And though local chapters of NARC targeted state legislatures and later the ACCD targeted the transit industry, it was these increasingly professionalized advocacy groups that monitored, participated in, and protested against federal government activity.

Early protest demonstrations almost certainly created a new sense of collective efficacy, helping diffuse protest across numerous cities.[34] Some cities acted as movement or protest centers: New York City saw some of the earliest protests in the form of unconnected events around education and Medicaid cutbacks in the 1960s, many coordinated by parents, the Committee on Aging and Disabled for Welfare, and social welfare groups and labor unions. In 1972, however, the New York-based DIA protested in Manhattan and later in Washington, D.C., against Nixon's veto of the Rehabilitation Act.

The Bay Area of California played home to the independent living movement of the late 1960s and early 1970s. Activists generated momentum surrounding deinstitutionalization and championed policy alternatives including rehabilitation. The Center for Independent Living made Berkeley a magnet for activists with disabilities when Ed Roberts, then a disabled student at UC Berkeley, challenged his university to provide access to people with disabilities across its campus. The activists at these centers, which emerged in other cities, considered existing client-service models as paternalistic and slow to incorporate a stronger civil rights focus. Centers for Independent Living operated, in their words, free spaces for young persons with disabilities to develop an "oppositional consciousness": a state of mind that understands membership in an oppressed group in relation to structures of domination contributing to a politicized collective identity.[35] Protests in the Bay Area peaked in the late 1970s and 1980s, when national disability groups like ADAPT, DIA, and ACCD became involved in coordinating demonstrations in the region.

The largest protests in the entire disability rights struggle occurred between 1972 and 1982 (see Table A.5 and Figure A.6 in the appendix).[36] The first wave of disability protest peaked just as other movements (e.g., race, abortion rights, LGBT, gender, human rights) saw a sharp decline in protest activity.[37] Disability activists mobilized around two key issues in the early part of the 1980s: threats to social services and civil rights by the new Reagan administration and equal access to transportation, with many protests held in the nation's capital. Of the fourteen major protests held in 1981 and 1982, eleven targeted the Reagan administration. While there were protests targeting transit agencies organized by ADAPT and protests at Gallaudet University, a large proportion of Washington protests targeted either Congress, the Supreme Court, or the administration, often coordinated by coalitions of groups including the NFB, Gray Panthers, and the ACCD.

In the second half of the 1980s, only about 10 percent of all disability protests targeted the federal government. By 1980, twenty-nine states had adopted disability rights laws, many modeled after Section 504;[38] not coincidentally, protests began to target state governments rather than federal agencies. Across the country, transit-related protests came to define disability protest.

Transit accessibility, as an issue focus, offered a concrete, proximate issue with a specific set of desired outcomes and a natural appeal. It continued to make intuitive sense, echoing early disability entrepreneurs' assertions that vocational training was of little use if a disabled person would be prevented, by discrimination, from getting a job. Pragmatic protesters could now assert that getting a job was of little use if a disabled person could not get to that job (see Chapter 2 for more on how actors in the disability policy network ultimately linked rehabilitation to discrimination). Further, the transit industry provided a more direct path for mobilizing grievances, as the federal government was increasingly portrayed as being unable or unwilling to do anything about disability rights. DIA and ADAPT created local short-term coalitions such as the September Alliance for Accessible Transit, and ADAPT was integral in bringing together activists in large cities like Los Angeles that, thus far, had only a scant history of disability-related mobilization.

ADAPT played a significant role in organizing protests first around public transit accessibility and then around in-home care in a "second wave" of protest (see Figure 5.1); while the group did target the federal government, they more often targeted transit companies and the nursing home industry (these combined represented about one-quarter of the protests in the period surrounding the ADA).

The uptick in this second wave coincided with the introduction of the ADA, but few protests between 1988 and 1992 directly (or at all) invoked the ADA. The policy may have had a general, indirect effect in generating buzz about disability issues, but only about 15 percent of the forty-nine protests during this period targeted the federal government, and only one protest (organized by ADAPT in 1990) sought to directly raise awareness about the ADA. About one hundred protesters were arrested at that event.

Despite the increase and sustained use of protest by the disability rights movement, these protests tended to be of small-to-medium size and short duration.[39] Few resulted in arrests (especially before the mid-1980s).[40] The number and frequency of arrests increased in the late 1980s and 1990s, partially as the result of the rise of disruptive transit protests (42 percent of transit-related protests led to arrests, but only 14 percent for protests overall). Of the thirteen protests coordinated by ADAPT in the 1980s, about half ended in arrests. ADAPT developed a reputation as a "militant advocacy group," reveling in its "role as agitator."[41]

Of course, arrests were not necessarily unwelcome. Organizers and protesters knew that arrests could be an important tool in increasing media attention and public interest. A Los Angeles Times reporter captured the interaction between disabled protesters and law enforcement, calling it an "odd orchestration of defiance and cooperation."[42] When ADAPT coordinated a protest of 131 wheelchair users against a public-transit conference in Los Angeles in 1985, there were eight arrests. Some protesters kicked and screamed, while others littered the streets with the shreds of their own organization's literature. One protester simply yelled, "Arrest me!"[43]

Police were generally reluctant to arrest disabled protesters. They knew the optics were bad and could create public relations nightmares. At Los Angeles protests in 1988, one arresting officer called it a "distasteful necessity," telling reporters, "We look bad no matter what we do." Police Captain Gregg Berg insisted, as protestors openly hoped to be arrested, "We don't have any intention of taking these folks into custody"[44] Throughout the 1980s, there would be arrests in transit disruptions across the country, from San Francisco to Atlanta to Cincinnati (see Table A.5 in the appendix).

ADAPT protests targeting the nursing home industry in the 1990s and 2000s generated few arrests. In 2003, ADAPT organized one hundred activists to protest the DOJ, demanding the agency force states to adopt policies favoring home care over nursing homes for the disabled. Police made a concerted effort not to arrest any of the protesters. An officer warily told reporters, "People look for us to do that sort of thing. And if we do make arrests, we wind up getting criticized." So "if there's some way we can try to let them get their point across but not make arrests, that's something we'll do."[45]

After the ADA was enacted, there was an overall decline in disruptive disability rights actions, and the federal government was seen as less and less relevant as a target of protest (see Figure 5.1). Of the seventy-four protests held between 1990 and 2006 (between passage of the ADA and ADARA), less than one-quarter targeted the federal government. With ADAPT refocusing its efforts away from transit to in-home care, DIA stepped in to organize a few transit accessibility-related protests. The second wave of protest lasted from the late 1980s to the early 2000s, with a waning in the disability protest cycle. However, the number and kinds of issues and targets the movement engaged with increased.

DIA, for instance, turned to dismantling negative and pitying images of disability by targeting the Jerry Lewis Telethon; the AIDS Coalition to Unleash Power (ACT UP) held several protests related to the treatment of people with HIV/AIDS (a 1990 protest featured the chant, "The disabled are proud. Say it out loud!"); and Not Dead Yet, a grassroots group of disability activists, opposed the legalization of assisted suicide and held protests, including several related to Terry Schiavo, who was in a persistent vegetative state after suffering cardiac arrest. Her husband and parents engaged in a protracted emotional and legal fight over whether to remove Schiavo's feeding tube. Between March 24 and 27, 2005, wheelchair users lay on the ground to the entrance of Schiavo's hospice, chanting, "We're not dead yet!" and telling reporters "that society needed to alter its attitude that a life of severe disability is not worth living."[46] The courts ultimately sided with Schiavo's husband, and her feeding tube was removed. Schiavo died March 31, 2005.

The rise of more militant groups like ADAPT clashed in the second wave, with long-established groups like PVA and their elite policy-maker advocates. The headline of a spring 1987 ADAPT newsletter, *Incitement*, read: "Paralyzed Veterans Declare War Against ADAPT." Apparently, PVA issued a statement prohibiting its members from any further associations with ADAPT, in which its executive director stated, "PVA, it seems, was more concerned with their 'professional' image and fundraising prowess than they were with the rights of people with disabilities."[47]

Protest did little to directly shape the policy agenda, but agenda-setting and policy-making processes shaped direct action (see the analyses in Table A.6 in the appendix). Policy dynamics—the world outside social movements—generated political opportunities for citizens to access the state. Contentious politics and extra-institutional activism showcase important institutional, organizational, and cultural dynamics in the evolution of the disability rights agenda, but they also point to that policies, disguised as political victories, may not always end up delivering the (public) goods.

Advocacy, Protest, and Policy in the "Third Wave of Civil Rights"

The political evolution of disability is a complicated interplay between policy making, disruption, and routine politics. As advocacy groups engaging in a mix of institutional and extra-institutional tactics were themselves shaped by institutional changes, their mobilization also became part of a broader effort that made disability policy in the 1980s a cornerstone in what Alan A. Reich, president of the National Organization on Disability, called America's "third wave of civil rights."[48]

In 1988, Reich outlined three important contributions of the joint efforts of movement activists and political entrepreneurs in the years leading up to the ADA.[49] The first was the construction of a collective identity uniting the disability community and tying their plight to that of other historically marginalized groups. Second, Reich pointed to increased visibility of the disability rights cause in the media and, finally, to "the participation of disabled people in the electoral process"—the identification of the disabled as politicized citizens.[50]

The optimism expressed by rights entrepreneurs belied a dark period in the civil rights struggle. Reagan's first term had been a nail in the coffin for Section 504 enforcement. The Office of Management and Budget (OMB) and the DOJ—two fairly conservative agencies[51]—grew more central in disability rights policy as the OCR became impotent and ineffective in enforcing disability rights legislation. The DOJ sought to rephrase Section 504 to limit requirements for accessibility to institutions and programs that directly received government funding, while the administration concurrently dismantled the requirements for transit accessibility so central to the disability rights struggle during the Carter years.

In 1981, Assistant Attorney General William Bradford Reynolds, who headed the Civil Rights Division under Reagan, established that the DOJ would "no longer insist upon, or in any respect support, the use of quotas or any other numerical or statistical formulae designed to provide to non-victims of discrimination preferential treatment based on race, sex, national origin or religion."[52] In other words, the administration was abandoning affirmative action. The DOJ also opposed applying Section 504 to people with communicable diseases, including HIV/AIDS.[53] The Consortium for Citizens with Developmental Disabilities, the Leadership Conference on Civil Rights, and the American Medical Association blasted the DOJ for its position.

Advocacy organizations such as DREDF, which provided important educational and legal resources to disabled Americans, joined groups such as PVA and the National Center for the Deaf in testifying against these institutional changes. In 1982, DREDF, the National Women's Law Center, and the NAACP criticized the failure of the Department of Education to enforce civil rights in regard to race, gender, and disability.

Efforts to court sympathetic elites in Congress brought some success. For instance, Congress enacted the Handicapped Children's Protection Act of 1986 (counteracting the *Smith v. Robinson* decision). Although Reagan signed the bill into law, he noted disapproval for its allowance of retroactive awards, claiming that it "permits the Congress to displace the judicial function by interfering with a final judgment. To do so disturbs the settled expectations of the parties and the traditional finality that our society has accorded court decisions."[54]

Political elites were further mobilized by judicial and administrative attacks on disability rights in the 1980s. Motivated by *Department of Transportation v. Paralyzed Veterans of America*,[55] for instance, in 1986 Sen. Bob Dole sponsored the Air Carrier Access Act (Pub. L. 99-435) prohibiting airlines from discriminating against disabled persons. The following year, Harkin and Rep. Edwin Madigan (R-IL) sponsored the Developmental Disabilities Assistance and Bill of Rights Act Amendments of 1987, seeking to empower disabled consumers of social services. UCP, the Epilepsy Foundation, and the Consortium for Citizens with Disabilities were heavily involved in the hearings leading up to the law.

Also in 1987, the Supreme Court, in *School Board of Nassau County v. Arline*, affirmed the 1985 lower-court decision that Section 504 applied to a schoolteacher with tuberculosis who had been fired by the board (Justices William Rehnquist and Antonin Scalia joined in the dissent).[56] The American Medical Association filed an amicus curiae brief, assuring the court that Section 504 did apply to irrational discrimination based on persons having communicable diseases such as tuberculosis or AIDS, and the ruling challenged the administration's position. The decision also stood in stark contrast to unfavorable judicial precedent set by the 1979 *Davis* case, one of the rare decisions to favor activists and rights entrepreneurs (alongside *Olmstead* in 1999).

In 1988, as the ADA was introduced, the Fair Housing Amendments Act strengthened enforcement of a twenty-year-old policy providing equal access to housing. The entire civil rights community gained with the passage of the Civil Rights Restoration Act (CRRA), previously vetoed by Reagan. In passing the CRRA, Congress revised the *Grove City College v. Bell* decision that only the division of a corporation to which an accessibility claim was brought had to comply.[57] Now that accessibility claims would affect entire corporations, noncompliance had greater consequences.

However, these policy developments also reopened debates about what constitutes disability, and the struggle over communicable diseases reemerged as a prominent issue in Congress as well as among disability activists and rights entrepreneurs. The CRRA amended the Rehabilitation Act's definition of "individual with handicaps" by excluding from Section 504 employment protections certain persons with contagious diseases or infections (those who would constitute a "direct threat" to the health or safety of others or who were not able to perform the duties of the job because of such contagious disease or infection).

The debate over whether people with HIV/AIDS, for example, were protected by disability rights legislation was important not only to AIDS activists but also to the disability rights movement. Activists were encouraged by the Senate's version of the proposed ADA, which signaled intent to include people with communicable diseases in the legislation, and by the Bush administration's support for the Senate version. The House was reluctant to act.

At a 1989 House Subcommittee on Health and the Environment hearing, James R. Allen, director of the National AIDS Program Office in HHS, urged the House to act on the Senate bill, calling it "a strong Federal antidiscrimination bill which will help persons with HIV as well as other handicapped people."[58] ACT UP, an important protest organization in the AIDS community, participated in the hearings, but only with regard to the treatment of HIV/AIDS, not the broader legislation.

By 1990, disability mobilization was peaking. Threats to rights by a growing number of opponents throughout the 1980s galvanized disabled activists and the disability policy community.[59] The years leading up to the ADA would see a shift from political threat to policy restoration, while activism evolved to include broader issues and newer targets.

New Political Opportunities in the "Emancipation Proclamation" for People with Disabilities

The controversy over Section 504 being akin to the 1964 Civil Rights Act finally seemed to be put to rest, as Jesse Jackson, of the Rainbow Coalition, reiterated at a 1989 hearing: "Americans with disabilities do not receive the protection of the Civil Rights Act of 1964, and the ADA would right that wrong."[60] Federal antidiscrimination legislation would directly address the separate and unequal system of civil rights policies that disability activists had been fighting against, arguing that discrimination based on disability is no different from discrimination based on other status characteristics. It was in this golden age of disability policy that momentum grew around a new bill of rights for the disabled—what Harkin called "their emancipation proclamation."[61]

One of the great triumphs of the ADA—as is often touted by its proponents—was the bipartisan support it received. Disability rights entrepreneurs, especially Republicans, worked to convince their party and the administration to support the ADA. Justin Dart,[62] believing strongly in the role of government in empowering citizens, headed the Disabled for Reagan campaign in 1984. He eventually became the RSA commissioner, but because of his civil rights advocacy was asked to resign.

Dart's role in championing the ADA came through his Reagan appointment to the National Council on the Handicapped. Dart was instrumental in convincing many in the Republican Party that a civil rights approach was necessary. Assistant Attorney General Reynolds, a persona non grata in the civil rights community, would ironically become a supporter, sympathizing with the plight of people with disabilities even as he argued against affirmative action and supported the *Grove* decision. Even Reagan, no friend of the disability rights struggle, appeared to be showing sympathy: "Our Nation's commitment to equal protection of the laws will have little meaning if we deny such protection to those who have not been blessed with the same physical or mental gifts we too often take for granted. I support Federal laws prohibiting discrimination against the handicapped, and remain determined that such laws be vigorously enforced."[63] His statement may have been vacuous and nonspecific, but it nevertheless marked a departure from a much stronger position against civil rights enforcement.

Thus, entrepreneurship within the Republican Party empowered elites and activists to work in support of the ADA. Dart was joined by notable figures such as John McCain, who regularly expressed his pride in being an original ADA cosponsor in 1988.[64] Moderate Rep. Steven Gunderson (R-WI) and McCain cosponsored the Telecommunications Accessibility Enhancement Act.[65]

Sen. David Durenberger (R-MN) perhaps best captured entrepreneurial efforts by members of his own party in describing colleague Bob Dole in 1990:

"His leadership in getting the Americans With Disabilities Act through this body with a very, very substantial vote against substantial opposition, his leadership in getting it to this point in the negotiations with the administration and his leadership now in trying to influence the House of Representatives to come to an agreement on a bill that the President can sign I think is a signal."[66] Durenberger suggested that these efforts would help the Republican Party shed its anti–civil rights reputation; along with Jeffords and Weicker, Durenberger had been among those Republicans of the 1980s who most often voted against the CC.[67]

George H. W. Bush had shown little support for Section 504 enforcement as Reagan's vice president, but he eventually became a strong advocate for the ADA and was viewed as an ally by many disability activists. Many explanations—some political, some personal—have been offered for his about-face, among them the loss of his daughter to leukemia and his son Neil's struggle with a learning disability. As Charles A. Riley wrote, the Bushes were members of disability's "silent army,"[68] fighting against unfair policy and public perceptions about disability.

The former vice president also had politically strategic reasons to distance himself from Reagan's ardent opposition to civil rights legislation. At first, Bush would not go out of his way to promote a civil rights agenda, yet his ambivalence signaled a loosening on the issue. For example, the 1991 Civil Rights Act, which recognized statistical discrimination (in defiance of Reagan's position) in addition to animus-based discrimination,[69] did not necessarily find support because of White House leadership; instead, it faced little opposition because there was no ideological battle around these policies. Things were getting easier for rights entrepreneurs to sway the Bush team on civil rights legislation. Bush's support for disability rights meshed nicely with his brand of "compassionate conservatism."

By the time the ADA was signed into law, the original legislation drafted by Dart and Robert Burgdorf had been watered down considerably. Lex Frieden, who chaired the National Council on Disability, believed that the compromises made since the 1988 draft risked producing an ineffective antidiscrimination policy. Although the law was hailed as a bipartisan achievement, vocal detractors showed that it was more compromise than consensus. Many of the arguments made against the ADA would resurface throughout the 1990s and 2000s as deep-seated opposition against any policy construed as interfering with or regulating the private sector gained dominance in government.

One major impediment involved the inclusion of HIV/AIDS as grounds for discrimination under the ADA. Rights entrepreneurs like Ted Kennedy, who in

1989 chaired the Senate Committee on Labor and Human Resources, strongly supported a definition of disability that included communicable diseases. Kennedy made an impassioned plea to his colleagues:

> Before this epidemic can be brought under control, it is essential to remedy the problem of discrimination against those infected with the virus. It is my hope that all members of this committee will cosponsor and support passage of the Americans With Disabilities Act in order to halt discrimination against any individual with a disability, including infection with the AIDS virus. In his campaign, President Bush pledged his support for this approach, and [I] am hopeful that the President and the Administration will join us in making clear that discrimination against people with AIDS is unacceptable.[70]

Kennedy, however, was preaching to the choir. The president, the administration, and the Senate were roughly on the same page in regard to the ADA. The House, however, acted far more cautiously. As a speech before the National Leadership Coalition on AIDS, later reprinted in the *Congressional Record* at the request of Orrin Hatch, President Bush insisted, "Today I call on the House of Representatives to get on with the job of passing a law—as embodied in the Americans with Disabilities Act—that prohibits discrimination against those with HIV and AIDS. We're in a fight against a disease—not a fight against people. And we won't tolerate discrimination."[71] Activists and advocates were impatient that the proposed amendments slowed the legislation's pace through Congress.

ACT UP and the Association of Black Psychologists called for activism in the March 1989 *AIDS Newsletter:*

ADVOCATE!

Write your Congressperson to support the Americans with Disabilities Act (ADA) which will establish broader antidiscrimination protections for persons living with AIDS or who are HIV positive.

Their efforts were reaching the public but changing few opponents' minds. The controversial Chapman Amendment was written, partially, as the result of National Restaurant Association pressure;[72] the interest group wanted the ADA to allow restaurants to reassign employees with AIDS to other comparable jobs, and their demand delayed House consideration of the final legislation. In his personal legislative notes, Bob Dole noted that the National Restaurant Association made similar claims about race in regard to the 1964 Civil Rights Act and that the amendment "resurrects groundless fears that AIDS can be spread through food, undermining years of public education efforts meant to calm people's fears about the disease."[73] PVA expressed its discontent to Rep. Steny Hoyer (D-MD).[74] The conferees dropped the amendment, but restaurateurs demanded it be reinserted. In vigorous debate, House members stipulated that they did not consider an employer refusing to assign food-handling jobs to an employee with an infectious disease as a violation of the ADA.[75]

The ADA also reinvigorated perennial concerns about housing and transportation, and the resulting tensions delayed its passage. Rights entrepreneurs saw an opportunity to finalize the twenty-year conflict around accessibility. Groups such as the Consortium for Citizens with Disabilities and Mental Health Law Project were heavily involved in these issues.[76] Citing a 1986 Harris Poll and study by the PVA finding that half of disabled respondents felt they could not get around due to lack of transit accessibility, Rep. Bill Owens (D-NY) testified that "discrimination in public transportation is one of the most destructive limitations facing disabled people. . . . The Americans with Disabilities Act of 1988 would bring about this vision of equality. It requires that bus systems gradually become completely accessible to mobility-impaired people who can't climb normal bus steps."[77]

Even Republican disability rights entrepreneurs were growing impatient. Once again, political elites turned to protesters to apply pressure on holdouts. When ADAPT occupied a federal building in Atlanta just before passage of the ADA, a call from President Bush himself allowed protesters to remain. Most likely, as Joseph Shapiro suggested in *No Pity*, supporters of the ADA (both inside and outside government) needed Republican holdouts to feel political pressure, and that had to come from outside government. In 1990, ADAPT held a protest in Washington, D.C., to raise public awareness surrounding the ADA, and Dole took notice: "And, now, citizens from throughout the Nation— as demonstrated during a recent gathering on the steps of the U.S. Capitol— are determined to see the Americans With Disabilities Act passed and signed into law."[78]

Disability rights activists, organizational leaders, and disability rights entrepreneurs found some measure of success, especially in forging new ties with policy makers and bringing the issue to the American public. ADAPT pointed to its success in organizing disruptive protests at one hearing, which happened to coincide with the twenty-fifth anniversary of the Urban Mass Transportation Act. When Harkin asked whether people with disabilities would actually prefer paratransit services over access to mainstream public transit, ADAPT's co-founder, Mark Johnson, responded: "They [attorneys] said in Phoenix, it is too hot, and people in Arizona prefer to be picked up at their door. Two weeks after ADAPT left Phoenix, AZ in 1987, they committed to total access."[79] ADAPT's newsletter trumpeted, "ADAPT Rides Again in Phoenix."[80] In addition to ADAPT's legal mobilization and discussion of the history of legislative mandates surrounding disability rights, Johnson stressed the importance of direct action:

> The American Public Transit Association, for years, has opposed total access. So I found it kind of enlightening to read their testimony that neither says we are for ADA or against ADA. . . . One reason why I am returning to the Atlanta area this evening is to continue my efforts in organizing a series of public protests aimed at the American Public Transit Association and the American Bus Association. ADAPT has followed APTA around for six years trying to get them to the point where they want to form a partnership. Year after year, they denied our appeals. Year after year, they have supported local option. Year after year, they have been as offensive as those questions were to me.[81]

APTA had become the chief antagonist in the rights struggle. To the pleasure of many activists, the media helped promote this narrative. For example, a *San Francisco Chronicle* article summarized the thrust of the protest wave: "For more than 10 years disabled people nationwide have pressed for wheelchair access to local buses and trains. However, APTA, in 1981, managed to overturn a federal mandate requiring wheelchair lifts on all new buses."[82] Other news outlets would echo this depiction of APTA's political influence over policy making.[83]

Protests raised public awareness about accessibility, and there were signs that this pressure around the pending ADA led to growing transit industry efforts to become more informed about how to conform to the legislation. The Architectural and Transportation Barriers Compliance Board testified in a 1990 ADA appropriations hearing that they received an increase in requests for technical information and assistance about compliance, claiming that "the increase can be attributed to the Board's outreach activities and increased interest in accessibility issues due to the pending Americans With Disabilities Act."[84] In response to the ADA, the board embarked on a public outreach campaign and held open meetings with groups, people with disabilities, public officials, employers, and other authorities.

On the eve of the House vote, two transportation amendments that neither the president nor the Democrats supported again stalled the legislation.[85]

A dismayed Hoyer fumed, "We ought to build in our society the psychology of accessibility to all people in our society."[86] To further complicate matters, the proposed Sensenbrenner Amendment would limit the remedies available to people with disabilities outlined in the 1990 Civil Rights Act.[87] Disability rights entrepreneurs adamantly opposed Sensenbrenner's proposal, but it had the support of the Bush administration.[88]

The ADA—the emancipation proclamation for people with disabilities, the product of political compromise reviewed and approved by four different committees, finally passed 403–20.[89] The 1980s began, as one representative of the National Spinal Cord Injury Association described, with "crushed aspirations" but with social movement work and the efforts of sympathetic political elites; the decade ended with significant political gains for those concerned with the civil rights of the disabled.

Political Victories and Deflating Hopes

The ADA was seen as a new opportunity to expand the momentum around civil rights to other legislative areas. Rights entrepreneurs like Harkin worked with the National Association of Developmental Disabilities Councils to study and improve public policies that affected people with developmental disabilities, as mandated by the 1987 Developmental Disabilities Act.[90] Policy makers worked on the Developmental Disabilities Assistance and Bill of Rights Act of 1990 and the Television Decoder Circuitry Act, which would increase telephone accessibility for deaf people.

The ADA also reenergized opponents mobilizing against what they saw as burdensome regulatory policy. Rather than settle a decades-old debate about what Congress meant when it enacted disability rights legislation, the ADA spurred innovative attempts to undermine civil rights for the disabled.

While the Chapman Amendment, for example, was unsuccessful,[91] critics would continue to raise concerns about the treatment of AIDS and other communicable diseases under the ADA. There was also plenty of ongoing discussion surrounding remedies, damages, and distinctions between intentional discrimination and disparate impact. In hearings regarding reauthorization of the Urban Mass Transportation Act, APTA lobbied against increasing funds, depicting the ADA as a "burden." The Senate in many ways legitimized complaints that the ADA was an undue hardship on employers, seeking to address any costs associated with accommodations through the use of tax credits that several Republicans opposed.

Given both the subtle and overt attempts by the administration and Congress to chisel away at the ADA, before and after its enactment, disability organizations became particularly vigilant around attempts to appease the business community, conservatives who worried about being criticized as regulating private interests, and liberals who feared that the ADA would not be taken seriously if they did not compromise. These groups had to be flexible in their advocacy efforts. ADAPT, for instance, coordinated protests targeting local authorities but also joined other groups in continued congressional lobbying efforts.

In the period between the introduction of the ADA and when it took effect (1988–1992), there were forty-nine disability protests. About 30 percent were related to transit accessibility, many targeting local authorities. However, activists saw new political opportunities in Bill Clinton's presidency, particularly in regard to health care, social services, and in-home care. In 1991, when Clinton was governor of Arkansas, disabled protesters chained themselves to the gates of his office until he agreed to restore program cuts and provide in-home care for people with disabilities.[92] Many hoped to parlay these more local efforts into successes at the federal level.

During the 1992 presidential electoral campaign, ADAPT organized a protest at Clinton's San Francisco headquarters. Wheelchair users blocked access for hours, successfully pressuring Clinton to include long-term care in his health-care platform. One newspaper declared, "Capitol Hill is the battleground now."[93] Clinton likely saw people with disabilities as an important constituency, lending credibility to his campaign promise to reform health care. Following Clinton's win, health-care reform generated both opportunities and uncertainties regarding inclusion of provisions directly affecting people with disabilities—including the attendant programs that make in-home care possible. Activists led a wheelchair processional across the Memorial Bridge with banners reading "healthcare for all," and Clinton encouraged activists to lobby Congress: "This is a battle that you may be able to lead for the rest of America. You can break through to those members of Congress. You can do it."[94]

ADAPT now turned its focus almost exclusively on in-home care, believing it was important to keep people out of institutions, and worked tirelessly in the late 1990s to influence legislation so that more funding would be earmarked for attendant programs. While ADAPT worked with legislators, it also drew from its extensive experience with direct action. In one large 1995 protest, which led to several arrests, 250 protestors blocked access to the Silver Springs headquarters of Manor Care. They wanted the head of the nursing home company to sign a letter to Congress demanding that 25 percent of Medicaid funding to nursing homes be transferred to home-care programs,[95] a defining issue for the movement even today. By the end of the decade, it had become clear that nursing homes and their industry associations were the chief adversary in the disability rights struggle. At a 1997 demonstration, protesters outside the National Home Care Association demanded that laws pertaining to home care require more input from the disabled.[96]

Disability-related issues were, however, finding an increasingly smaller audience. Largely the result of less diverse committee jurisdictions and the shrinkage of venues dedicated to addressing disability, there was a sharp decline in congressional hearings. The ADA was seen as *the* governmental solution to most of the problems people with disabilities face. For many people, that meant the ADA had settled and closed the books on the issue of disability rights.

The Senate Subcommittee on the Handicapped—a committee central to expanding interest in disability rights on the policy agenda in the 1970s—became the Subcommittee on Disability Policy. Although the committee was chaired by rights entrepreneurs like Harkin and its members included supportive legislators like Jeffords, Dodd, and Hatch, the committee was disbanded by the end of the decade. Between 1990 and 1995, it worked on the Developmental Disabilities Assistance and Bill of Rights Act, reauthorization of the Rehabilitation Act of 1973, and reauthorization of IDEA. However, over five years, the committee held only ten hearings, many fewer than in the 1970s and 1980s.

The new institutional context of the 1990s has contributed to the current state of unsettled disability politics. The debate over in-home care, for instance, is still raging in 2018, just one example of a bipartisan policy plagued by entrenchment problems.

In-home care has a lengthy history in the independent living movement of the 1970s and, to some extent, in earlier rehabilitation policies. In the 1990s, direct systematic efforts led by Republicans like House Speaker Newt Gingrich produced the Medicaid Community Attendant Services Act (also known as MiCASA), increasing disabled Americans' input in long-term care policies and emphasizing care in the community or home.

Gingrich proposed amendments to the Social Security Act to allow individuals eligible for Medicaid services and living in nursing homes to use the funds covering these services to pay instead for qualified community-based attendant services. ADAPT, seizing the opening, demanded that hearings be held on the issue of home care so that the disability community's voice could be heard. After sixty-four protesters tied themselves to the White House gate (many were arrested), Rep. Michael Bilirakis (R-FL), chair of the House Commerce Committee's Subcommittee on Health and Environment, agreed to arrange a hearing in March 1998. Considered a highly productive congressman, Bilirakis had a strong conservative voting record (an average CC score of about 90). He was a complicated figure concerning disability: he received a score of 0 percent from the American Public Health Association (APHA),[97] yet he was also strongly against doctor-assisted suicide and voted against the Pain Relief Promotion Act of 1999 in a move that appealed to many disability activists.

Clinton's administration supported MiCASA, testifying in Congress that it had been working with disabled constituents and advocates over the last few years to further develop community-based care. Indeed, bipartisan work on the proposed legislation was reminiscent of the bipartisanship that had motivated midcentury rehabilitation policies. Many conservatives framed their support of attendant programs as a way to help the disabled help themselves rather than turn people with disabilities into tax burdens by institutionalizing them. As Newt Gingrich proposed, "Our goal should be to replace the caretaker-dependency model with a model of empowerment and independent living. We should seek to use the means at our disposal to encourage and maximize personal independence," or what Rick Lazio (R-NY) called "unleashing the shackles of institutional care." In his testimony, Justin Dart called on Congress and Clinton to "translate the rhetoric of free enterprise into action that will give real choices to people with disabilities and older Americans who participate in the American dream."[98]

It helped that the policy was framed to fit with the Clinton-Gingrich bipartisanship so often heralded as a hallmark of the Clinton presidency (and used to facilitate Clinton's controversial welfare reform, the 1996 Personal Responsibility and Work Opportunity Reconciliation Act). While the president supported the policy in the broadest sense, he also preferred states to take the lead: "States should help each other move forward."[99] Those working on health care at the state level sympathetic to attendant home care worried that without federal government leadership, the nursing home industry's powerful influence over state legislatures would undermine their efforts.

The Bilirakis-led hearing allowed activists to voice their opinions about the proposed legislation. One of the Denver cofounders of ADAPT, Michael Auberger, testified, "Across the Nation the call is ringing. We are tired of waiting.

Needing personal attendant services is not a crime, but thousands of people with disabilities are locked away in institutions because there are very few real options in the United States' long-term care system."[100] ADAPT requested that six additional field hearings be held across the United States to facilitate participation of the disability community. However, as a result of cuts to committee resources, Bilirakis did not hold these hearings.

The hearing demonstrated to policy makers the importance of this issue in the disability community as well as activists' technical expertise in addressing community-based care through federal legislation. Auberger and ADAPT cofounder Wade Blank highlighted the critical role of activists in the political process. Rep. Diana DeGette (D-CO) called on activists at the hearing "to make sure that their local elected officials, from their city council all the way up to Congress, come and see what happens in nursing homes, come and see what happens in community-based organizations. Because that is the only way we, as your elected officials, will truly understand the importance of this kind of legislation."[101]

ADAPT was joined by Voice of the Retarded and National Alliance of the Disabled, among other groups, in writing to the subcommittee in support of MiCASA. Alongside independent living centers, NARC, the Brain Injury Association, and the Association for the Severely Handicapped (TASH), the letter reminded legislators of the disability community's heterogeneous needs and warned that, while they supported the legislation, they believed this and other policies continued to promote a bias toward institutional care and lacked quality-assurance measures for personal caregivers.

Disability groups brought up contentious elements in the proposed policy, including the quality of health-care workers, but these points were moot. The Congressional Budget Office (CBO) delivered a blow to the entire project, claiming in a report that the policy would be prohibitively expensive: "This new entitlement will place enormous strain on federal and state budgets."[102] The nursing home industry vigorously opposed the amendment, worried that this would lead to funding cuts to their institutions. The law never made it out of committee and died with the 105th Congress. In 1998, hundreds of protesters again blocked HHS offices in Washington over policies seen as favoring institutionalization.[103]

Disability activists and rights entrepreneurs in Congress did have new ammunition in promoting in-home care: *Olmstead v. L.C.* In 1999, the Supreme Court ruled that the state of Georgia had violated the ADA when it required two women with learning disabilities to live in a mental hospital. When Harkin reintroduced the Medicaid Community-Based Attendant Services and Supports Act (MiCASSA, now festooned with two "S's") in 2001, Rep. Danny K. Davis (D-IL), cosponsor, told his House colleagues on the twelfth anniversary of the ADA:

> On July 26, 1990 President George Bush signed the Americans with Disabilities Act into law. This landmark civil rights legislation . . . established a new social compact that seeks to end the paternalistic patterns of the past that take away our rights if we become disabled. . . . Much like the promise of the 1965 Civil Rights Act, however, the promise cannot become a reality until we roll up our sleeves and do the work necessary to eliminate the barriers, which still hinder its full implementation. While some recent decisions of the Supreme Court have threatened the scope of the ADA, I would like to call our attention to a Supreme Court ruling that reaffirms the fundamental principle that people with disabilities have the right to be active participants integrated into the everyday life of society. In 1999, the Court ruled in the Olmstead case that states violate the Americans with Disabilities Act when they unnecessarily put people with disabilities in institutions.[104]

Throughout the 2000s, ADAPT coordinated protests against the nursing home industry while seeking ways to work with Congress on policy initiatives like MiCASSA. But unlike the original 1997 House bill, the Senate bill had, among its smaller list of cosponsors, only two Republicans. John Shimkus (R-IL), considered a reliable social and fiscal conservative,[105] sponsored the House version in 2002 (resulting in sixty-nine Democratic and fifteen Republican cosponsors). In it, legislators at least partially responded to disability organizations by including quality-assurance programs.

Danny Davis again insisted on what disability activists had pointed out years earlier: without federal government leadership, states and the nursing home industry would not change. Indeed, by 2002, only twenty-seven states had adopted a policy under Medicaid that provided some personal care, and even across these states, there was wide variation. Like other backers of the bill, Davis saw the federal government as critical in removing the bias toward institutionalization. Davis concluded: "I can think of no better way to honor the memory of our departed disability rights leader, Justin Dart, who died on June 22nd and was known by many as the father of the Americans with Disabilities Act than to support passage of H.R. 3612."[106]

Neither the House nor Senate bill left its respective committee. In 2003, Harkin again reintroduced MiCASSA, and the bill was sent again to the Senate Finance Committee in 2004. The committee held one hearing, likely at the behest of George W. Bush's administration, which wanted to make the main objectives of MiCASSA part of the New Freedom Initiative (closely resembling the Senate's Money Follows the Person bill [MFP]). This new version of the bill called for few changes to Medicare, seeking only to provide up-front money to states to encourage attendant care programs. It was an election year, and Medicare and Medicaid were hotly political. Harkin reiterated that, compared to other parts of the health-care reform proposals, MiCASSA had "no 'politics' on this whatsoever."[107] Sympathetic policy makers still saw an uphill battle. Sen. Max Baucus (D-MT) called it a "challenging" issue in an election year.[108]

Again dismayed by delays, ADAPT organized a protest at the Old Courthouse in St. Louis. It was part of a larger campaign that had begun as a fourteen-day march of about twenty thousand protesters from Philadelphia to Washington, D.C. Protesters held signs reading "There's no place like home."[109] The organization pressured policy makers by citing widespread support for MiCASSA: "In fact, 92 national organizations are MiCASSA supporters. An additional 255 state or regional organizations also support the bill, as well as 306 local groups. . . . ADAPT is working with children's advocates and senior advocates. Supporting organizations represent people with all types of disabilities: people with cognitive disabilities, people with sensory disabilities, people with mental health labels and/or people with physical disabilities."[110]

Democrats sought solutions, including shifting the focus away from amending existing Medicare law. Coming up short in support from the Congress, the Democrats may have seen an opportunity in the Republican administration's initiative to advance the policy. Baucus outlined the strategy: "Senator Harkin is also pragmatic. He is advocating bipartisan support for an administration proposal called Money Follows the Person. The Money Follows proposal will set us on the right path in the short term, giving a few States incentives to allow people to return home from nursing homes if they so choose."[111] ADAPT ultimately supported Harkin's efforts in enacting MFP as a more attainable short-term goal than the original MiCASSA. It was policy making through "satisficing"[112]—accepting a less than desirable policy to facilitate output but undercutting more significant (and intended) reform.

Disappointingly, but perhaps not surprisingly to longtime activists, nothing really came from the efforts of rights entrepreneurs on this issue. In-home care quickly became another example of deflated hopes in the disability community. MiCASSA was once again reintroduced by Harkin in 2005 and again, it got stuck in committee. In his speech about the sixteenth anniversary of the ADA, Harkin pleaded with members of Congress. The same year, Harkin reintroduced the Money Follows the Person Act. Ultimately, MFP was included as a demonstration program in the Deficit Reduction Act, which awarded states funds to begin transitioning individuals from institutional care back to the community. Harkin introduced the Promoting Wellness for Individuals with Disabilities Act in 2006 and 2007 with no Republican cosponsors on either occasion. The proposals, which would improve medical diagnostics and promote well-being, were referred to committees where they died.

Disability activists and rights entrepreneurs were hopeful when the Democrats regained control of Congress after a twelve-year drought in 2008. Davis and Harkin reintroduced the Community Choice Act (CCA), and two hearings were held in 2007 and 2008. While no disability organization formally participated in the 2007 Senate hearing, Sen. Chuck Schumer (D-NY) interrupted hearing protocol to acknowledge activists in attendance, "the more than 50 constituents who got on a bus yesterday from Rochester, NY. [Applause.] They are from the Center for Disability Rights and the Regional Center for Independent Living."[113] Harkin also acknowledged ADAPT in its efforts over the years and pointed to Newt Gingrich as the original sponsor and a continued supporter of the legislation. Harkin hoped he could appeal to the Democratic promise to work with Republicans in the 110th Congress. Echoing the rhetoric from the 1990s, Baucus said in his opening remarks, "Americans value freedom. . . . Many low-income people with disabilities pay for Medicaid services with their independence. They lose the right to decide when they use the phone, they lose the right to decide what food they eat and when they eat it, and they lose the right to decide what time to wake up or to go to bed."[114]

In 2008, ADAPT participated in a House hearing and listed the numerous civil rights groups supporting the law from outside the disability community, including the NAACP and the National Organization for Women (NOW).[115] The proposed legislation was supported by then-senator Barrack Obama. In 2009, when the Democrats regained control of both chambers and the administration, Davis and Harkin reintroduced CCA, with Harkin pointedly citing President Obama's senatorial support and cosponsorship of the proposal.[116]

Many disability groups, including the Center for Disability Rights, would become highly critical of what they saw as the Obama administration's failed promise to pursue the CCA when its principles were stripped from health-care reform proposals. For institutional activists, "the President had backed out of his commitment to help us pass CCA in this Congress!"[117] ADAPT activists chained themselves to the White House fence, with one saying of Obama's administration, "All they wanted to talk about was them implementing Money Follows the Person and all of those things—that was the last administration, what is this administration going to do? Our message in there, to the president, was this is a civil rights issue and we want you to FREE OUR PEOPLE and they're [*sic*] response was NO!"[118]

The Senate Committee on Health, Education, Labor, and Pensions, chaired by Harkin, held a hearing in 2010 titled *The ADA and Olmstead Enforcement: Ensuring Community Opportunities for Individuals with Disabilities*. Participants commemorated the now eleven-year-old *Olmstead* ruling, with Assistant Attorney General Thomas E. Perez saying, "We had hoped that the *Olmstead* decision would be more or less the *Brown versus Board* of the disability rights movement, catalyzing very quick and effective transformation from the institutional bias to the community biases. Undeniably, many States have made great strides in that effort, but we have undeniably a long way to go."[119]

The CCA was ultimately abandoned in compromises over the Affordable Care Act (ACA, a.k.a. Obamacare). Although disability groups applauded that ACA encouraged at-home care (Community First Choice established a consumer-driven care model in agreement with the *Olmstead* decision, but the program remained optional),[120] analyses by disability rights groups such as the American Association of People with Disabilities (AAPD) concluded the CCA had been taken off the table because of costs.[121] Conflicts around in-home care persist. In 2017, activists protested against President Donald Trump and the Republicans' proposal to replace Obamacare, in which the GOP favors institutional over in-home care.

Politics Is Pressure in the Government and in the Streets

Disability was more than a policy issue; it was a political issue. The politicization of disability from the 1988 Bush-Dukakis campaign, in which both candidates pledged support for disability rights, to the work of Republican and Democratic members of Congress in making the ADA the centerpiece of a third wave of civil rights, had important effects on the disability community. Rep. Gus Yatron (D-PA) claimed, "The exciting thing is that for the first time people with disabilities are identifying with common goals and concerns as a more united minority group—the largest minority in the country (37 million people)."[122]

The disability community developed a loud political voice, helped change attitudes about disability, and increased awareness among elites and everyday citizens about the plight of people with disabilities. They also held vigil over three important policy areas: mainstreaming in education, at-home caregiving, and equal access to public transportation.

There was a prevailing sense that protest remained a necessary and legitimate tactic for countering exclusion, marginalization, and oppression. Its viability had been demonstrated in some direct success where protest organizers had modest and immediate goals: demanding an audience with authorities, access to hearings, and statements of support (which they often received) from authorities in their broader policy efforts.

For example, ADAPT protesters at a demonstration against the Metro in Washington, D.C. (Auberger was in attendance) called off their protest once the Metro general manager met with them.[123] At a 1985 Trailways bus protest, demonstrators and Auberger negotiated with the terminal manger and closed the protest.[124] An article titled "Disabled Protesters Achieve a Partial Victory in Atlanta" described how activists at a DOT protest who did not receive a summary order for immediate accessibility *did* obtain a "pledge of government support" that buses purchased with federal funds would be accessible.[125]

Groups saw protests not as antithetical to institutional politics but as complementary to those efforts. Most advocacy organizations lobbied Congress and also coordinated disruptive protests. Disability and AIDS activists joined in protesting Washington, D.C., mayor Marion Barry's proposed cuts to social services, sparking "extraordinary community interest" and gaining access to an appropriations hearing regarding the budget.[126] Activists sought access to municipal governments, including in Los Angeles, where activists fighting for representation in municipal policy making obtained a commitment from the deputy mayor for the creation of a formal commission to advocate for the disabled.[127]

Disability activism—institutional and grassroots—is best understood within a cycle of broken political promises. As policies raised expectations and political threats deflated hopes, the disability rights struggle of the past forty years has adapted and secured (partial) victories.

The policy making of the 1990s illustrates particularly important links between the political process and social movement mobilization. First, the struggles over policy retrenchment, then policy restoration, saw the emergence of a new set of political entrepreneurs, including Weicker, McCain, Dole, Stafford, Hoyer, Coelho, and Harkin. These legislators continued to pursue disability rights even when government momentum slowed to a near halt. MiCASSA is a key example: legislators and activists pursued the policy for years, but change had not catalyzed quickly. Tenacity and perseverance would mark even the most partial policy victories.

Second, institutional activism throughout the 1980s and 1990s transcended party ideology. No doubt, party affiliation and platforms mattered broadly in setting the agenda. But across the ideological aisle, disability rights entrepreneurs worked to promote disability policy even when their respective parties and administrations were either unsupportive or uninterested in expending political resources or capital on the issue.

Third, rights entrepreneurs facing institutional obstacles relied on the efforts of disability advocacy organizations to not only pressure legislators but also energize everyday Americans on issues of inequality and discrimination. They held the federal government to high standards, insisting that it become the disability rights leader it claimed to be. Disability advocacy groups translated political promises into local, everyday examples of persistent physical and attitudinal barriers and their rectification. Activists did what politicians of the period could not.

Their mobilization would become more salient in a context of issue decline and ongoing political roadblocks. To the chagrin of advocates, the struggle over policy entrenchment and threats to existing civil rights would remain central to twenty-first-century disability politics. In those very areas in which protest had led to small success, partial victories and incremental back-stepping would continue to undermine educational mainstreaming, equal access to transportation, and the right to care within the community.

6 Empowering the Government

The late Senator Hubert Humphrey spoke about the moral test of
government being how it treats those in the shadows of life, the sick,
the needy, and the handicapped. For too long, the disabled have lived
in the shadows of American life. They have been denied rights and
opportunities afforded to others in our society. They have had a vague
and imperfect imitation of the rights we take for granted—the right to
work, the right to communicate, the right to live in the community—
without fear of discrimination.

**—Representative Bruce Vento (D-MN), statement during
congressional proceedings, May 22, 1990**

POLITICS DO NOT END with policy. Rather, policies transform politics by redefining
the rules governing interactions between policy makers, voluntary associations,
constituents, and other policy stakeholders. Policies can create new political
opportunities for everyday citizens to mobilize the law. As Subcommittee on
Select Education chairman Major Robert Owens reflected on early political
entrepreneurship, "When we resolve to fully use the Federal Government's authority and resources to better protect and expand the rights of any group, we
stimulate the processes of the empowerment within that group."[1]

Disability rights entrepreneurs empowered citizens through policy making.
They helped direct the evolution of disability politics and policy; no doubt,
without their institutional work, disability rights would not have entered the
political landscape as early as it did. But the kinds of politics that followed
agenda expansion and "legislative victories" signaled uncertainty for disability
rights. It points to more deep-seated "policy-elite perceptions" about the disability rights struggle.[2] Despite institutional activism to extend minority civil
rights to the disabled, institutional and cognitive barriers persist. Policy makers, policy stakeholders (including employers), and even everyday Americans
find it hard to see the disability community as they do other historically marginalized and oppressed groups.

Vento's statement, read in this light, reveals political inauthenticity. Almost twenty years after Hubert Humphrey proposed amending the 1964 Civil Rights Act to include disability, Vento noted, despite disability rights entrepreneurs' good intentions, the federal government had almost institutionalized the view that rights for people with disabilities were not the same as the civil rights afforded to other groups. For many, this seems the key reason that disability rights continue to face threats decades after civil rights were enshrined into law, a problem made more salient by the current political climate, leading many groups to be concerned about the stability of rights legislation.

Present-day efforts by Republicans and the Trump administration to undermine the ADA prompt scholars and activists to question whether anything would be different had Humphrey and Vanik succeeded in amending the Civil Rights Act to preclude the establishment of a so-called separate-and-unequal system of rights for the disabled. Compromises between policy stakeholders that facilitated enactment of rights-based policies may, in fact, prevent attitudinal and behavioral shifts—for example, the belief that "rational discrimination" is justifiable in denying work to people with disabilities.[3] Is political entrepreneurship—which generated policy change, helped bring people with disabilities into the political process, and increased Americans' stake in federal disability policies and programs—unintentionally detrimental to profound social change?

The ADA would not have passed without the compromise process orchestrated by political elites. However, these compromises watered down the legislation, allowing ongoing retrenchment efforts and political disputes over its objectives. Consequently, disability policy remains unsettled; the issue of disability rights to many is treated as closed—a done deal. Yet it continues to be in flux, open to attacks and rollbacks. Americans with disabilities today struggle for social services and civil rights, just as they did in the 1970s and 1980s, when the disability rights movement helped make their struggles known to all Americans.

The (Not So) "Quiet Revolution"

The failure to implement and enforce antidiscrimination legislation was—and is—symptomatic of the reluctance of policy stakeholders like school officials, transit authorities, and employers to accept disability rights as so many had accepted civil rights for African Americans and women. Weak enforcement of laws such as Section 504, meant to change attitudes and behaviors to recognize the immorality of discrimination, has contributed to that policy's inability to provide a bottom-up legitimacy to disabled rights.

On the sixteenth anniversary of the ADA, Tom Harkin commemorated a quiet but profound revolution that led to important political and social change. By "quiet revolution," Harkin alluded to often slow and incremental transformations of institutions, organizations, and professions—the kind of change that generates few splashy headlines. Actors seeking change in this way use regular political channels, including institutional advocacy, to advance policy agendas. The term "quiet revolution" was first applied to disability politics in 1973 by Paul R. Dimond, who referred to the litigation leading up to IDEA and observed that this landmark policy was being driven not by riots and protests but by parents and organizations lobbying legislators to outlaw the denial of mainstream education for disabled children.[4]

But is "revolution" even the best way to characterize the sociopolitical changes resulting from the introduction of rights onto the disability policy agenda? "Revolution" theoretically and empirically masks the processes defined by a policy-participation cycle that created a demand for political advocacy and generated the kinds of collective action (including disruptive protest) associated with the disability rights movement. This book describes instead a political *evolution* from small, piecemeal efforts emanating from an expanding disability policy network, which eventually gave rise to a civil rights policy frame. It conceives of political opportunities as providing institutional access and encouraging the rise of new mobilizing structures. *Policies* created political opportunities to frame grievances in terms of minority oppression. They also generated *new* grievances when the government backed away from its promises to implement disability rights, in a protracted period of political threat. The federal government, that is, actively shaped the political unfolding of disability rights.[5]

The disability rights movement is not independent of, or entirely exogenous to, the institutional arrangements and political entrepreneurship characterizing the dynamic social-change landscape within which activism is situated. Understanding disability activism thus requires understanding the confluence of variables, including changing interactions between disabled citizens and the state, new demands for political advocacy and rights monitoring, and ongoing efforts to undermine legislation. With these in mind, I provide an explanation about how and why social movements develop, especially with reference to their long-term efforts, goals, and outcomes. Contextualizing mobilization in a broader landscape helps illustrate what Andrea Campbell calls an "upward policy trajectory,"[6] in which a constituency, motivated by political threats, mobilizes new policy tools, transforms existing mobilizing structures, and generates innovative advocacy coalitions to rectify political inequalities.

The "burst" of disability rights onto the policy agenda was part of a longer evolution of a policy framework exclusively tied to social services (such as rehabilitation) to one including civil rights. Many have written on this important shift—"from goodwill to civil rights," as Richard Scotch put it—and many have pointed to the importance of a grassroots social movement,[7] contentious politics,[8] and collective identity and oppositional consciousness in transforming disability rights in the United States.[9] Yet we must not overlook the important institutional side in providing additional explanatory insight regarding the long-term consequences of this movement for policy legacies, the voluntary sector, and grassroots mobilization.

Further, advocacy mobilized around civil rights while simultaneously continuing to promote, develop, and expand social welfare provision. The policy-participation model provides a context for understanding institutional isomorphism in the convergence around this hybrid service-rights policy context. When the government was seen as back-stepping on both rights and social-service provision, the demand for hybrid organizations grew. As mobilizing structures defended against multifront political threats, they gained legitimacy. These organizations interacted with policy makers on a host of disability-related issues, but their use of disruptive action in the 1980s and 1990s around the intersection of rights and service provision, including the protracted political conflicts over Medicaid and in-home care, demonstrated that the disabled could also be a powerful, politicized protest constituency.

On the ADA's twenty-seventh anniversary, Sen. Robert (Bob) Casey (D-PA) testified, "We should be celebrating the liberty and freedom of people with disabilities, but instead of having a celebration of the Americans with Disabilities Act on this anniversary day, the Senate Republican bill—which, I guess, is basically the House bill that we are on right now—threatens that freedom and threatens that liberty that was accorded in the Americans with Disabilities Act with regard to those with disabilities."[10]

"Repeal and Replace," first undertaken in 2017, generated mobilization reminiscent of the 1990s, in which key advocacy organizations used both direct action and work with sympathetic political elites to change the Medicaid funding bias in long-term care. Casey specifically charged that "Trumpcare" would

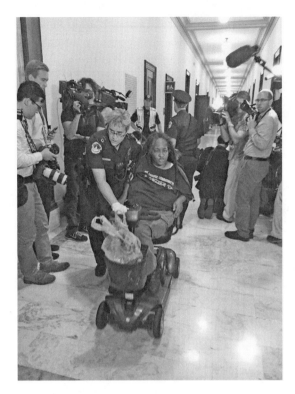

Figure 6.1 A protester being removed by Capitol police, June 2017, from a crowd chanting "No cuts to Medicaid" outside Senate Majority Leader Mitch McConnell's office. *Source:* Photo by Andrew Desiderio. Reprinted with permission.

undermine the civil rights of people with disabilities, eroding the slow-won improvements of the last fifty years. He lauded the advocacy work of ADAPT, National Council on Independent Living, ARC, Easter Seals, the Association of University Centers on Disabilities, and the Autistic Self Advocacy Network in keeping vigil over, and mobilizing against, retrenchment threats.

Veteran disability activist and ADAPT member Dawn Russell summarized the interconnectedness of rights and social welfare when she referred to the Better Care Reconciliation Act as a bill so damning to people with disabilities "that none of any of the [disability rights] work matters with the passing and the gutting of our Medicaid long-term services and supports."[11] In a replay of the conflict that sustained disability rights mobilization in the 1990s, ADAPT protested the Republican health-care bill at Majority Leader Mitch McConnell's office in June 2017 (Figure 6.1). One activist proclaimed, "Our lives and liberty shouldn't be stolen to give a tax break to the wealthy. That's truly un-American."[12] Forty-three protesters were arrested and forcibly removed by police; one was dropped to the ground in the process.

Linking disability rights to health-care reform in part reshaped the politics of disability as well as the context of mobilization. Disability consequently gained attention on the policy agenda alongside the considerable political baggage any health-care reform in the United States carries. Disability rights—an issue once described as among the most nonpartisan and noncontroversial in Congress—became part of a debate framed in increasingly partisan terms.

Casey, along with Sen. Patty Murray (D-WA), saw the Democratic Party as allies and champions for disabled constituents in the conflict over health care: "Again, the Democrats are here. We are not giving up, and we going to fight any effort to pass TrumpCare until the last possible moment because that will probably be the result. We are going to speak out for families nationwide—children, parents, patients, people with disabilities, seniors, and people who have called and tweeted and marched and filled our office halls."[13] Reminiscent of the ADA critics in decades past, Casey asked that the proposed health-care reform legislation be brought back to its committee of jurisdiction (the Finance Committee) for hearings and "some regular order . . . [to] really consider the issue seriously."[14] The political fight over in-home care and other disability issues in the health-care reform effort draws attention to the role of social movements and everyday citizens in the long-term political struggle to protect civil rights and mitigate a backlash.

To some, the quiet revolution was *too* quiet. Its early policy gains fostered a particular kind of relationship between policy elites and institutional advocacy groups such that movement leaders had routine access to the policy agenda. When the politics of elites and activists are highly aligned, relationships like those seem largely positive.[15] But when institutional activism reaches its limits, groups must rely on their ability to challenge the state, even when it turns allies into opponents. Sidney Tarrow, for instance, once warned that movement organizations that become too imbued in the logic of institutional elites prevent mobilizing structures from growing the oppositional consciousness necessary to effectively challenge the status quo.[16] Get too close to those who hold power, that is, and you will have constrained your own strategic and tactical repertoires, as well as the ways in which grievances are politicized.

The link between political entrepreneurship and social movement mobilization in disability rights is more nuanced than that. The disability rights movement may not be highly identified with large sustained protest waves generating congressional attention or policy change or, perhaps, have its complex and intricate issues garner the same kind of public and media attention as other social movements.[17] While the disability rights struggle *has* seen periods of heightened mobilization, disruptive action, and grassroots efforts, most often disability organizations have engaged in a variety of institutional and extra-institutional activity—monitoring policy and working with elites while coordinating protests.

The disability rights struggle showcases how everyday politics turns into disruptive action as the relationship between the two ebbs and flows under various institutional conditions: in periods of issue punctuation and in periods of decline; in mobilization for policy change and in mobilization against threats to existing policy. Indeed, the politics of retrenchment tells us a lot about how Coelho's so-called hidden army of activists and advocates emerges from political institutions and from the voluntary sector against new perceived threats. Policy and social movements evolve together within a social-change landscape of political elites and everyday citizens, embedded in a variety of institutional and organizational venues.

The cyclical nature of politics and mobilization also tends to highlight episodes of contention. Persistent institutional attempts to undermine rights following the ADA generated little public attention in the 1990s and 2000s; the disability rights movement, finding itself in a new political and organizational climate, had trouble maintaining and mobilizing over an issue seen as resolved. The landmark ADA was, after all, hailed as *the* definitive political resolution to the problem of social exclusion and persistent inequality. In a post-ADA world, some wondered what the disabled could possibly have left to fight about.

The Post–Disability Rights Era?

> ADA, now. Empowerment, now. Services to be fully human, now.
> —Justin Dart, statement at *Oversight Hearing on H.R. 4498,*
> *Americans with Disabilities Act of 1988,* 1988

The ADA is already seen as the product of a bygone era of congressional bipartisanship, when supposedly people of different political persuasions could still come together to do the right thing. But even in its passage, people in both parties, such as Franklin Goodling (R-PA) and Bill Lipinski (D-IL), thought disability rights entrepreneurs were "charging" through the ADA in a "cavalier" fashion and overlooking its potential consequences.[18] The ADA, they insisted, could potentially overlap with and even contradict portions of the National

Labor-Management Relations Act and the Age Discrimination in Employment Act, and only careful study could mitigate such problems.

Others simply framed the ADA as an attack on the business community. They situated the act among social programs and "expensive" regulations conservatives already heavily disliked. Rep. Mel Hancock (R-MO) told the Speaker that employers were under attack: "From the mandated increase in the minimum wage, to the mandated parental leave bill, to the clean air bill, to the Americans With Disabilities Act, the employer is being confronted with the stark reality of the 1990's—that is, if the liberals cannot get the Government to fund their new programs—they will require businesses to fund them."[19] William Dannemeyer, who had become quite critical of the ADA, asked when the troops would be sent in—"when U.S. small businesses are besieged by the clean air regulators and the Americans with disabilities' lawyers?"[20]

Even at the ADA's signing, President George H. W. Bush recited some of the negotiations that had led up to the bill. Conservatives worried it was ill conceived and hurried, and Bush sought to assuage any fears that the ADA was a marked departure from the familiar and nearly twenty-year-old Rehabilitation Act: "Fears that the ADA is too vague or too costly and will lead to an explosion of litigation are misplaced. The Administration worked closely with the Congress to ensure that, wherever possible, existing language and standards from the Rehabilitation Act were incorporated into the ADA. The Rehabilitation Act standards are already familiar to large segments of the private sector that are either Federal contractors or recipients of Federal funds."[21]

Republicans and Democrats with vested interests in decades-old disability rights policy politically negotiated for the ADA's success. Instead of being charged through, the ADA was a product filtered through hearings, committee reports, amendments from both Republicans and Democrats, and iterative Senate and House conference committee reports meant to resolve differences between the two chambers.

Political Compromise and the "Great Renegotiation"

The balancing act that made so many call the ADA a success involved framing the legislation as ushering in a new civil rights era but not a *terribly* revolutionary one (so policy stakeholders inclined toward the status quo would not be upset). After all, legislators like Goodling and Lipinski were right in one respect: The ADA interacts with a diverse set of fields, including the labor market. One need look only to the conflicting views expressed by disability advocacy organizations and employers and businesses (and their powerful lobby groups). Policy makers sought a middle ground that seemed to satisfy neither side in the long run.

Two specific issues had already helped organize and focus opposition to the entire disability rights project: HIV/AIDS and the perennial transit accessibility issue. Some in Congress went as far as to testify that the "gay lobby" was using the ADA to include HIV/AIDS and perhaps even sexual orientation as grounds for discrimination. Rep. Dan Burton (R-IN) testified concerning what he called the "chilling effects" of the ADA: "Homosexual lobbyists, AIDS activists, and their Congressional allies in Washington, D.C., realize that a Federal law which directly prohibits discrimination based on 'sexual orientation' or 'HIV infection' would be unpalatable to the majority of Americans and unlikely to pass. Instead, they have devised a masterpiece of legislative subterfuge which would effectively achieve their goals without using terms which raise a red flag in the minds of the public."[22] Sen. Jesse Helms (R-NC), a leader of the conservative movement, tapped into a widespread belief that the ADA was trying to protect people from discrimination that resulted from their own reckless behavior. He argued that ADA's Senate cosponsors "have done their level best to ensure that AIDS is treated politically rather than confronted head-on as a public health issue."[23]

Regarding public transit, the House Subcommittee on Surface Transportation raised concerns that the ADA threatened public-transit operators. Rep. Tom Petri (R-WI), recognizing that the issue of equal access came with political baggage, worried that the ADA signaled an effort to entrench equal accessibility requirements that had been, to the pleasure of those who saw disability rights as burdensome, undermined by the Reagan administration. As Petri put it, "Some advocacy groups are insisting that all public transit equipment should be equipped to meet the needs of all disabled persons. Politically, this is difficult to oppose, but it is not the best way to go."[24]

Even the most vocal supporters of the law raised concerns about this "sweeping" legislation. Very early in the process, Sen. John McCain expressed fears to President Bush regarding proposals to remove the term "undue hardship" in reference to the burdens accommodations would impose on public and private entities.[25] In regard to accommodations, Orrin Hatch believed that the ADA went beyond the 1964 Civil Rights Act and worried that the ADA would not find enough support in Congress.[26]

Tony Coelho thought Hatch might introduce his own version of the ADA, and he reminded the senator that the original ADA had been put together by a committee struck by Reagan: "We very much want you on board and very much need your support," Coelho testified. He was looking to "reach an accommodation" to ensure the ADA's enactment.[27] Even with strong bipartisan support, disability rights entrepreneurs were made nervous by these delays. The Sensenbrenner and Chapman Amendments had already stalled the legislation. By 1989, the ADA reflected compromises, and by 1990, it still underwent two conference bills to work out differences between the House and Senate (for example, Chapman's food-handler issue was a major sticking point later worked out through a compromise via the Hatch Amendment directing the HHS secretary to compile a running list of communicable diseases thought to be transmitted through food handling).

Policy makers like Steny Hoyer recognized these as "weakening amendments,"[28] while Owens expressed outright suspicion of the negotiations between the administration and Congress: "That is an act we started in 1987, I think, and continued in 1988, and in 1989 there was a great renegotiation that took place. That is the Tony Coelho bill. Tony Coelho was a sponsor, and he led the negotiations. The Senate, the House, the president agreed, a bill was passed in the Senate in 1989 fairly early in the session, and then it was referred to four committees in the House."[29]

Many have written about the open American political process in which multiple veto points can reshape legislative intentions.[30] Policy making becomes more susceptible to compromises between opponents, including actors outside the government, because political entrepreneurs working to build a coalition of support in a given area are incentivized to find majority support to increase the likelihood of policy enactment. Compromise can therefore take precedence over intended outcomes when policy makers think their coalition is threatened by the introduction of new proposals and/or delays.[31]

Anticipating his opponents' criticisms, Ted Kennedy supported an amendment that would restrict punitive damages and eliminate the possibility of quotas.[32] Then, when the ADA generated enough widespread support in the government, an original cosponsor, Bob Dole, refused to cosponsor subsequent proposed bills. Ruth Colker speculated that Dole was confident the ADA would ultimately pass and hoped to use this as an opportunity to renegotiate the law, given his particular quibbles, including what he saw as expanding definitions of disability and the watering down of the undue hardship clause (both of which he believed deviated from the spirit of the Rehabilitation Act).[33]

In the 1990s, disability rights hinged on a "fragile compromise." Colker described the ADA as a "one step at a time" approach. In regard to Title III, in the section on public accommodations, "ADA proponents traded expanded coverage for limited relief."[34] They hoped to address these issues once the policy was close to passing or already enacted. Given the opposition to the law, they fretted that any unwillingness to compromise would derail the project.

The ADA is an example of how compromise can generate outcomes in which neither proponents nor detractors are satisfied. This can decrease a policy's legitimacy, facilitating future attempts to undermine the law under the auspices of improving it. Owens and others knew this was a possibility and hoped that "Congress will act to produce a bill which is not shackled by weakening amendments, damaging compromises or gross distortions. . . . We all have good reason to believe that a bill will pass. But when the process is completed, we want to celebrate a final product as great as the proposal we have initiated."[35] Twenty years later, the ADARA of 2008 was meant to address failures stemming, in part, from the political compromises inherent in the ADA's passage. Its partial successes were simply not enough to settle the disability rights question.

The New Political Realities of Restoring Disability Rights

> It really is a scar on our society, and it's just the one thing that we've, just, again, I thought ADA would start moving us in that direction, and we haven't made the strides we should make in that area, we just haven't done it. And it's very frustrating.
> —Tom Harkin, statement at *Restoring Congressional Intent and Protections Under the Americans with Disabilities Act* hearing, 2007

In the early 2000s, activists began turning their attention to the landmark policy that was supposed to have entrenched civil rights. Decades earlier, advocates had cautioned against the trajectory disability rights policy was taking, signaling concern over enforcement and the court's interpretation of "reasonable" accommodations. Now the ADA appeared in need of restoration.

To the extent that many saw the ADA as a failed policy, it was especially so in regard to eradicating economic inequality. As Figure 6.2 illustrates, employment rates among people with disabilities had been declining before the ADA took effect and continued to decline afterward. By the time Congress initiated "restoration" hearings in 2006, disability employment rates had dropped by about 50 percent and earnings levels had stagnated since 1988, returning in 2012 to 1988 levels. Something had to be done to revitalize federal training programs, and even some conservative policy makers like Sen. Mike Enzi (R-WY)

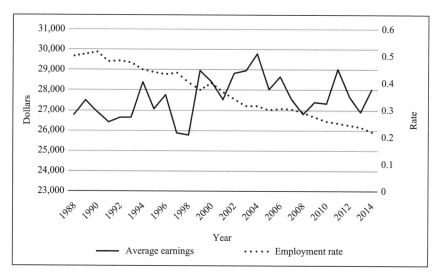

Figure 6.2 Employment and earnings among people with disabilities, 1988–2014.
Source: Maroto and Pettinicchio, "The Limitations of Disability Antidiscrimination
Legislation."

saw new legislative remedies as necessary to provide more resources and flexibility in improving job training and marketable skills.[36]

Rights entrepreneurs with close ties to the ADA hailed its successes, but it was very difficult to defend its record regarding economic outcomes. Harkin drew the attention of the Senate Committee on Health, Education, Labor, and Pensions to the problem of employment: "That's the one thing that has bedeviled me since the passage of the ADA, we made wonderful strides in accommodations and transportation, a lot of the things, and that coupled with IDEA, mainstreaming it, getting kids into school. But we really haven't cracked that nut on employment, what is it, 63 percent of people with disabilities are not employed, and of those, I don't know the percentage but a high percentage are underemployed. In other words, they may be working, but they're not working at their full potential for one reason or another."[37] Those arguing in favor of and against the law had different opinions about the reasons for these policy failures.

A limited number of public hearings on ADARA began shortly after the reauthorization of IDEA. Proponents and detractors were again embroiled in a debate that had defined the conflict over disability rights in the late 1970s and again surrounding the 1990 ADA: the ways civil rights policies are supposed to positively shape policy stakeholders' preferences and behaviors.[38] Champions of disability rights claimed the ADA never had a chance to effect change among employers; opponents argued that the law disincentivized hiring people with disabilities, since even those in the business community who sought to hire them would fear lawsuits over accommodations. At a hearing, Rep. Darrell Issa (R-CA) called on a small-town contractor to testify how the ADA had hurt small-business owners in his state.

Detractors not only echoed criticisms made against the ADA twenty years earlier, such as those made by Dannemeyer in 1990, who warned of the ADA's "horrors" and its "perverse and unintended results,"[39] but also, like their predecessors who claimed the ADA went beyond the Rehabilitation Act, argued that "the 'ADA Restoration Act of 2007' would radically expand the ADA's coverage by redefining the term 'disabled.' By changing the definition of 'disability' the proposed legislation, in turn, alters the scope of the ADA so as to make it almost unrecognizable."[40]

Although the US Chamber of Commerce eventually came to support the House bill, it had been adamantly against ADARA when it was first introduced.[41] The disability community, along with institutional activists, wanted to broaden the definition of disability as a way to counter restrictive court rulings. After all, the major impetus for ADARA was to address the issue of courts throwing out cases based on standing. The business community, however, was insistent about not altering the ADA definition of disability, by which disability *substantially limits a major life activity*. Again, stakeholders reached a compromise that largely retained the existing ADA framework while providing some guidelines about how it should be interpreted.

On the eve of the bill's 2008 enactment, a roundtable hearing held by Ted Kennedy, chair of the Committee on Health, Education, Labor, and Pensions, saw the conservative Heritage Foundation claiming that ADARA only generated uncertainty in already-uncertain economic times. The foundation pointed to what it saw as an expanding definition of disability so that "everyone is disabled" and articulated a concern that ADARA would shift the burden of proving that an individual alleging discrimination is not "a qualified individual with a disability" from the disabled person to the employer.[42]

In an attempt to answer the decades-old call that more should be done to bring disability rights law closer to the 1964 Civil Rights Act, lawmakers in the Senate affirmed that a person should not be discriminated against because of a *disability*, not as an *otherwise qualified person*—the term "otherwise qualified" is not, for example, found in the Civil Rights Act. As one attorney put it, "This entire brouhaha about the change of burden of proof, is because the language is now going to look just like Title VII [of the Civil Rights Act]. I'm really curious as to whether now under title VII no one has to prove that they're qualified as part of their prima facie case."[43]

Others argued that the courts' narrowing of the scope of Section 504 and the ADA in the 1990s and 2000s had actually clarified legislative intentions. Thus, as senior Republican member of the committee, Howard (Buck) McKeon of California, testified, the business community had come to accept that ADARA would destabilize the detente between the disabled and other policy stakeholders established by the ADA. Even the senior vice president of the American Council on Education clamored for assurance that the precedent set in cases such as *Davis*—that institutions need not provide an accommodation when doing so would fundamentally alter the essential aspects of programs or diminish the academic standards set by the institutions[44]—would not be upset by any proposed legislation. Lawrence Lorber of the US Chamber of Commerce claimed that ADARA would replace "the long experience under the Rehabilitation Act of 1973 and the ADA" with a "litigation regime not focused on the universally lauded goal of full inclusion of qualified individuals with disabilities into the mainstream of American life."[45] McKeon, referring to both the ADA and ADARA, explained that "even the best of legislative intentions often produce harmful unintended consequences. Sometimes measures such as this may even harm the very individuals they seek to help."[46]

For sympathetic policy makers and disability rights activists, however, what allowed employers to accept the ADA had been a lax enforcement system whereby the courts protected employers from the ADA rather than the ADA protecting people with disabilities from discrimination. Champions of the ADA claimed the law was ineffective in part because of compromises made to get it passed, but *mostly* because the courts had rendered the ADA impotent in shaping economic outcomes.

Judicial resistance gave employers few incentives to implement the law; there was little consequence if they did nothing. According to a law firm that saw ADARA as an attack on employer-employee relations, "Some employers have not offered ADA training in years because of the relatively restrictive view that courts took of the ADA."[47] To disability rights activists, these opponents were actually proving their point: "tortured" judicial interpretations had taken the bite out of the ADA, rendering it useless in its intended goals.[48] Opponents and backers essentially agreed on the situation but disagreed about whether and how anything should be done to change it.

In this context Harkin and Arlen Specter (R-PA) proposed what was originally called ADARA in the Senate (S. 1881) and Steny Hoyer and Jim Sensenbrenner proposed in the House (H.R. 3195). Harkin and Sensenbrenner had, of course, been key players in the enactment of the ADA in 1990. Harkin set the tone: the country was moving backward on disability rights. Motivated by the belief that the ADA had been jeopardized by the courts (though, interestingly, not by weakening amendments in Congress), Harkin asked for commonsense remedies to improve the lives of disabled Americans. To him, this meant upholding and protecting their civil rights by intervening to address devastating judicial inter- pretations. As Harkin testified, "We cannot go back to the old days of denial, dis- enfranchisement and discrimination, and that's why we need a common-sense remedy." [49] At the same time, disability organizations were also turning to the courts—to legal mobilization—hoping to settle the disability rights question.

The Rise of Court-Centered Activism

I always am interested when we see a bill called the so-and-so restoration act, because it means we think the Supreme Court has misinterpreted what Congress said, which it often has.
— **Representative Jerrold Nadler (D-NY), statement at**
ADA Restoration Act of 2007 **hearing, 2007**

Over the last fifty years, a pattern of judicial interpretation of disability civil rights laws emerged distinct from those related to gender and race discrimina- tion. The Supreme Court has overturned liberal lower-court rulings that origi- nally sided with disabled plaintiffs; in these reversals, disability discrimination cases were almost 70 percent more likely to lead to a ruling against the disabled plaintiff than in gender-discrimination cases and 30 percent more likely than race, national origin, age, and religion cases.[50] Their moves negatively affected disabled workers, but they also pointed to a more troubling concern: justices do not see disability discrimination as analogous to race- or gender-based dis- crimination. Activists charge that Supreme Court rulings plainly demonstrate that discrimination and minority rights neither institutionally nor cognitively extend to the disability community. For opponents, these cases appropriately contained the federal government. Conservative attorney Stephen McCutch- eon aptly summarized the cases: "We believe it goes far in helping to restore the Constitution's limits on Congress's power. Congress isn't omnipotent, and states are more than mere subdivisions of the United States."[51]

A *Los Angeles Times* article captured the sentiments of advocates: "Congress giveth. . . . The Supreme Court taketh away."[52] Congress in this period retained some of its reputation as a place of redress for disability activists. The very first hearing about ADARA held by the Judiciary Committee in 2006 opened with the Subcommittee on the Constitution chair, Steve Chabot (R-OH), pointing to the "trilogy" of Supreme Court case decisions handed down in 1999 that, in his opinion, had severely undermined the ADA. In *Sutton v. United Airlines*, *Murphy v. UPS*, and *Albertson's v. Kirkingburg*, the Supreme Court restricted the ADA by limiting who can qualify for rights.[53] In narrowing standing to file suit, the court terminated litigation before it could address cases involving reasonable accommodation and undue hardship.

Robert Burgdorf, the attorney who had been responsible for drafting the original ADA, testified that "95 percent of the lawsuits that are filed under Title I of the ADA are thrown out of court based on the restrictive definition of disability. So we haven't given Title I a chance to see if there were a broad definition would there be enough prohibition of discrimination and employment that these statistics would begin to change. But right now we don't know."[54] In a back and forth with former attorney general Thornburgh, with whom he agreed wholeheartedly, Harkin remarked, "It almost seems to me that the Court is just kind of taking a standard that disabled means that you're not able to do anything. That's sort of the standard. You're disabled and you're not really able to do something, you're not really able to work."[55] These were attitudes and beliefs entirely antithetical to the policy objectives established by rehabilitationists in the 1940s and 1950s.

Judicial decisions generated some disruptive collective action. A 2001 protest organized by ADAPT fought against the decision in *Board of Trustees of the University of Alabama v. Garrett*,[56] which disallowed state employees to collect damages from their states for offenses under the ADA. Simultaneously, a core set of professional disability advocacy groups with the resources and knowhow shifted advocacy efforts to the judiciary. Their contemporaneous use of disruption and court-centered activism showcased their tactical flexibility. Established organizations like NARC, DIA, and UCP acted as amici—friends of the court—filing amicus curiae briefs summarizing organizations' positions with the intention of influencing judicial decisions even as they, to varying degrees, helped coordinate and participate in protests.

Acting as amici has become one of the most significant ways in which groups participate in court-centered activism.[57] Modeling themselves after DIA and ACCD, ADAPT, which had coordinated some of the most intense protests against the nursing home industry, served as amicus curiae in *Olmstead v. L.C.*, one of the few favorable disability Supreme Court cases. Although disability groups hoped targeting the courts would bring some measure of success as part of a multipronged effort to ward off retrenchment, the relationship between the use of this tactic and favorable court outcomes is tenuous.[58] Congress was increasingly unable to intervene in what activists saw as the courts gutting civil rights, so organizations had little choice. As an ADAPT representative told a *New York Times* reporter following the *Garrett* decision, "Disability rights lobbyists and policy makers had been in conference calls all day discussing what they could do and had reached no conclusion. The prevailing view in Washington was that Congress was left with little room to act."[59]

Organizations adapted to these political realities. New expectations from advocates and lawmakers encouraged increasingly professionalized disability groups to engage directly with the courts. In turn, court-centered activism gained legitimacy as a tactic for social change.[60] The AAPD, headed by Cheryl Sensenbrenner (wife of Jim Sensenbrenner of the famed Sensenbrenner Amendment), was among the newest advocacy groups, but it had already become the largest national nonprofit disability group. The organization filed an amicus brief in the infamous 2002 *Chevron v. Echazabal* case, in which the Supreme Court upheld an ADA regulation allowing employers to make hiring decisions based on their perception of whether a given candidate's disability would cause harm to the business.[61]

Andrew Imparato relayed AAPD's court-centered activism back to Congress. During the ADARA hearings, he told the House Committee on Education and Labor that "the ADA Restoration Act is the top legislative priority for AAPD. . . . Because of what the courts have done to the ADA, I no longer believe that I can count on the law to protect me against employment discrimination. . . . Do we want to send 18 years after the Americans with Disabilities Act the message that you should be careful not to achieve to your full potential, be careful not to live as independently as possible, or you may lose your federal civil rights protections?"[62]

Political elites' rallying around blaring judicial resistance finally created an opportunity to do right by disability rights. But again, policy makers believed that bipartisanship was the only way to secure a congressional policy response. Ted Kennedy chaired the Senate Committee on Health, Education, Labor, and Pensions, which historically had the most proximate jurisdictional legitimacy over disability rights, and he emphasized the legacy of bipartisanship on disability rights, noting that ADARA was no different.

Like the ADA, ADARA would involve agreements between the disability and business communities with players in both political parties. Ironically, although the motivation behind the law was to restore what had been retrenched, political compromise would see the word "Restoration" dropped from the title. Now, it was the "Amendments Act" (Americans with Disabilities Act Amendments Act, or ADAAA). Compromise also weakened the burden of proof placed on employers and, to assuage continued concerns about "everyone being disabled," sought to ensure that not all impairments would be automatically considered disabilities (in part, by removing a list of medical conditions defined as disabilities). The politics surrounding ADAAA revealed an even greater chasm between proponents of disability rights and detractors. While activists thought court cases like *Garrett* jeopardized civil rights, especially by questioning the constitutionality of laws like the ADA, and the ADAAA sought to restore Congress' intent when it came to the ADA, opponents saw these cases as victories for states' rights.

Today, almost a decade since "rights were restored," many, if not all, of the concerns the ADAAA sought to remedy—bridging the gap between conflicting policy stakeholders, enforcement and compliance problems, and retrenchment—persist. Under pressure from the Trump administration, particularly the Office of the Solicitor General, and Coca-Cola, the Supreme Court declined a case about inaccessible vending machines (*Magee v. Coca-Cola*) and upheld a restrictive view of public accommodations issued by the Fifth District Court of Appeals.[63] The court also declined to hear an appeal regarding IDEA's "stay put" rule (*N. E. v. Seattle School District*),[64] leaving the Ninth Circuit Court's rather odd interpretation of the rule intact. The legal and legislative challenges are again mounting against disability rights as enforcement is relabeled as burdensome and over the top.

Success and Failure: "Whither the Disability Rights Movement?"

The disability rights movement has made some inroads even in regard to the perennial challenges of equal access and educational desegregation. Today, for instance, many take accessible spaces for granted. The National Council on Disability notes that the ADA had made remarkable progress in local public transit,[65] while APTA confidently reports that almost all American buses are accessible (with lower levels for light rail and commuter trains).[66] However, for many disabled individuals, local options for public transit are often limited or unavailable,[67] and there are continuing conflicts between increasing accessibility in mainstream transit and improving paratransit services (the latter seen as perpetuating the separate-but-equal approach early institutional and movement activists worked against).[68]

Disability transit accessibility received periodic attention in Congress throughout the 2000s. In 2006, ADA noncompliance by bus operators was awkwardly tacked on to a conversation mainly initiated by curbside operator safety concerns. ADA compliance was treated as "an inconvenience" in relation to bus operator safety.[69] It also became clear that enforcement of the ADA in the transport industry was seriously lacking. In her testimony, Annette Sandberg of the Federal Motor Carrier Safety Administration (FMCSA) publicly acknowledged the slow progress in transit accessibility, reporting, "Non-compliance with the ADA regulations is an issue throughout the bus industry."[70]

To make matters worse, the FMCSA would not consider ADA compliance when issuing licenses to bus carriers, defying DOT regulations and the 2006 DC Circuit ruling in *Peter Pan Bus Lines* requiring it to do so.[71] Legislators such as Peter DeFazio (D-OR) and Jim Oberstar (D-MN) expressed concern with weak enforcement and rule making. In 2008, Congress enacted the Over-the-Road Bus Transportation Accessibility Act, which had two original Republican and one Democratic cosponsor.

In 2011, the House and Senate held hearings in which Easter Seals and AARP participated. These hearings were about the economic recession's disproportionate effects on low-income people with disabilities' access to public transit,[72] as well as the problems facing seniors and people with disabilities who lived in areas where public transit options did not exist.[73]

The Obama administration supported the idea that getting around was a civil right. Nonetheless, policies such as the 2012 Moving Ahead for Progress in the 21st Century Act (MAP-21) perpetuated a separate-but-equal system.[74] Ultimately, lawmakers were interested in "practical" solutions that were increasingly seen as antithetical to securing civil rights. As Irving Zola aptly put it, "On a social level, systems like this, no matter even if operated more efficiently on all these dimensions, will always have a negative consequence; for, by their very nature, they promote and sustain segregation, not integration."[75]

The nearly fifty-year-old debate about transit accessibility provides a case example of how issues evolve as a result of elite entrepreneurship; undergo decades of compromise and threat, extensive claims making, and frame contestation; develop into social movement issues, targets of mass mobilization, and institutional advocacy; and achieve some common ground between policy stakeholders. These processes have shaped the kinds of partial victories to which the disability rights movement has grown accustomed and policy stake-holders are reluctant to embrace.

Similarly, integrating students with disabilities into mainstream educational settings has created fundamental change in the lives of the disabled in spite of opposition that is nearly as old as efforts to end educational segregation itself. The work of political elites, advocacy groups, and everyday activists has been effective. According to the National Center for Education Statistics, about 60 percent of children between six and twenty-one years old served by IDEA spend more than 80 percent of their time in general or regular school classes. Since the 1990s, the number of students spending more than 80 percent of their time in regular classes increased by about 93 percent.[76] Disabled students in mainstream education have better educational outcomes and, subsequently, better labor-market outcomes; IDEA helps reduce inequality.

When Congress worked to reauthorize IDEA in the early 2000s, the law was already nearly three decades old and had become entangled with Bush-era education policy the No Child Left Behind Act (NCLB). NCLB was disliked by liberals for not going far enough to strengthen the federal government's role in education and hated by conservatives, who envision zero federal government involvement in education. Many Democrats and key disability policy elites saw reauthorization as an opportunity to strengthen the federal government's commitment to the rights of people with disabilities,[77] and many Republicans saw it as a political opportunity to quietly diminish the government's role in education.

The House Committee on Education and Workforce and the Senate Committee on Health, Education, Labor, and Pensions held no hearings directly on this matter. If hearings are an indicator of the amount of interest and resources Congress is willing to expend, then educational mainstreaming was not high on the list of priorities. In 2002, two years before IDEA was reauthorized, the House Subcommittee on Education Reform held a generic hearing on special education.[78] Not a single disability rights group testified at the hearing. DREDF, in part concerned that the Republican-controlled House might weaken the law and in part looking for new political opportunities to potentially bolster IDEA, quickly established the IDEA Rapid Response Network to monitor policy developments and disseminate information to the public.

Reauthorizing IDEA opened a can of worms, reinvigorating debates over big government, costs versus rights, definitions of disability,[79] and classroom discipline. One key issue was schools' authority to suspend/expel children with behavioral problems under the guise of a "code of conduct."[80] Many who disliked federal education policy and IDEA specifically publicly fretted that, if teachers and schools were afraid to take action when children were behaving dangerously in classrooms (presumably, the schools would not want to face discrimination lawsuits), all kids were in danger. Jeff Sessions specifically claimed that IDEA contributed to the decline of civility in American classrooms. In response to H.R. 1350, ARC, National Down Syndrome Congress, and Easter Seals held a National Call-in, Write-in, and Visit Your Representative Day.

The Senate compromised on IDEA, ultimately repealing the "stay put rule." Regardless, groups like ARC and UCP called it a "marked improvement" over the House bill, which had divided Democrats and Republicans over whether federal funding should be mandatory or discretionary.[81] Constrained by the policy options put forth by political elites, disability groups gave lukewarm support for the lesser of two evils.

When Congress reconvened in 2004, senators undertook a bipartisan effort to reconcile differences and pass the law. But as a *New York Times* article noted, these efforts were entirely "behind the scenes negotiation."[82] As very few public hearings or consultations were undertaken; the recently created League of Special Education Voters (mostly parents and guardians of children with disabilities) publicly worried that the Senate would give too much away to get the bill passed and promised to hold demonstrations like Hands Across America.

Congress reauthorized IDEA, but without full mandatory funding. The result of political compromise, IDEA funding kept some policy makers busy for the next ten years. ARC, UCP, the National Association of Protection and Advocacy Systems, and TASH all charged that the federal government had never delivered on its promise to do whatever possible to mainstream children with disabilities in the thirty years since IDEA was enacted. Sympathetic policy makers agreed. Rep. Sheila Jackson Lee (D-TX) thundered, "Congress has slipped backward in its commitment to fully fund IDEA, from a high of 18.6 percent in fiscal year 2005 to the proposed level of 17 percent in President Bush's fiscal year 2007 budget proposal instead of the promised 40 percent,"[83] disappointments that were nothing new to activists.

Between 2006 and 2017, the conversation surrounding special education largely excluded the voices of constituents, beneficiaries, and advocates, and it generated little public interest. Discourse instead revolved around reforming NCLB under the broad umbrella of childhood education, health, and safety, and, as in the case of public transit, the focus was much less about disability rights per se. Policy makers and activists were hopeful that the Democratic president Barack Obama and the Democratic-controlled 111th Congress would go a long way in reinforcing and expanding a law seeking to prevent educational (and social) segregation based on disability. But bills to increase funding to IDEA (e.g., IDEA Full Funding Act, Full Funding for IDEA Now Act, and Keep Our PACT Act, which proposed mandatory funding) and to recover expert witness fees in IDEA due process hearings (i.e., Harkin's IDEA Fairness Restoration Act) were made in virtually every congressional year, and all were unsuccessful.[84]

During Obama's presidency, Republicans such as Jim De Mint (R-SC), Scott Garrett (R-NJ), and Buck McKeon sought to cut back IDEA. The conservative think tank, the Thomas B. Fordham Institute, argued that "special education has largely been insulated from considerations of cost and cost-effectiveness."[85] Disability advocacy organizations were largely absent from the politics of IDEA cutbacks, perhaps because there was so little public and political space available to contest the issue. Disability rights framing was shunted aside for educational reform, cost cutting, and small government as IDEA was reauthorized and funding hearings moved forward. Nonetheless, the National Education Association (NEA), Council for Exceptional Children, and other education-related associations came out in full support of federal mandatory funding to special education, forming the IDEA Funding Coalition.[86]

In a recent attempt to limit federal funding, Illinois Republican Tim Walberg sponsored the Building on Local District Flexibility in IDEA Act of 2015 (BOLD), supported by the Association of Educational Service Agencies, allowing districts to reduce their special education funding during tough economic circumstances "without penalty."[87] The Every Student Succeeds Act (ESSA), which replaced NCLB, was another result of a compromise in which Democrats accepted that states, not the federal government, would determine accountability criteria related to performance and Republicans accepted that schools would be held accountable for student performance. Groups such as the National Down Syndrome Congress saw this compromise giving an unacceptable and "unprecedented level of discretion" to states.[88]

Both the transportation and education sagas reveal the shifting institutional arrangements, the work of political elites, and the efforts of advocacy organizations hoping to effect policy change. Actors and policy venues shape policy trajectories, opening or closing opportunities for groups to have a place at the table. Importantly, these lengthy processes showcase a back-and-forth or nonrecursive trajectory rather than linear policy progression. Policy innovations struggled to develop enforcement and implementation mechanisms, faced protracted periods of threat and rollbacks, generated institutional and extra-institutional activism, saw new policy attempts to restore intent, and were faced with recurring efforts by detractors to undermine the law.

The evolution of disability rights periodically brings together those for and against these policies. For example, the Rehabilitation Act (1973), ADA (1990), and ADAAA (2008) each represents a specific mood and climate in the life course of disability rights. Partly the result of developments within the disability policy domain and partly the result of exogenous forces shaping US politics, including the rise of a distinctive brand of conservativism, a growing tolerance of inequality and antiwelfare attitudes, party polarization, and antiestablishment/antielite sentiments, progress is never guaranteed.[89]

The periods also reflect distinct institutional spaces. Just after the Rehabilitation Act was passed, positive feedback generated increased issue salience and the expansion of disability on the policy agenda. For three decades, lawmakers paid attention to disability, and the disability rights movement ramped up its mobilizing efforts. After passage of the ADA and ADAAA, it appeared that negative-feedback processes were at work, closing the issue of disability. Throughout much of the 2000s, attention to disability issues hovered at pre-1960 levels, a time when disability had been narrowly defined by a settled disability policy monopoly. Fewer venues meant fewer hearings, declining political opportunities, and declining political will to pursue the disability rights struggle.

In turn, institutional realities impacted how advocacy and social movement organizations sought to influence federal policy making. Disability rights, which had coalesced into a comprehensive policy area between 1968 and 1990, experienced a sort of Balkanization as civil rights became less significant in framing education and transportation policies. Even though these specific issues touched on civil rights, they were filtered through policy communities that kept these issues separate and often uncoordinated. A core set of disability advocacy groups divided and concentrated their efforts in different policy domains. At the same time, the disability rights movement was aging into a context in which the federal government had become less relevant in affecting rights and social services. The voluntary sector increasingly targeted local and state agencies to improve social services for their constituents.

In an article for the American Bar Association's *Human Rights Magazine*, Eve Hill summarized the political climate focused on states' rights, small government, and declining bipartisanship and wondered if they had withered the disability rights movement and its impact on disability rights legislation.[90]

Like issue salience, social movement mobilization, too, eventually declines, often following policy settlement. Political activity declines when a high level of consensus is reached (usually facilitated by bipartisan compromise) around policy responses like the ADA. Or it declines if no clear policy path emerges from claims-making activity around problems and solutions like the issues of in-home care, transit, and educational mainstreaming. They may even decline because oppositional forces push the issue off the agenda or reframe the issue, as occurred when civil rights became less relevant in defining the problems faced by disabled Americans in different policy arenas.[91] All of these explanations shed some light on the politics of disability following passage of the ADA.

If social movement mobilization is both a consequence and cause of policy change, then a movement's life course should be shaped by issue expansion and decline. Social movement scholars Herbert Blumer and Charles Tilly outlined movement stages: grievances emerge, are translated into collective action, and become more institutionalized as formalized and professionalized organizations seek to define goals, strategies, and targets of action.[92] Demobilization may be the result of success, failure, co-optation, repression, or going mainstream. Whatever the case, the policy-participation cycle posits that policy making and mobilization influence each other over the long run. Internal-movement dynamics (activism, collective identity, organizational change, targets, etc.) are therefore influenced by institutional forces, as the macro portrait of the disability rights struggle in Figure 6.3 illustrates.

Following passage of the ADA, the organizational field contracted for the first time in at least forty years. The number of active disability groups began a steady decline from 1993 onward (with a decrease of almost 20 percent after 1990). Fewer organizations were being created. Existing groups were disappearing (as Figure 6.3 illustrates, the organizational mortality rate increased quite significantly). Consolidation saw flexible professional advocacy groups coordinating protests as well as working with lawmakers in Congress and engaging in court-centered activism. Protests declined, and events became more sporadic. Did the ADA—a struggling policy touted as victory—demobilize parts of the disability rights movement by making the issue seem "settled"? If so, did the ADA jeopardize the ability of a community to fight against powerful opposition?

Asked another way, is the kind of demobilization in the disability rights movement the result of co-optation? As a partial policy, "appropriation via inclusion" may have come with costs.[93] If the efforts and goals of the movement were overly institutionalized, perhaps they were also inoculated against grassroots grievances and political threats. To "outflank challenges" inside and outside the state, communities seen as challenging the status quo are brought

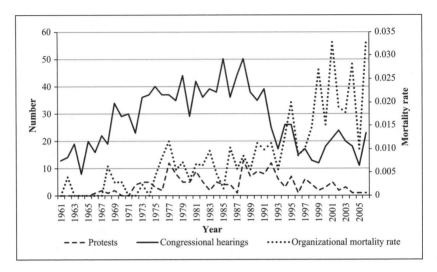

Figure 6.3 Demobilization: A shrinking policy agenda, declining protest, and contracting organizational field.

into the decision-making process either by incorporating part of their ideas and demands or by bringing organizations directly to the policy table—they may even be conferred elite status—to minimize and manage disruption.[94]

Philip Selznick's thesis about how the Tennessee Valley Authority co-opted local citizen groups to further its objectives and fulfill its "need for control and consent" presents a classic illustration of how elites manage and anticipate potential future challenges.[95] Indeed, social movement scholars have confirmed that the appropriation of movement discourse—in principle but not necessarily in practice—is a form of social control; granting access to professional advocacy groups minimizes more radical challenges, Timothy Hedeen and Patrick Coy hypothesized, ultimately transforming social movement mandates.[96]

Co-optation has a "complicated pedigree." On the one hand, institutionalizing key elements of a movement can generate new opportunities for challengers to effect progressive (if often incremental) policy change. Ongoing access certainly encourages the kind of advocacy transformation that rippled through the disability nonprofit sector.[97] On the other hand, activists who become policy elites may be forgoing future mobilization, especially when positive change does not come about.

The parallel system of civil rights for the disabled reflects an imperfect policy solution. Policy "half solutions" undercut the political push for more effective policies, contributing to movement demobilization. As Andrea Campbell noted, "We often get partial solutions because they are politically feasible—how many times has a lawmaker said a piece of legislation 'isn't perfect but we'll fix it later'—but the act of having done something to address a problem undermines mobilization around the issue and results in the political agenda moving on to other pressing needs."[98]

Republicans and Democrats wanted to have done something on disability rights,[99] and political elites believed that making that happen required the participation of all policy stakeholders in compromise between their competing interests. Reminiscing with Hatch about the ADA, Harkin alluded to the tedious process of negotiating: "It took a long time to work out. But through the good faith of people on all sides with whom we worked—the disability rights community, all the different disability groups, and the chamber of commerce supported the bill—in the end, we worked together to bring everybody together. But it was a long process, as the Senator remembers."[100]

The ADA *is* a significant piece of civil rights legislation. It has also been paradoxically followed by an era of growing inequality among disabled Americans. Institutional arrangements have facilitated back-stepping and unfinished policy entrenchment. To what extent can we attribute the current state of affairs to the disability rights movement?

We know a lot less about what social movements do and whether they are successful at doing it during periods of stable or declining mobilization and issue interest.[101] Although the disability rights movement may not look like it did in the 1970s and 1980s, neither do our political arrangements. There are a few issues to bear in mind in regard to evaluating the efficacy of the movement.

First, disability organizations have been quite resilient and adaptable. When resources are few and political opportunities closed, organizations grapple with sustainability.[102] Professional hybrid service-advocacy organizations formed political coalitions around issues touching on both rights and social services, diversifying their targets and engaging in numerous tactics. ADAPT, for instance, survived by bending with political shifts, gained legitimacy as representative of a political constituency, and carved out a niche as an important player in the political process.

Second, groups more readily come in and out of protest campaigns as they also directly engage with political elites. Organizations' use of both institutional and extra-institutional tactics helps keep co-optation in check. Even when disability groups had institutional access during the Carter years, that access did not preclude the groups' criticizing the government's policy proposals.[103]

Finally, disability organizations can and do have multiple goals and objectives. Some may not target policy making or may only indirectly target policy making by shaping cultural beliefs and values. But when they do target legislative activity, when they are seeking to shape the policy agenda,[104] it becomes all the more important to investigate how movements interact with policy-making institutions and with lawmakers and how these relationships change over time. Eve Hill concludes, "The long-term future of disability rights law remains uncertain. . . . While legal and policy changes may challenge these efforts, and disability rights advocates and attorneys, as well as state agencies, may have to take on additional responsibilities to maintain and continue progress, the power of the disability rights movement, on individual, community, and societal levels, will continue."[105]

History Repeats Itself

> You've come a long way, baby . . . but there's still a very long way to go.
> Democracy is always unfinished business.
> —**Alan Reich (National Organization on Disability), statement during**
> **congressional proceedings, September 13, 1988**

Disability rights represents the last frontier in America's so-called minority rights revolution. The fetishization of bipartisanship in ongoing political struggles around failed entrenchment, according to Eric Patashnik and Julian Zelizer, points to the fact that "the fragility of inherited policy commitments, and that the capacity of reforms to remake politics is contingent, conditional, and contested."[106] Disability rights entrepreneurs may have traded big plans for more limited action, leaving disability rights an unfinished project. Like Reich, as quoted in this section's epigraph, Harkin told us years ago, "We have come a long way. We have some more things to do. We are at it and we are going to keep at it."[107]

The disability rights struggle shines light on societal limits—how far or not politicians, the courts, employers and public and private corporations, social movement and civil rights activists, and the American public are willing to extend civil rights, both in its understanding of the plight of a historically disadvantaged group and in policy implementation.

In the wake of the 2008 Restoration Act and throughout Obama's presidency, disability rights meant fighting familiar battles. The Bush-era Medicaid debate (including the Community Choice Act) carried over with little progress. Attempts to weaken the ADA's public accommodation requirements of commercial facilities continued (for example, the initiative sponsored by Rep. Chris Cannon [R-UT] in 2011) as detractors sought to extend accommodation compliance times to which the Epilepsy Foundation strongly objected. Others, particularly in the business community, simply sought to undermine the legitimacy of the ADA by framing it as a policy serving the interests of unscrupulous ambulance-chasing lawyers (a charge DREDF has publicly criticized).[108] Meanwhile, because no monetary damages were available to disabled people experiencing accessibility obstacles, businesses faced few negative sanctions for their noncompliance.

Given the story this book tells, it is no surprise that many worried over disability rights during the 2016 presidential campaign and assumed the ADA would, again, come under attack. The 2017 ADA Education and Reform Act proposed relaxing requirements for businesses to provide reasonable accommodations. Title III provisions were undermined when the Trump administration placed efforts to improve ADA website accessibility regulations on the inactive list, signaling a retreat by the DOJ on equal access. The administration has proposed cuts to legal services and protection and advocacy services, making it increasingly difficult for victims of employment discrimination to access and mobilize their rights. It has also sought to roll back the use of fines against nursing homes charged with mistreatment (efforts to which the Center for Medicare Advocacy referred as emasculating already weak enforcement).[109]

The past, in sum, shows us where the disability rights struggle in the United States is going. The devolution of legislative intent; the quiet, insidious attempts to undermine the law through attention-resistant rule making and enforcement; the growing partisan divide over disability rights; the business community's lobbying against regulations of all kinds—none of this is new to the disability rights movement. Policies are *never* settled.

This book seeks to uncover how policies that "everyone agrees with" face ongoing political threats. Part of the answer involves detractors' persistent efforts, but more potent are the extant policy commitments and legacies governing the interaction between disability rights entrepreneurs and the venues within which they operate. Policy pathways touching on various issues like education, health, and transportation have both encouraged backlash and limited proponent's abilities to seek new political solutions. In their efforts to do the morally and economically right thing, political entrepreneurs may have also "loaded the dice,"[110] shaping the future of disability rights such that even when policy pathways appeared to be a done deal, there would be plenty of subsequent opportunities for retrenchment.

Early on, political entrepreneurs sought alternative political opportunities to enact disability rights—the parallel rights system that, in the ultimate compromise, evolved leading up to the ADA. Their efforts unfortunately precluded the inclusion of sufficient self-reinforcing mechanisms to protect rights from backlash and retrenchment. Compromises that allowed policy enactment may very well have prevented rights entrenchment. This has placed a tremendous burden on disability activists and advocacy groups to change negative attitudes about disability among policy stakeholders and the general public. Widespread beliefs among detractors that these are "special efforts," burdens, and unfair redistribution have worked against institutionalizing civil rights, subsequently leading to downstream reversals. It may have been worthwhile, although perhaps somewhat ironic, for disability rights entrepreneurs to take lessons from the rehabilitationists of the 1940s and 1950s, who were considerably more successful in ensuring self-reinforcement and aggrandizement of their policy domain. Considering how institutional layering can work to undermine legislation,[111] political entrepreneurs may not have done enough, for a variety of institutional, ideological, and professional reasons, to "stack the deck" by embedding their policies in enduring structures, particularly rule making and enforcement, so that policies withstand erosive elements.[112]

Returning to the tortoise-and-hare analogy of innovation and retrenchment in American policy making, one cannot help being reminded of the moral of Aesop's fable: slow and steady wins the race. Political entrepreneurship was critical in jump-starting the conversation about civil rights for the disabled. It carved out spaces within institutional settings for a community that had traditionally been left out of political decision making. However, how political elites went about pursuing disability rights legislation exposed the political drawbacks of their approach and the limitations of institutional activism in entrenching policy.

Backlash and organized opposition have frequently mobilized citizens by reminding them that nothing—not even their civil rights—can be taken for granted. Now, as in the past, advocates and activists are seeking to empower political elites. They aim to make the United States a world leader in disability rights, not just in its capacity to move policy forward but also in the assurance that those policies have an actual, positive impact on citizens' everyday lives.

Reference Matter

Appendix

Chapter 2

Ideological positioning scores. These scores ("nominate" variable) are assigned to each member of Congress (see the *Voteview congressional roll-call database at* https://voteview.com). The scores are based on two dimensions: liberal and conservative preferences on "fundamental" issues (e.g., taxation) and liberal and conservative preferences on social issues (e.g., civil rights). For average committee ideological position, I obtained the individual scores for each committee member at a given point in time and averaged the scores.

CC scores. These are based on the Conservative Coalition (CC scores) provided in the *Congressional Quarterly Almanac* each year for each member of Congress.[1] As Nelson Polsby explains, CC scores capture the percentage of roll calls on which a legislator voted with the CC.[2]

Committee stability and turnover. This is the committee membership composition over time that considers those exiting the committee (in part because they were voted out of office) and those joining a committee (through assignment, for example). Committee members are reported regularly in the *CQ Almanac*, as well as on all committee hearing documents. This also allows for an analysis of committee membership size over time.

CQ issue salience. I use the number of disability-related stories in the *CQ Almanac* to gauge issue salience within government. Typically, an article on an issue in the main chapters of the *CQ Almanac* is related to a particular legislative initiative. That is, it tracks intensity (not content) of legislative activity in

Congress on a given topic.[3] These data were obtained from the Policy Agendas Project (a.k.a. Comparative Agendas Project) using the five disability-related codes (see the Chapter 3 section of this appendix for more information on the Policy Agendas data). Like content analyses of newspaper articles meant to operationalize media interest, *CQ* stories can be either a function of government response to a problem (i.e., a response to crises, public pressures, or other exogenous factors) or government-led initiatives in tackling those problems (i.e., more supply-side factors, including personal and professional motivations, shifting political interests, etc.).

Organizational data.   Information about organizational membership size and structure was obtained from my content analysis of organizational entries in the *Encyclopedia of Associations* (published by Gale Research; see the Chapter 4 section later in this appendix for more information about these data). These entries include information about founding year, budget, number of local and state chapters, and number of members. Information about disability organizations testifying before Congress (typically groups serving as witnesses) was obtained from a content analysis of all disability-related hearings held between 1946 and 1960.

Chapter 3

Hearings (and hearing-days), bills, and laws.   The Policy Agendas Project (a.k.a. Comparative Agendas Project; see https://www.comparativeagendas .net) was developed to capture system-level stability and change in policy agendas, especially, as Bryan Jones and Frank Baumgartner articulate, "how institutional procedures constrain policy reactions to information flows."[4]

Disability-related hearings, bills, and laws were gathered using Lexis-Nexis/ Proquest Congressional and the *Congressional Record.*[5] Following Paul Burstein and Elizabeth Hirsh,[6] I found all 393 public laws and relevant bills related to disability by scouring books, law reviews, and archives, as well as legislative information provided by numerous disability organizations.

I found a total of 1,275 hearings: 875 House hearings and 400 Senate hearings. Note that I do not rely on laws or bills to locate hearings, as this truncates the number of hearings by excluding those unattached to specific legislative activity (that is, there are many hearings that are unaffiliated with bills).

Table A.1 Disability policy makers of the 1950s

Policy maker	Party	State	First elected	Professional background	Additional congressional activity
Dominick Daniels	D	NJ	1959	Lawyer	Championed educational policies; strongly supported organized labor; supported policies to help historically disadvantaged groups
Paul Douglas	D	IL	1949	Economics professor	Joined the "liberal coalition"; strongly supported black civil rights; coauthored Consumer Credit Protection Act
Carl Elliot	D	AL	1949	Lawyer	Voted against the 1957 and 1964 Civil Rights Acts; authored the Library Services Act; involved in "space race" policies
Edith Green	D	OR	1955	Education lobbyist	Championed higher education policies; involved in "space race" policy; worked on Title IX legislation to prohibit sex discrimination in education; supported Library Services Act; worked on mental health legislation
Ernest Greenwood	D	NY	1949	Educator; supervisor, Federal Board of Vocational Education	Unsuccessfully ran as a Republican; worked on educational policy
Augustine B. Kelley	D	PA	1941	Superintendent of a coke and coal company	Chaired House Committee on Invalid Pensions; worked on problems of health and air pollution
Herbert H. Lehman	D	NY	1950	Governor of New York	Considered a very liberal senator; strongly supported civil liberties and was vocal critic of Joseph McCarthy
Samuel McConnell	R	PA	1944	Investment banker; township commissioner	Replaced Barden as chair of House Committee on Education and Labor; criticized the Federal Employment Practices Committee; supported Joseph McCarthy's efforts
Carl D. Perkins	D	KY	1949	Lawyer	Strongly supported federal educational programs; chaired Committee on Education and Labor in the 1960s; played a significant role in the Head Start and War on Poverty programs
Wint Smith	R	KS	1947	Lawyer	Supported Joseph McCarthy's initiatives; voted against a bill that would provide aid to China
Stuyvesant Wainwright	R	NY	1952	Lawyer	Supported a bill that made Fire Island a national park; supported the Powell Amendment to withhold aid to school districts that did not comply with *Brown v. Board of Education* only if it contained the Republican distributional formula
Roy W. Wier	D	MN	1949	Member MN House of Representatives	Strongly supported federal aid to education

TABLE 3.—*Total expenditures from Federal and State funds for vocational rehabilitation, fiscal years 1943–52*

Year	Expenditures			Percent	
	Total	Federal funds	State and local funds	Federal funds	State and local funds
1943	$5, 629, 923	$2, 761, 748	$2, 868, 175	49. 1	50. 9
1944	6, 371, 992	4, 051, 551	2, 320, 441	63. 6	36. 4
1945	9, 855, 544	7, 135, 441	2, 720, 103	72. 4	27. 6
1946	13, 749, 488	10, 002, 239	3, 747, 250	72. 7	27. 3
1947	19, 313, 344	14, 188, 933	5, 124, 411	73. 5	26. 5
1948	24, 568, 814	17, 706, 843	6, 861, 971	72. 1	27. 9
1949	25, 818, 839	18, 215, 683	7, 603, 156	70. 6	29. 4
1950	29, 346, 824	20, 340, 142	9, 006, 682	69. 3	30. 7
1951	30, 272, 854	21, 001, 388	9, 271, 466	69. 4	30. 6
1952	32, 689, 353	22, 122, 437	10, 566, 916	67. 7	32. 3

Figure A.1 Table of total expenditures from federal and state funds for vocational rehabilitation, presented at a congressional hearing by Mary Switzer of the RSA. *Source: Assistance and Rehabilitation of the Physically Handicapped*, 83rd Cong. 6 (1953).

Additionally, knowing the length of each hearing, I constructed a hearing-days variable that is the product of the number of days and the number of hearings in a given year.

Accounting for hearing-days rather than just a count of hearings over time corrects for holding fewer but longer hearings. Jerold Auerbach notes that committee chairs may have preferences in holding fewer multiple-day hearings, while others prefer more, but shorter, hearings.[7]

After I assigned unique identifiers to each of the disability-related hearings included in my sample, I linked them to the Policy Agendas Project data of all congressional hearings held between 1961 and 2006. Unfortunately, given the magnitude of the scale of their data-gathering effort, they tend to underestimate or coded differently those hearings that have important disability-related implications. However, the benefit of linking my data to theirs is that it allows me to situate disability within the broader policy agenda across time.

Policy domains.   The nineteen major topics in the Policy Agendas data are macroeconomics; civil rights; health; agriculture; labor; education; environment; energy; transportation; law, crime, and family issues; social welfare; community development and housing; banking and finance; defense; science; foreign trade; international affairs; government operations; and public lands.

There are five disability-relevant codes: handicap/disease discrimination (205); mental health/retardation (333); long-term care, home health, terminally

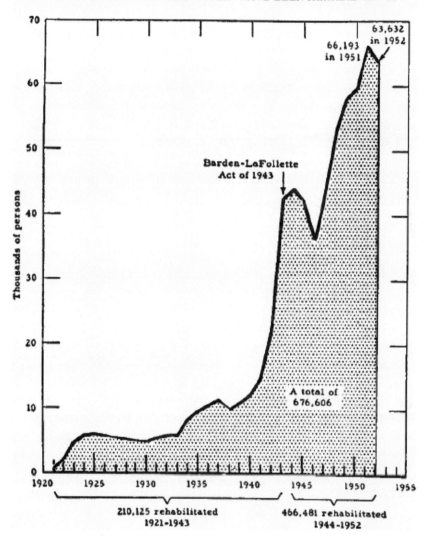

Figure A.2 Chart of number of rehabilitated people, presented at a congressional hearing by Mary Switzer of the RSA. *Source: Assistance and Rehabilitation of the Physically Handicapped*, 83rd Cong. 8 (1953).

ill, and rehabilitation services (334); special education (606); and assistance to disabled/handicapped (1304).

Entropy (informal committee jurisdictions). Entropy is a measure of the "congressional opportunity structure."[8] It is based not on what committees are formally expected to but actually do hold hearings about. Like a Herfindahl-Hirschman Index (HHI) of concentration, entropy is thus a measure of congressional committee issue concentration (that is, how wide or narrow committee informal jurisdictions are).

Entropy is calculated using the following formula:

$$\sum_i p_{ij} \times \log\left(\frac{1}{p_{ij}}\right)$$

where p is the share of hearings held on topic i by committee j. For each committee in every year included in the sample, an entropy score was calculated based on the nineteen major topic codes in the Policy Agendas data set.

Formal/statutory committee jurisdictions (jurisdictional proximity). This is a measure of the formal or statutory jurisdiction of a committee and is based on content analysis of committee descriptions published in *Rule X of the Rules of the House of Representatives* and *Rule XXV of the Standing Rules of the Senate.*[9] I assign a value of 1 for each committee using the following criteria: handicap/disease discrimination/rights (employment, education, etc.); access/physical barriers; mental health/retardation; long-term care/rehabilitation services; special education; social welfare/housing/community services for "vulnerable" groups; social security/disability insurance; work programs/vocational services. This variable therefore ranges from 0 (e.g., Committee on Agriculture) to 7 (Senate Committee on Health, Education, Labor, and Pensions).

Chapter 4

Organizational data. Data on disability organizations are based on my content analysis of information in the *Encyclopedia of Associations* volumes over a forty-five-year period. Except for very early editions, volumes are published yearly. To locate disability organizations, I and three research assistants manually scanned each physical page of every yearly volume. No online search engines were used; nor were the headings provided by the *Encyclopedia* to categorize organizations because many nonprofit groups include people with disabilities as a constituency that the *Encyclopedia* does not categorize as a disability group.

Table 4.1 ... ; leaders in Congress, 1960s–1970s

Policy maker	Party	State	First elected	Professional background	Additional congressional activity
Bella Abzug	D	NY	1971	Lawyer and activist	Strongly supported Equal Rights Amendments; pushed strongly for the 1974 Equality Act
Bob Bartlett	D	AK	1945	Alaska politician; chair of Unemployment Compensation Commission of Alaska; president of the Alaska Tuberculosis Association	Sponsored the Alaska Mental Health Enabling Act of 1956; involved in health and safety policies, increases in minimum wage, and federal aid extensions to education
Mario Biaggi	D	NY	1968	Police officer and lawyer	Worked mainly in policy areas of transportation, law and order, and social welfare, including child support policies
John Brademas	D	IN	1959	Served in navy; Rhodes Scholar	Sponsored creation of the National Endowment of the Arts; sponsored the Alcohol and Drug Abuse Education Act; worked heavily in education policy, including student aid
Alan Cranston	D	CA	1968	Served in army; author and reporter	Involved in EEOC-related legislation, affirmative action monitoring, and labor legislation; supported amendments to increase federal funds to planned parenting
Kenneth Gray	D	IL	1954	Served in air force; founded the Walking Dog Foundation for the Blind	Heavily involved in public works, including the interstate highway system; advocated for senior citizens and veterans
Hubert Humphrey	D	MN	1949	Pharmacist; mayor of Minneapolis	Introduced the first Peace Corps bill in 1957; involved in nutrition programs of various kinds; involved with unemployment compensation and the Work Hours Standards Act; played a pivotal role in passing the Civil Rights Act in 1964
Jacob Javits	R	NY	1947	Lawyer	Supported the 1957 Civil Rights Act; supported the 1964 Civil Rights Act and many of Johnson's Great Society programs
Robert Stafford	R	VT	1961	Lawyer; governor of Vermont	Worked in education policy with particular interests in student loan programs; worked in foreign aid, sponsoring the Staffer Disaster Relief and Emergency Assistance Act
Charles Vanik	D	OH	1955	Lawyer; served in naval reserve	Involved in housing legislation, minimum wage increases, and civil rights expansion in the 1950s; supported student aid expansion in 1958; involved in civil rights, economic opportunity, urban renewal, and environmental issues in mid-1960s; supported the Full Opportunity Act in 1969
Harrison Williams	D	NJ	1953	Lawyer; served in naval reserve	Sponsored legislation that created the Occupational Safety and Health Administration and the 1964 Urban Mass Transportation Act; involved in issues of the elderly, including Employee Retirement Income Security Act
Jim Wright	D	TX	1954	Served in air force; Texas politician; mayor of Weatherford	Voted for the 1957 Civil Rights Act; did not support the 1964 Civil Rights Act; heavily involved in public works; succeeded Tip O'Neil as Speaker of the House

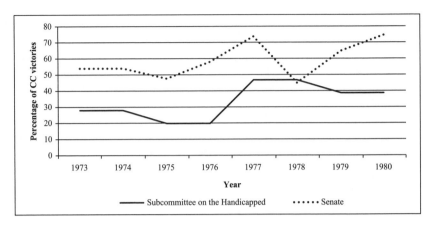

Figure A.3 Conservative voting in the Subcommittee on the Handicapped and the Senate.

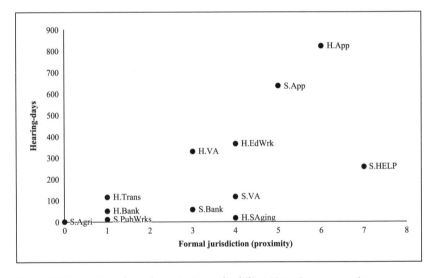

Figure A.4 Committee formal proximity to disability. *Note:* Some committees are excluded from the graph for readability. H.App = House Committee on Appropriations; H.Bank = House Committee on Banking and Currency; H.EdWrk = House Committee on Education and Workforce; H.SAging = House Permanent Select Committee on Aging; H.Trans = House Committee on Transportation and Infrastructure; H.VA = House Committee on Veterans' Affairs; S.Agri = Senate Committee on Agriculture, Nutrition, and Forestry; S.App = Senate Committee on Appropriations; S.Bank = Senate Committee on Banking, Housing, and Urban Affairs; S.HELP = Senate Committee on Health, Education, Labor, and Pensions; S.PubWrks = Senate Committee on Environment and Public Works; S.VA = Senate Committee on Veterans' Affairs.

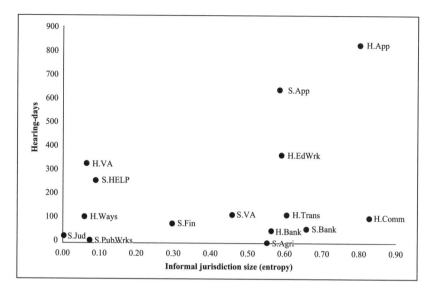

Figure A.5 Committees holding disability hearings based on their informal jurisdictions. *Note:* Some committees are excluded from the graph for readability. H.App = House Committee on Appropriations; H.Bank = House Committee on Banking and Currency; H.Comm = House Commerce Committee; H.EdWrk = House Committee on Education and Workforce; H.Trans = House Committee on Transportation and Infrastructure; H.VA = House Committee on Veterans' Affairs; H.Ways = House Committee on Ways and Means; S.Agri = Senate Committee on Agriculture, Nutrition, and Forestry; S.App = Senate Committee on Appropriations; S.Bank = Senate Committee on Banking, Housing, and Urban Affairs; S.Fin = Senate Finance Committee; S.HELP = Senate Committee on Health, Education, Labor, and Pensions; S.Jud = Senate Committee on the Judiciary; S.PubWrks = Senate Committee on Environment and Public Works; S.VA = Senate Committee on Veterans' Affairs.

Once all editions were processed, I compiled a master list of all groups in the sample (including those founded before 1961 and those that disbanded between 1961 and 2006). Organizations were also tracked to account for name change. Each organization received a unique identifier used throughout its life course in my time frame of interest.

Following Debra Minkoff, I coded organizational entries provided by organizations to the *Encyclopedia* by using an adapted version of Minkoff's codebook to content-analyze women's, ethnic/racial, and African American organizations.[10] This allowed me to track key variables related to organizational size and structure, tactics, and core strategies over time.

Table A.3 Estimating attention to the disability civil rights issue, using panel data, 1961–2006

	Effects of committee entropy	Agenda setting	Level of consideration
Entropy	0.28 (1.3)	1.39** (0.69)	−2.11 (2.68)
Proximity	0.51*** (0.15)	0.41*** (0.12)	0.05 (0.24)
Democratic control	−1.59** (0.77)	−1.60** (0.7)	3.38 (2.23)
Prior legislation	0.08** (0.03)	0.07 (0.04)	−0.04 (0.1)
Prior hearing days	−0.02 (0.04)	−0.08** (0.03)	−0.01 (0.11)
Prior civil rights hearing days	0.03 (0.1)	0.24** (0.07)	0.17 (0.24)
Democratic × Entropy	3.73** (1.45)	3.63*** (1.01)	−0.8 (3.77)
Democratic × Proximity	−0.13 (0.13)	−0.11 (0.14)	−0.09 (0.25)
Constant	−3.73*** (1.06)	−5.13*** (0.75)	−3.7 (18.2)

Note: Robust standard errors are in parentheses. A likelihood-ratio test revealed that negative binomial regression is more appropriate than a Poisson model. The "Effects of committee entropy" column uses a fixed-effects model and shows whether committees with broader, less concentrated jurisdictions hold more hearings. The "Agenda setting" column uses a Hurdle logit model to test agenda setting (whether a committee will ever hold a hearing), and the "Level of consideration" column uses Hurdle negative binomial regression to test the level (or intensity) of consideration. The models control for prior bills, prior civil rights bills, and chamber (Senate/House), but these never reached significance. Data are based on disability-related hearings, bills, and laws and are structured as a times-series cross section of all existing committees, including both select and standing committees (forty-seven committees) over a forty-five-year period, producing a maximum sample size of 2,115 cases.

$*p < 0.01, ** p < 0.05, ***p < 0.001.$

Organizational formation/founding. For each organizational entry, the *Encyclopedia* reports the date of organizational formation. Where no date is available, I either conducted further research to locate the organizations' founding date through books, databases, and Internet searches or, as Minkoff does, use the year of first appearance in the *Encyclopedia* as the year of formation.

Organizational density. The density of disability organizations is the number of existing active organizations at the end of a given year plus the number of new organizations minus those that became inactive or defunct.[11] Note that organizational density is also sometimes used as a measure of movement or organizational capacity—what Erik Johnson refers to as "movement infrastructure."[12]

Core organizational strategy (service, advocacy, hybrid). Following Minkoff,[13] each organizational description (which is submitted by the organization itself) is content-analyzed using a series of activities that are then, in their total, used to determine the core strategy for each organization in a given year.

For example, a service-provision organization often works to provide any number of services and types of aid, including electoral/political, legal, educational economic, community, financial, and religious services. Legal services can include free or reduced-fee services or legal resource referral. Educational services include financial aid or educational/vocational counseling. Economic services include employment/career services and job-placement programs.

Advocacy organizations might engage in lobbying, policy/program development, reform efforts, legal mobilization, direct action, voter registration, or leadership training. Specific advocacy-group activities can include lobbying, coalition formation, policy development and monitoring, research dissemination, general political reform efforts, and community organizing/mobilizing.

Table A.4 Favorable environments for organizational expansion, 1961–2006

Predictors	Founding rate
Entropy (informal committee jurisdictional expansion)	18.6**
	(7.29)
Democratic Senate	−0.28**
	(0.13)
Democratic House	1.61***
	(0.41)
Hearing-days	0.005**
	(0.002)
Legislative activity	0.022**
	(0.01)
Organizational density	−0.005***
	(0.001)
Constant	−8.16
	(1.22)
Wald test (χ^2 [6])	177.82***

Note: Coefficients obtained from negative binomial regression models. Robust standard errors are in parentheses. All independent variables are lagged one year. Organizational density is the number of active groups at $t - 1$ + new entrants − defunct groups. See Hannan and Freeman, *Organizational Ecology*; Hannan and Carroll, *Dynamics of Organizational Populations*; Minkoff, *Organizing for Equality*. Wald test χ^2 is significant, rejecting the null hypothesis that all the coefficients are equal to 0. Democratic Senate and House are dummy variables accounting for whether the Democrats control those respective chambers in a given year. Hearing-days control for the total number of disability-related hearing-days (not the hearing count) held in the year prior, and legislative activity is also a lagged measure of the number of disability-related laws enacted. $N = 45$ years.

*$p < 0.05$, **$p < 0.01$, ***$p < 0.001$.

Using the dozens of activity types to code the entries (I coded up to five activities for each group), I then used a matrix to determine the single most appropriate organizational strategy, including a service-advocacy hybrid if the organization engaged in a mix of these activities.

Chapter 5

Protest events.   These data were obtained by coding four newspapers—the *New York Times*, *Los Angeles Times*, *Washington Post*, and *San Francisco Chronicle*—across a forty-five-year period (1961–2006) with the help of research assistants. These newspapers by and large report on regional and national events. I include the *San Francisco Chronicle* because the Bay Area is a known protest center in the disability rights struggle.

No doubt, my content analysis might exclude smaller protests or protests in small towns and cities. However, it is important that newspaper coverage be available consistently for my entire time period. While the *Los Angeles Times* and *New York Times* were available electronically for my entire period of interest, this was not the case at the time of data collection for the *Washington Post* and *San Francisco Chronicle*. In the early years, I had to content-analyze articles on microfiche.

While Newsbank and Newsbank Retrospective at the time of data collection seemingly provided a searchable longitudinal database of thousands of national and local newspapers, each newspaper included in the search did not have the same digital availability. That is, the coverage year for individual newspapers was inconsistent. For instance, whereas coverage of the *Washington Post* at the time of data collection began in 1977, coverage of the *Dallas Morning News* began in 1984. I individually reviewed eleven of these major newspapers, and it appears that the coverage dates for these newspapers in Newsbank reflect the year in which the newspaper content became digitized. Lexis-Nexis had the same limitation. At the time of my data collection, only eleven major metro newspapers in Newsbank consistently began coverage in 1985.

This means that the use of these databases, like Newsbank, without properly controlling for the denominator (that is, the number of newspapers becoming digitized), inflates the number of protest events.[14] My distribution of protests, however, still resembles Sharon Barnartt's distribution (although with far fewer protests) and is consistent with what others have found in regard to disability protest events.[15]

Mean protest size.   Based on the estimated number of protesters reported in newspaper articles, I use a convention similar to the one of Pamela Oliver and

Daniel Myers: small/modest (less than 99), medium (100–499), large (500–999), very large (greater than 1,000).[16]

Duration.   Duration was the number of hours the protest lasted (as reported in the article): short (less than 1 day/5–24 hours), moderate (1 day/24 hours), long (2–3 days/48–72 hours), very long (4 days or more/ >96 hours).

Targets and goals.   Targets were coded into three main types: local and state government (e.g., Anaheim City Council, Virginia State Chamber of Commerce), federal government (e.g., Reagan administration, HEW), and private/public corporations (e.g., Greyhound Lines, US Airways, New York Metropolitan Transit Authority). Protest goals are sometimes explicitly noted in the article, although often goals had to be inferred. There were six main types of protest goals: securing equality/civil rights; increasing representation in social institutions; removing barriers/increasing access/resources; increasing public awareness of discrimination; maintaining access/programs/services; and raising awareness of social problems and portrayal of disability.

Organizations.   Information about organizational involvement in protest events is based on a newspaper article directly reporting one or more organizations as having coordinated the event or indirectly through interviews with protesters who stated organizational affiliations as relevant to the protest.

Chapter 6

Disability percent employed and average earnings.   In prior work, my colleagues and I have shown that employment rates among disabled Americans has declined since 1988 and wages stagnated.[17] Figure 6.2 is based on analyses

Table A.5 Description of disability protests

Description	Overall	1961–1971	1972–1979	1980–1992	1993–2006
Mean number of protests per year	4.00	0.60	5.00	6.50	3.20
Mean size (number of protesters)	489.92	141.60	768.16	415.13	382.05
Duration (days)	3.90	7.04	7.02	2.93	1.67
Mean number of protests with arrests	0.15	1.00	1.00	1.00	4.86
Mean number of people arrested	37.50	27.00	5.00	32.00	53.88
Mean of events with organization involvement	0.51	0.50	0.45	0.54	0.53

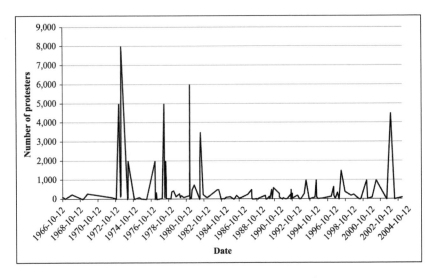

Figure A.6 Disability protest size over time, 1961–2006. *Note:* There were no protests before 1966 and none after 2004.

Table A.6 Simultaneous equations predicting hearings, public laws, and protest, 1961–2006 (three-stage least squares regression)

Predictors	Model 1		Model 2		Model 3	
	House hearings	Protest	Senate hearings	Protest	Public laws	Protest
House hearings (lagged)		0.28*** (0.07)				
Senate hearings (lagged)		−0.08 (0.11)				
Public laws (lagged)		0.1 (0.09)				
Protest (lagged)	0.14 (0.23)		0.02 (0.26)		−0.1 (0.18)	
Rehabilitation Act		2.66** (1.32)		3.58** (1.44)		3.87*** (1.42)
ADA		−0.16 (1.32)		0.1 (1.51)		−0.33 (1.49)
Constant	19.9 (3.24)	−2.82 (1.35)	0.61 (4.53)	−0.63 (1.4)	6.05 (1.77)	−0.83 (1.39)

Note: Coefficients based on three-stage regression testing for nonrecursivity between institutional change and protest. See Costain and Majstorovic, "Congress, Social Movements and Public Opinion." These models show that hearings and policies shaped protest, but protest did not directly shape hearings or policy enactment (that is, the relationship between institutional change and protest is recursive). Models control for congressional committees, civil rights as the most important problem (lagged), party control, and disability as a congressional issue (results not shown). Standard errors are in parentheses. $N = 45$.

*$p < 0.1$, **$p < 0.05$, ***$p < 0.01$.

of 1988–2014 Current Population Survey (CPS) data for working-age people (twenty-five to sixty-one years of age) with and without work-limiting disabilities. Estimates show the average percentage of employed based on disability status. For earnings, estimates show the average earnings in 2014 dollars based on disability status. Estimates control for age, education, marital status, the presence of children, sex, race, the receipt of government assistance, and state of residence.

In subsequent work, we explain how growing inequality is in part the result of occupational segmentation or ghettoization into lower-paying precarious jobs, as well as the overlapping systems of oppression that especially disadvantage women of color with disabilities and contribute to their economic insecurity.[18]

Organizational mortality.   Like organization founding, organizational mortality is similarly based on the *Encyclopedia of Associations*' reporting of whether the organization has ceased operations. In certain cases, the organization is repeatedly listed as either inactive or having an unknown address (in some cases, for more than five years). I treat these organizations has having disbanded. On a very small amount of cases, the *Encyclopedia* inexplicably drops the entry in subsequent volumes. I further investigated those organizations to determine whether they have disbanded or become inactive. In situations where it is impossible to determine the whereabouts of the organization, I use the last year of appearance in the *Encyclopedia* as the year of disbanding.

Resources

Policies

ADA Education and Reform Act of 2017 (H.R. 620)

ADA Restoration Act/ADA Amendments Act of 2008 (ADARA/ADAAA, Pub. L. 110-325)

Additional Aid for the American Printing House for the Blind (Pub. L. 82-354)

Affordable Care Act (a.k.a. Obamacare, Pub. L. 111-148)

Age Discrimination in Employment Act (Pub. L. 90-202)

Air Carrier Access Act of 1986 (Pub. L. 99-435)

Amendment to the Charter of the Columbia Institution for the Deaf (Pub. L. 83-420)

Americans with Disabilities Act (ADA, Pub. L. 101-336)

Architectural Barriers Act (ABA, Pub. L. 90-480)

Better Care Reconciliation Act (H.R. 1628)

Biaggi Amendment (adopted during House discussion, Cong. Rec. 34,180)

Building on Local District Flexibility in IDEA Act (BOLD, H.R. 2965)

Chapman Amendment (H.R. 2273)

Civil Rights Act of 1964 (Pub. L. 88 352)

Civil Rights Restoration Act of 1988 (CRRA, Pub. L. 100-259)

Civil Services Act Amendment (Pub. L. 80-617)

Community Choice Act (S. 799)

Developmental Disabilities Assistance and Bill of Rights Act Amendments of 1987 (Pub. L. 100-146)

Developmental Disabilities Services and Facilities Construction Act (Pub. L. 91-517)

Developmentally Disabled Assistance and Bill of Rights Act (Pub. L. 94-103)

Economic Opportunity Act (Pub. L. 88-452).

Education Amendments of 1974 (Pub. L. 93-380)

Equal Employment Opportunity Act (Pub. L. 92-261)

Equal Employment Opportunity for Handicapped Individuals Act (S. 446)

Every Student Succeeds Act (ESSA, S. 117)

Fair Housing Act (Title VIII of the Civil Rights Act, Pub. L. 90-284)

Fair Housing Amendments Act (Pub. L. 100-430).

Federal-Aid Highway Act 1970 (Pub. L. 91-605)

Federal-Aid Highway Act Amendments 1974 (Pub. L. 93-643)

Full Funding for IDEA Now Act (H.R 1829, H.R. 823, H.R. 1107, H.R. 526)

GI Bill (a.k.a. Servicemen's Readjustment Act of 1944, Pub. L. 78-346)

Handicapped Children's Protection Act (Pub. L. 99-372)

Housing Act of 1954 (Pub. L. 83-560)

IDEA Fairness Restoration Act (S. 2790, H.R. 1208, S. 613, H.R. 2740, H.R. 4188)

IDEA Full Funding Act (S. 88)

Individuals with Disabilities Education Act (IDEA); Education for All Handicapped Children Act of 1975 (Pub. L. 94-142)

Keep Our PACT Act (H.R. 864).

Mass Transit Amendments/Transit Assistance Act of 1981 (S. 1160)

Maternal and Child Health and Mental Retardation Planning Amendments (Pub. L. 88-156)

Mental Retardation Facilities and Community Mental Health Centers Construction Act (Pub. L. 88-164)

Moving Ahead for Progress in the 21st Century Act (MAP-21) of 2012 (Pub. L. 112-141)

National Labor-Management Relations Act (Pub. L. 74-198)

National Mass Transportation Assistance Act Amendments of 1975 (S. 662)

National Mass Transportation Assistance Act of 1974 (Pub. L. 93-503)

National Technical Institute for the Deaf Act (Pub. L. 89-36)

No Child Left Behind Act (NCLB, Pub. L. 107-110)

Over-the-Road Bus Transportation Accessibility Act (Pub. L. 110-291)

Randolph-Sheppard Act (Pub. L. 74-732)

Rehabilitation Act of 1973 (Pub. L. 93-112)

Sensenbrenner Amendment (H.R. 2273)

Smith-Fess Act of 1920 (Pub. L. 66-236)

Smith-Hughes Act of 1917 (Pub. L. 64-347)

Smith-Sears Act of 1918 (Pub. L. 65-178)

Social Security Act Amendments of 1956 (Pub. L. 84-880)

Social Security Act Amendments of 1967 (Pub. L. 90-248)

Social Security Act of 1935 (Pub. L. 74-271)

Telecommunications Accessibility Enhancement Act (Pub. L. 100-542)

Urban Mass Transportation Act of 1964 (Pub. L. 88-365)

Urban Mass Transportation Assistance Act of 1970 (Pub. L. 91-453)

Vocational Rehabilitation Act Amendments of 1965 (Pub. L. 89-333)

Vocational Rehabilitation Act Amendments of 1967 (Pub. L. 90-99)

Vocational Rehabilitation Act Amendments of 1968 (H.R. 15827, H.R. 16134, H.J. Res. 811)

Vocational Rehabilitation Act Amendments of 1972 (S. 3690)

Vocational Rehabilitation Act of 1954 (Pub. L. 83-565)

Voting Rights Act Amendments of 1982 (Pub. L. 97-205)

Court Cases

Albertson's, Inc. v. Kirkingburg, 527 U.S. 555 (1999)

Board of Trustees of Univ. of Ala. v. Garrett, 531 U.S. 356 (2001)

Brown v. Board of Education of Topeka, 347 U.S. 483 (1954)

Chevron U.S.A. Inc. v. Echazabal, 536 U.S. 73 (2002)

Department of Transportation v. Paralyzed Veterans of America, 477 U.S. 597 (1986)

Griggs v. Duke Power Co., 401 U.S. 424 (1971)

Grove City Coll. v. Bell, 465 U.S. 555 (1984)

Magee v. Coca-Cola Refreshments USA, Inc., 143 F. Supp. 3d 464 (2015)

Murphy v. United Parcel Service, Inc., 527 U.S. 516 (1999)

N. E. v. Seattle School District, No. 15-35910 (9th Cir. 2016)

Olmstead v. L.C., 527 U.S. 581 (1999)

Pennhurst State Sch. v. Halderman, 465 U.S. 89 (1984)

Peter Pan Bus Lines, Inc. v. FMCSA, No. 05-1436 (D.C. Cir. 2006).

School Bd. of Nassau County v. Arline, 480 U.S. 273 (1987)

Smith v. Robinson, 468 U.S. 992 (1984)

Southeastern Commun. Coll. v. Davis, 442 U.S. 397 (1979)

Sutton v. United Air Lines, Inc., 527 U.S. 471 (1999)

Trageser v. Libbie Rehab. Center, Inc./Convalescent Home, 442 U.S. 947 (1979)

Wards Cove Packing Co. v. Atonio, 490 U.S. 642 (1989)

Organizations

AIDS Coalition to Unleash Power (ACT UP)

Alexander Graham Bell Association for the Deaf

American Association of People with Disabilities (AAPD)

American Association of Workers for the Blind

American Association on Mental Deficiency (a.k.a. American Association on Mental Retardation, American Association on Intellectual and Developmental Disabilities)

American Coalition of Citizens with Disabilities (ACCD)

American Council of the Blind

American Council on Education

American Federation for the Blind
American Foundation for the Blind
American Institute of Architects
American Instructors of the Deaf
American Medical Association
American Nurses Association
American Occupational Therapy Association
American Printing House for the Blind
American Psychiatric Association
American Public Health Association (APHA)
American Public Transit Association (APTA)
American Servicemen's Union
American Speech-Language-Hearing Association
American Veterans (AMVETS)
Association for Children with Learning Disabilities (ACLD)
Association for the Blind
Association of Black Psychologists
Association of the Deaf
Association of University Centers on Disabilities
Autistic Self Advocacy Network
Barrier Free Anaheim
Blind Veterans Association
Brain Injury Association
Catholic Guild for All the Blind
Center for Concerned Engineering
Center for Independent Living
Center for Medicare Advocacy
Children's Defense Fund
Committee on Aging and Disabled for Welfare
Conference of Executives of American Schools for the Deaf
Consortium Concerned with the Developmentally Disabled (CCDD)/Consortium for
    Citizens with Developmental Disabilities/Consortium of Citizens with Disabilities
Council for Exceptional Children
Council for the Retarded
Council of Chief State School Officers
Council of State Administrators of Vocational Rehabilitation
Deafpride
Disability Rights and Education Defense Fund (DREDF)
Disability Rights Center

Disabled American Veterans

Disabled in Action (DIA)

Easter Seals (a.k.a. National Easter Seal Society, Easterseals)

Epilepsy Foundation of America

Goodwill

Gray Panthers

Heritage Foundation

IDEA Funding Coalition

IDEA Rapid Response Network

International Association of Parents of the Deaf (a.k.a. American Society for Deaf
    Children)

Joseph P. Kennedy Jr. Foundation

Leadership Conference on Civil Rights

League of Special Education Voters

Mainstream, Inc.

Mental Disability Legal Resource Center

Mental Health Law Project

Mothers of Young Mongoloids (a.k.a. Parents of Down Syndrome Children)

Muscular Dystrophy Association

National AIDS Program Office

National Alliance of Blind Students

National Alliance of the Disabled

National Art and Handicapped Information Service

National Association for Mental Health

National Association of College and University Business Officers

National Association of Developmental Disabilities Councils

National Association of Private Residential Facilities for the Mentally Retarded (a.k.a.
    American Network of Community Options and Resources)

National Association of Protection and Advocacy Systems

National Association of Retarded Children (NARC/ARC)

National Association of Social Workers

National Association of the Deaf

National Association of the Handicapped

National Association of the Physically Handicapped

National Center for Law and the Handicapped

National Center for the Deaf

National Council of the Blind

National Council on Independent Living

National Down Syndrome Congress

National Education Association (NEA)
National Epilepsy League (later merged with Epilepsy Foundation)
National Federation of the Blind (NFB)
National Foundation for Neuromuscular Disease
National Home Care Association
National Legislative Council for the Handicapped
National Mental Health Association
National Multiple Sclerosis Society
National Organization for Mentally Ill Children
National Organization for Women (NOW)
National Paraplegia Foundation
National Parents and Teachers Association
National Parkinson Foundation
National Recreation Association
National Rehabilitation Association (NRA)
National Society for Autistic Children (a.k.a. Autism Society of America)
National Spinal Cord Injury Association
National Tay-Sachs Association
National Urban League
National Women's Law Center
Not Dead Yet
Paralyzed Veterans of America (PVA)
Parents' Campaign for Handicapped Children and Youth
Rainbow Alliance of the Deaf
Rainbow Coalition
Rehabilitation, Inc.
San Diego's Community Service Center for the Disabled
September Alliance for Accessible Transit
The Association for the Severely Handicapped (a.k.a. The Association for Persons with
    Severe Handicaps) (TASH)
United Cerebral Palsy Association (UCP)
Voice of the Retarded

Notes

Preface

1. Abrams, "Our Lives Are at Stake."

Chapter 1

1. As Richard Scotch notes, "The concept of rehabilitation was at the core of the ideology of the emerging American welfare state." Scotch, *From Good Will to Civil Rights*, 24. This, in turn, supports Theda Skocpol's challenge to Harold Wilensky's characterization of the United States as a "welfare laggard," fitting more closely with Ann Orloff's 1988 "belated welfare state" narrative. See Skocpol, *Protecting Soldiers and Mothers*; Wilensky, *The Welfare State and Equality*, 118; and Orloff, "The Political Origins of America's Belated Welfare State."

2. A policy monopoly, also known as an iron triangle, refers to a tightly bounded network including congressional committees, agencies in the Executive Branch, and interest groups governing a policy area and excluding outside actors. See Givel, "Punctuated Equilibrium in Limbo"; True and Utter, "Saying 'Yes,' 'No,'"; and McCarthy, "Velcro Triangles."

3. Barbara Altman and Sharon Barnartt use this term in regard to moral entrepreneurship in the politics leading up to the ADA. See Altman and Barnartt, "Moral Entrepreneurship and the Promise of the ADA." As I show throughout this book, *political* entrepreneurship explains the much longer legacy of disability politics and broader civil rights.

4. *Special Education and Rehabilitation*, 86th Cong. 621 (1960) (statement of Judge Kenneth Griffith).

5. For more on the medical model and social model of disability, see Shakespeare, "The Social Model of Disability."

6. Berkowitz in effect blames rehabilitationists for blocking alternative conceptualizations of disability (presumably including civil rights) from emerging. See Berkowitz, *Disabled Policy*. While partly true, this is not a complete picture when we take into account the broader political and institutional context that limited the ability for dramatic policy innovation to emerge during much of the middle part of the last century.

7. In *Protecting Soldiers and Mothers*, Skocpol argues that the distinction between deserving and undeserving is the major fault line running through American social policy.

8. Institutional activism has been used to describe the proactive behavior by those with access to power and resources—political entrepreneurs—championing causes that may overlap with social movement efforts. See Pettinicchio, "Institutional Activism"; Pettinicchio, "Strategic Action Fields"; and Pettinicchio, "Elites, Policy and Social Movements."

9. In his work on biotechnology policy agenda setting, Adam Sheingate describes entrepreneurs as transforming a policy issue by creatively combining different ideas endogenous or exogenous to a policy domain. In doing so, political entrepreneurs can "change the flow of politics," which is part of Mark Schneider and Paul Teske's definition of a political entrepreneur. See Sheingate, "Political Entrepreneurship," 185; and Schneider and Teske, "Toward a Theory of the Political Entrepreneur," 737.

10. 119 Cong. Rec. 24,553 (1973). See also Bill 92, S.3987 (1972).

11. In his thesis on citizenship and social class, Alfred T. Marshall distinguished between civil citizenship (respect for individual rights), social citizenship (the provision of services to maintain a basic quality of life), and political citizenship (direct and/or indirect inclusion in the policy-making process), explaining that these develop sequentially. In many ways, disability policy blurred these forms of citizenship in that the focus on the political and civil followed from the social. See Marshall, *Citizenship and Social Class*.

12. 119 Cong. Rec. 16,401 (1973).

13. *Effectiveness of the Architectural Barriers Act of 1968 (P.L. 90–480)*, 94th Cong. 1 (1975).

14. Many have referenced Humphrey's statement in their congressional testimony over the years, including Betty Duskin of the National Council of Senior Citizens, who said that "a society may be judged by how it treats three groups in its population: Those in the dawn of life, its young; those in the twilight of life, its elderly; and those in the shadows of life, its disabled." *President Carter's Social Security Proposals, Part 2*, 95th Cong. 646 (1977).

15. Skrentny, *The Minority Rights Revolution*.

16. In *Personal Roots of Representation*, Barry C. Burden argues that life stories and legislators' personal lives shape not only why they enter politics but also why and how

they pursue particular issues. Burden argues that these personal roots ultimately shape policy outcomes as much as if not more so than party ideology and voter preferences.

17. For a discussion of the relationship between preferences, values, and decision making, see Hechter, Nadel, and Michod, *The Origin of Values*.

18. Kaufman, "Time to Ratify the Global Disabilities Convention."

19. *Implementation of the Helsinki Accords: Disability Rights and U.S. Foreign Policy*, 103rd Cong. 79 (1994) (statement of Rep. Steny H. Hoyer).

20. These were formally known as the American Association on Mental Retardation and the National Society for Autistic Children, respectively.

21. I use the term "field" to encompass several related usages in field theory. Pierre Bourdieu explains that fields are where actors with varying social positions are located and interact in some meaningful way, vying to establish dominance or incumbency by acquiring resources, including social capital. Fields also overlap and intersect—a policy community is in effect a strategic action field composed of actors such as politicians, bureaucrats, industry professionals, and interest groups, which are themselves embedded in their own respective fields; for instance, an interest or social movement group is also located in an organizational field and/or social movement sector. Their leaders may interact with state actors as well as actors within their specific sectors. This understanding complements what Debra Minkoff calls the "institutional ecology of organizational development," whereby voluntary associations respond to field-level changes, which explains why service-provision organizations turn to political advocacy. See Bourdieu, *Distinction*; Fligstein and McAdam, "A Theory of Fields"; and Minkoff, *Organizing for Equality*, 119.

22. For a classic outline of resource mobilization theory, where social movement sector (SMS) refers to the social change field that includes all social movement organizations transcending issues and constituencies, see McCarthy and Zald, "Resource Mobilization and Social Movements."

23. Paul Pierson defines retrenchment as "policy changes that either cut social expenditure, restructure welfare state programs to conform more closely to the residual welfare state model, or alter the political environment in ways that enhance the probability of such outcomes in the future." See Pierson, *Dismantling the Welfare State?*, 17.

24. Southeastern Community College v. Davis, 442 U.S. 397 (1979).

25. Campbell, *How Policies Make Citizens*, 4.

26. The premise of McAdam and Boudet's work is that social movement scholars have overemphasized the role of movements in social change while ignoring broader factors that are independent of social movements but that can also shape that change—what Sydney Tarrow and David S. Meyer have called the world outside social movements. See McAdam and Boudet, *Putting Social Movements in Their Place*; Tarrow, *Power in Movement*; and Meyer, "Social Movements."

27. 134 Cong. Rec. H2800 (1988).

28. *Transportation: Improving Mobility for Older Americans*, 94th Cong. 50 (1976).

29. Califano, *Governing America*, 259.

30. *National Mass Transportation Assistance Act of 1977*, 95th Cong. 480 (1977). At the hearing, Shapiro was representing the concerns of other disability groups as well, including Paralyzed Veterans of America (PVA), National Paraplegia Foundation, and UCP.

31. Ibid., 241.

32. *Implementation of the Rehabilitation, Comprehensive Services, and Developmental Disabilities Amendments, 1979*, 96th Cong. 71 (1979).

33. This included, for instance, the Air Carrier Access Act of 1986, Developmental Disabilities Assistance and Bill of Rights Act Amendments of 1987, and the Civil Rights Restoration Act of 1988.

34. 134 Cong. Rec. E9604 (April 1988).

35. Owens would again refer to the ADA as the "next great struggle in the American civil rights movement." 138 Cong. Rec. E2298 (July 1992).

36. 134 Cong. Rec. H6969 (August 1988).

37. For in-depth interviews with disability activists and policy makers, see Pelka, *What We Have Done.*

38. 109th Cong. 11 (2006).

39. Kaufman, "News Journal."

40. 150 Cong. Rec. 8122 (2004).

41. Alan Reich also served in the National Paraplegia Foundation and other disability groups.

42. 150 Cong. Rec. 8123 (2004).

43. Thornburgh, "Respecting the Convention on the Rights of Persons with Disabilities."

44. On the limitations of disability antidiscrimination legislation, lack of enforcement, and judicial resistance, see Maroto and Pettinicchio, "The Limitations of Disability Antidiscrimination Legislation."

45. Steinhauer, "Dole Appears."

46. Kaufman, "Time to Ratify the Global Disabilities Convention."

47. Moyers and Winship, "Do-Nothing Congress Gives Inertia a Bad Name."

48. Countries such as Great Britain, Canada, and Sweden began to develop policies specifically aimed at improving the lives of people with disabilities only in the 1960s and 1970s, well after the United States had done so. In Canada, disability policy aimed at providing rehabilitation and employment insurance emerged in the 1960s. In the United Kingdom, the Chronically Sick and Disabled Persons Act of 1970 defined the government's role in regard to people with disabilities until the mid-1990s. British legislation dealt mainly with access to medical and social services for people with disabilities. It did seek to address physical barriers, "but only if practicable." In

Sweden, despite having a very well-developed and comprehensive welfare state, there was no specific provision for people with disabilities until the 1960s and 1970s, when new disability-specific policies emphasizing vocational rehabilitation were enacted. In regard to minority rights, the British Disability Discrimination Act of 1995 and Australia's disability rights legislation were modeled on the ADA.

49. Cowen, "Don't Mistake This for Gridlock."

50. For a discussion of environmental policy, see Lundqvist, *The Hare and the Tortoise*; on sexual harassment, see Zippel, *The Politics of Sexual Harassment*.

51. Cowen, "Don't Mistake This for Gridlock."

52. Maroto and Pettinicchio analyzed the impact of the ADA on labor-market outcomes and noted that since 1988, employment rates among people with disabilities have declined virtually every single year despite the ADA's recent twenty-fifth anniversary. See Maroto and Pettinicchio, "The Limitations of Disability Antidiscrimination Legislation."

53. Senate Bill 3406, sponsored by Tom Harkin, had forty-two Democratic and thirty-three Republican cosponsors.

54. See Disability Rights Education and Defense Fund, "The ADA Is Under Serious Attack!"

55. Elsewhere, I have described the importance of revising the insider-outsider dichotomy in relation to activism as scholars increasingly view social movements as part of "everyday politics." See Pettinicchio, "Institutional Activism."

56. In other policy arenas, see Costain, *Inviting Women's Rebellion* (women's groups); Skocpol, "State Formation and Social Policy" (welfare organizations); Campbell, *How Policies Make Citizens* (the "grey lobby"); and Johnson, "Social Movement Size" (environmental groups).

57. For use of the term "advocacy explosion," see Berry and Wilcox, *The Interest Group Society*, 15.

58. For similar process in the pro-choice movement, see Staggenborg, *The Prochoice Movement*, and in women's organizations, see Minkoff, "The Sequencing of Social Movements."

59. I am borrowing from Anne Costain, who argues that congressional activity generated mobilization by the women's movement. See Costain, *Inviting Women's Rebellion*.

60. Richard Scotch characterizes the development of Section 504 of the 1973 Rehabilitation Act as a movement in the government. See Scotch, *From Good Will to Civil Rights*.

61. For examples of supply-side or top-down explanations for policy change, see Sabatier, "Top-Down and Bottom-Up Approaches"; Pulzl and Treib, "Implementing Public Policy"; and Pierson and Skocpol, *The Transformation of American Politics*.

Chapter 2

1. *Vocational Rehabilitation of the Physically Handicapped*, 81st Cong. 403 (1950).

2. *To Create a Bureau for the Deaf and Dumb in the Department of Labor and Prescribing the Duties Thereof*, 65th Cong. 4 (1918).

3. Ibid.

4. Education and vocational rehabilitation was provided through policies such as the 1917 Smith-Hughes Act and 1918 Smith-Sears Act.

5. 58 Cong. Rec. 1016 (October 1919).

6. Note that this was the pre–Great Depression, pre–New Deal, Democratic Party of fiscal conservatives dominated by Southern members. Sen. Hoke Smith, Fess's co-sponsor on the 1920 law and a Southern Democrat from Georgia, was, however, also considered an "activist member of Congress." He likely saw vocational and educational rehabilitation as well as agricultural reforms he was proposing as strengthening and modernizing the South's economy. See Grant, "Senator Hoke Smith," 113.

7. *Charges Against the Federal Board for Vocational Education, Part 7*, 66th Cong. 353 (1920).

8. For instance, the 1944 GI Bill (Pub. L. 78-346).

9. *Assistance and Rehabilitation of the Physically Handicapped*, 83rd Cong. 9 (1953).

10. Skocpol, "State Formation and Social Policy"; and Pierson, "When Effect Becomes Cause."

11. This occurred following the 1953 reorganization of the Executive Branch.

12. In *Visions of Social Control*, Stanley Cohen discusses the ways in which the policies and programs championed by experts create new clients that serve to further expand their profession—what he called "iatrogenesis" (169).

13. Orloff, "The Political Origins of America's Belated Welfare State."

14. See accounts by Meyer, "Protest and Political Opportunities"; Carmines and Stimson, *Issue Evolution*; and Stimson, *Tides of Consent*.

15. Burns, *The Deadlock of Democracy*.

16. This was part of an analysis of alleged political polarization in America. See Fiorina, Abrams, and Pope, *Culture War?*

17. Some amendments and appropriations were addressed in the Ways and Means and Civil Service Committees, but usually with no public discussion.

18. "President Eisenhower Presents Largest Peacetime Budget."

19. Democrats lost control of the House and Senate twice in the 1950s.

20. Note that positive values indicate increasing conservatism and negative values indicate increasing liberalism.

21. Polsby, *How Congress Evolves*, 16.

22. CC scores are based on the percentage of times politicians voted with the Conservative Coalition.

23. For an analysis of the role of the federal government in public education following World War II, see Munger and Frenno, *National Politics and Federal Aid to Education*.

24. Barden voted 82 percent of the time with the CC.

25. Elliot had a CC score of 36. The special subcommittee was created under the House Committee on Education and Labor in the late 1950s.

26. Polsby, *How Congress Evolves*, 17.

27. Ibid., 17, 180.

28. Pub. L. 83-420 was enacted in 1954.

29. Pub. L. 82-354 was enacted in 1952.

30. Pub. L. 83-565: "An Act to amend the Vocational Rehabilitation Act so as to promote and assist in the extension and improvement of vocational rehabilitation services, provide for a more effective use of available Federal funds, and otherwise improve the provisions of that Act, and for other purposes."

31. Ideological-positioning scores are based on roll-call-vote data for each member. Negative values indicate liberalism, and positive values, conservativism (see *Voteview* database, at https://voteview.com; and the appendix).

32. Among the more conservative members of the Senate Committee on Education and Public Welfare were Republicans Barry Goldwater (AZ) and John Sherman Cooper (KY), who had a CC score of 72 and 47, respectively. However, Cooper also voted against the CC as many times as he voted with them and was widely considered a moderate Republican.

33. Jennings Randolph had been a House member in 1936 when he sponsored the Randolph-Sheppard Act. It is considered the first piece of affirmative action legislation ever enacted. The law gave blind people preference in federal contracts for food-service stands on federal properties. He lost the 1946 election but was reelected, this time to the Senate, in a special election in 1958.

34. In 1959, Douglas had a CC score of 7 and voted against the CC 82 percent of the time.

35. His father, Mayer Lehman, was one of the cofounders of the investment bank Lehman Brothers, which famously declared bankruptcy in the 2008 Great Recession.

36. Eisenhower, "Special Message to the Congress," 69–70.

37. Ibid., 74.

38. Bill S. 2759.

39. On disability, work, and cash benefits, see Berkowitz, *Disabled Policy*.

40. "Vocational Rehabilitation."

41. "Record of 84th Congress."

42. Policy monopolies have been identified across numerous policy domains: on public works, see Maass, *Muddy Waters*; on defense, see Adams and Cain, "Defense

Dilemmas in the 1990s"; on health care, see Peterson, "Institutional Change"; and on nuclear energy, see Baumgartner and Jones, *Agendas*. Frank R. Baumgartner and Bryan D. Jones credit the ubiquity of monopolies in the 1950s for agenda stability and explain why institutional arrangements in the 1960s largely obviated such monopolies.

43. Polsby provides a detailed analysis of committee assignments in his account about the liberalization of Congress. See Polsby, *How Congress Evolves*.

44. In addition to biographical characteristics and ideological positions, preferences of committee chairs and whether assignments help members get reelected play a central role in influencing committee assignments. See Bullock, "Freshman Committee Assignments"; and Clapp, *The Congressman*.

45. Kentucky Career Center, "Carl D. Perkins Vocational Training Center."

46. Both would support civil rights. However, they did not do so unconditionally, and Frelinghuysen would be a critic of the War on Poverty programs.

47. Jones and Baumgartner use *CQ* reports as a measure of salience—the extent to which legislation in different policy arenas is considered "important" within the government. See Jones and Baumgartner, *The Politics of Attention*.

48. These include the Special Subcommittee to Promote Education of the Blind, the Special Committee on Special Education, the Subcommittee on the Education of Physically Handicapped Children, the Special Subcommittee for Establishing a Federal Commission for Physically Handicapped, the Subcommittee on Vocational Rehabilitation of the Physically Handicapped, and the Special Subcommittee on Assistance and Rehabilitation of the Physically Handicapped.

49. Bullock, "Freshman Committee Assignments."

50. Numerous scholars have suggested that voters appreciate politicians who are seen as "doing something," often regardless of their ideological position on those issues. See Miller and Stokes, "Constituency Influence in Congress"; Kingdon, "A House Appropriations Subcommittee"; and Sulkin, *Issue Politics in Congress*.

51. The board was created by the 1917 Smith-Hughes Act, which separated vocational education from regular secondary school education.

52. These are some of the few years in which conservative Democrat Barden did not chair the committee because the Democrats had lost control of the House in the 83rd Congress.

53. On policy monopolies as iron triangles, see Adams, *The Politics of Defense Contracting*, 24; Givel, "Punctuated Equilibrium in Limbo"; McCarthy, "Velcro Triangles"; and True and Utter, "Saying 'Yes,' 'No.'"

54. This is not unusual in other policy areas. For instance, see Campbell, *How Policies Make Citizens*, for discussion on the Social Security Administration, Grey Lobby, and the elderly; and Johnson, "Social Movement Size," which traces the rise of

environmental advocacy groups following the creation of the Environmental Protection Agency (EPA).

55. In 1947, President Harry Truman created the Commission on Organization of the Executive Branch; Eisenhower implemented many of its recommendations in 1953.

56. While their motivation remains ambiguous, Rep. John F. Kennedy (who later as president, signed into law several important bills related to mental health/cognitive disability) and Rep. Augustine Kelley introduced a bill that would establish this commission. Some groups supported the bill, but it is unclear whether they did so specifically because of the federal commission or because of the other components of the bill related to the expansion of services. Notably, Richard Nixon was present at these hearings; as president, he would twice veto the Rehabilitation Act. *Federal Commission for Physically Handicapped*, 81st Cong. 29 (1949).

57. Ibid., 63.

58. *Vocational Rehabilitation of the Physically Handicapped*, 69.

59. Jones was arguing against full federal control over service provision and administration at the aforementioned hearing about establishing a federal commission. Ibid., 56.

60. Smith and Lipsky, *Nonprofits for Hire*, 3.

61. *Special Education and Rehabilitation, Part 7*, 86th Cong. 1766 (1960).

62. *To Promote the Education of the Blind*, 84th Cong. 15 (1956).

63. Other groups, for example, included the American Association of Workers for the Blind, American Foundation for the Blind, Association of the Deaf, and Blind Veterans Association.

64. In *The Strategy of Social Protest*, William Gamson distinguished between incumbent and challenging social movement organizations and noted that the former have disproportionate influence on social change.

65. Debra Minkoff used the term to describe strategic adaptation among women and racial-minority organizations. See Minkoff, "Bending with the Wind."

66. *Gallaudet College*, 83rd Cong. 12 (1954).

67. Isomorphism is the process by which organizations, facing similar environmental constraints, converge to look similar. For a discussion of the "iron cage" thesis about how isomorphic processes produce organizational conformity and homogeneity, see DiMaggio and Powell, "The Iron Cage Revisited"; see also Meyer and Rowan, "Institutionalized Organizations"; Zald and Berger, "Social Movements in Organizations"; and Minkoff, *Organizing for Equality*.

68. Membership is based on the data reported by organizations to the *Encyclopedia of Associations* in a given year.

69. Charlton, *Nothing About Us Without Us*.

70. Bill S. 1066.

71. *Vocational Rehabilitation of the Physically Handicapped*, 404.

72. Oddly, in his early years in the House, Baring was considered a liberal. However, a staunch segregationist, he became exceptionally critical of the 1964 Civil Rights Act, associating the law with communism.

73. *Education and Assistance to the Blind*, 86th Cong. 8 (1959).

74. For a description of the kind of information typical in interest-group testimony at government hearings, see Burstein and Hirsh, "Interest Organizations."

75. *Assistance and Rehabilitation of the Physically Handicapped*, 258.

76. *Special Education and Rehabilitation, Part 1*, 86th Cong. 24 (1959).

77. Ibid.

78. *Special Education and Rehabilitation, Part 5*, 86th Cong. 1813 (1960).

79. Ibid. 1241.

80. Ibid.

81. *President's Health Recommendations and Related Measures, Part 1*, 83rd Cong. 38 (1954).

82. On instrumental and immanent values, see Hechter, "The Role of Values."

83. Much of this understanding developed in the late 1800s and subsequently resurfaced following World War I in relation to rehabilitating disabled soldiers and providing assistance to their wives and children. In hearings held in 1919 and 1920, it was readily apparent that those working in vocational rehabilitation and public welfare were especially concerned about returning veterans who were unable to provide for themselves and their families.

84. *Federal Commission for Physically Handicapped*, 15 (statement of Rep. Leroy Johnson of California).

85. Ibid.

86. For a discussion of "critical policy analysis," see Gottweiss, "Rhetoric in Policy Making," 238; for a discussion of "narrative policy analysis," see van Eeten, "Narrative Policy Analysis."

87. *Physically Handicapped Children's Education Act of 1950*, 81st Cong. 18 (1950).

88. *Assistance and Rehabilitation of the Physically Handicapped*, 83rd Cong. 6 (1953).

89. Emery Roe's work on narrative policy analysis shows how policy "stories" that incorporate the points of view of participants shape the policy-making process. See Roe, *Narrative Policy Analysis*.

90. *Special Education and Rehabilitation, Part 1*, 55.

91. *Special Education and Rehabilitation, Part 7*, 1736.

92. Experts draw from "powerful supporting ideas," policy images "so positive that they evoke only support or indifference by those not involved," helping ward off challengers and maintain policy stability. See Baumgartner and Jones, *Agendas*, 7; see also Rose and Davies, *Inheritance in Public Policy*.

93. Howard, *The Welfare State Nobody Knows*. Christopher Howard sought to debunk the myth of America's pale imitation of the true welfare state.

94. *Social Security Act Amendments of 1954*, 83rd Cong. 92 (1954).

95. Criticisms of asylums had already emerged in the 1920s and 1930s, but the proliferation of these institutions continued until the 1950s. By the 1960s and 1970s, professional, political, and social movement efforts converged to undermine the so-called practice of warehousing (and often mistreating) individuals with disabilities.

96. *Mental Health*, 84th Cong. 32 (1955) (statement of Leo H. Bartemeier, chairman of the AMA Council of Mental Health).

97. *Special Education and Rehabilitation, Part 1*, 33 (statement of Rep. John E. Fogarty of Rhode Island).

98. Ed Roberts, seen as the father of independent living, established the first Center for Independent Living in Berkeley, California, in 1972. Its creation was motivated mainly by the lack of housing for students with disabilities, which forced disabled students into infirmaries. See Pelka, *What We Have Done*.

99. Shapiro, *No Pity*, 61. Shapiro examines the evolving relationship between policy (particularly the ADA), the public, and people with disabilities, especially changes in the ways in which disability was understood.

100. *Federal Commission for Physically Handicapped*, 12.

101. For a description of the demeaning nature of "Jerry's kids," see Shapiro, *No Pity*, 57.

102. According to Neil Fligstein and Doug McAdam, socially skilled actors bring about routinized order in fields by fashioning consensus around issues that describes the disability policy monopoly of the period. See Fligstein and McAdam, *A Theory of Fields*.

103. Jacobus TenBroek was appointed to the California Social Welfare Board by then-governor Earl Warren, who later became Chief Justice of the US Supreme Court. See TenBroek and Matson, *Hope Deferred*.

104. In 1946, TenBroek provided testimony at a Committee on Ways and Means hearing about the Social Security amendments. He pushed for increased spending to help get blind Americans out of poverty but emphasized that they should not be "lumped" with dependents, as they are fully capable of working and being self-sufficient. See *Amendments to Social Security Act, Part 8*, 79th Cong. 1021 (1946). He reiterated the NFB's goal of making blind Americans productive citizens at a 1949 hearing about amending the Social Security Act—referring to the "normality of blind people." See *Social Security Act Amendments of 1949, Part 1: Public Assistance and Public Welfare*, 81st Cong. 517 (1949). He testified in several hearings throughout the 1950s in favor of rehabilitation programs and policies.

105. Few legal actions regarding this legislation (Pub. L. 80-617) were taken subsequent to its enactment, and activists and scholars rarely cite it. See Feldblum, "Definition of Disability."

106. The legislation's sponsor, James Hobson Morrison (D-LA), was a Southern Democrat who later voted against the 1964 Civil Rights Act.

107. Establishing how issues get discussed is at the heart of agenda setting. See Baumgartner and Jones, *Agendas*; Kingdon, *Agendas, Alternatives, and Public Policies*; and Fligstein and McAdam, *A Theory of Fields*.

108. *Vocational Rehabilitation of Persons Disabled in Industry*, 65th Cong. 10 (1918).

109. *Special Education and Rehabilitation, Part 3: Cullman, Ala.*, 86th Cong. 621 (1960).

Chapter 3

1. In his testimony before the subcommittee in 1960, Monroe Sweetland of the Oregon State Senate Board claimed that the "mildly retarded or educable" represent a vast majority of the retarded. See *Special Education and Rehabilitation, Part 7*, 86th Cong. 1730 (1960). At the hearing, evidence was submitted to the Subcommittee on Special Education by a representative of the Pennsylvania Department of Public Instruction regarding funding authorization for special education and rehabilitation programs for physically and mentally handicapped persons.

2. "Congress Enacts New Mental Health Programs."

3. "Kennedy's Key Votes in House and Senate Since 1947." Kennedy had also proposed important (but failed) legislation, for instance, laws to promote self-expression of the blind. See *Education and Assistance to the Blind, Part 1*, 86th Cong. 27 (1959).

4. "Congress Enacts New Mental Health Programs."

5. 109 Cong. Rec. 1941 (February 1963).

6. In response to Kennedy's requests, Congress enacted two pieces of legislation in 1963: one that provided federal grants to help states and local governments construct community mental health and retardation facilities (Pub. L. 88-164, Mental Retardation Facilities and Community Mental Health Centers Construction Act) and another that helped furnish medical services for the prevention and treatment of mental retardation (Pub. L. 88-156, Maternal and Child Health and Mental Retardation Planning Bill).

7. "President's 'War on Poverty' Approved."

8. *Economic Opportunity Act of 1964, Part 3*, 88th Cong. 1279 (1964) (statement of Alfred DeGrasia).

9. "President's 'War on Poverty' Approved."

10. The House Committee on Education and Labor held six hearings regarding H.R. 10440 and H.R. 10459 (bills intended to combat poverty in the United States) in the spring and summer of 1964.

11. *Economic Opportunity Act of 1964, Part 3*, 1210.

12. Entropy measures how concentrated (or narrow) and spread out (or complex) a committee's jurisdiction is. Higher entropy means more spread. See Sheingate, "Structure and Opportunity"; and Baumgartner, Jones, and MacLeod, "The Evolution of Legislation Jurisdictions." See also the Chapter 3 section in the appendix for more information.

13. Levitan and Taggart, *The Promise of Greatness*, 29.

14. "Major Investigations Undertaken by 86th Congress."

15. *Model Secondary School for the Deaf*, 89th Cong. 2 (1966).

16. Bill H.R. 17190, which became Pub. L. 89-694.

17. *Model Secondary School for the Deaf*, 3.

18. Pub. L. 89-36.

19. *Model Secondary School for the Deaf*, 2.

20. Levitan and Taggart, *The Promise of Greatness*, 9.

21. Until the 1960s, most programs were permanently authorized. However, with a greater push by appropriations committees for greater control over the process, as well as the push for more oversight in spending (which continued into the 1970s), authorizations were now more temporary and extended for a limited number of fiscal years. See Oleszek, *Congressional Procedures*.

22. Pub. L. 89-333.

23. Pub. L. 90-99 and H.R. 15827, respectively.

24. *Vocational Rehabilitation Act Amendments*, 89th Cong. 36 (1965).

25. Ibid.

26. Bill H.R. 6476.

27. Bill S. 1525.

28. "Congress Enacts New Mental Health Programs."

29. Celebrezze is seen as instrumental in aligning HEW's interests with those of President Lyndon Johnson's Great Society initiatives.

30. Bill H.R. 5888, which became Pub. L. 88-136.

31. This has often been referred to as the unfunded or unfinanced mandate in American policy making. See Posner, *Politics of Unfunded Mandates*.

32. For an account of congressional policy making in the middle of the last century, see Polsby, *How Congress Evolves*.

33. Pub. L. 90-248.

34. Pub. L. 90-99.

35. "Congress Extends Vocational Rehabilitation Act."

36. Bill H.R. 16819.

37. The bill focused on the poor and those living in "urban ghettos" who underachieved because of lack of social, psychological, and economic resources.

38. "New Vocational Rehabilitation Program Established."

39. Ibid.

40. Patterson, *America's Struggle Against Poverty*, 182.

41. Pratt, *The Gray Lobby*.

42. Cohen served as undersecretary for both Secretaries Celebrezze and Gardner.

43. Berkowitz and DeWitt, *The Other Welfare*.

44. Hughes, *The Vital Few*, 500.

45. President Truman originally established the President's Committee on National Employ the Physically Handicapped Week in 1947, and Eisenhower's 1955 executive order made it a permanent organization (renamed President's Committee on National Employ the Physically Handicapped) whose purpose was to work with state and local officials to implement the 1954 Vocational Rehabilitation Act Amendments. Kennedy's 1962 Executive Order 10994 officially renamed it the President's Committee on Employment of the Handicapped.

46. Russell enlisted in the army following the attack on Pearl Harbor. He lost both his hands diffusing an explosive while filming a training video. Russell won the Academy Award for best supporting actor in *The Best Years of Our Lives* (1947) for his portrayal of a sailor who lost his hands during the war.

47. *Accessibility of Public Buildings to the Physically Handicapped*, 90th Cong. 8 (1967) (statement of Harold Russell).

48. "Political and Legislative Highlights of 1960."

49. *To Amend the Vocational Rehabilitation Act*, 89th Cong. 90 (1965).

50. Bill H.R. 6476.

51. *Vocational Rehabilitation Act Amendments*, 11 (statement of Harry A. Sohweikert Jr., executive secretary of PVA).

52. *Accessibility of Public Buildings to the Physically Handicapped*, 2. Russell testified before Congress on numerous occasions as chair of AMVETS, mainly regarding disabled veterans, HEW appropriations, and operation of vending stands by the blind.

53. Bill S. 222.

54. Pub. L. 90-480.

55. Katzmann, *Institutional Disability*, 20.

56. His testimony also reflected impatience with the slow pace at which the federal government addressed architectural barriers.

57. *Accessibility of Public Buildings to the Physically Handicapped*, 3.

58. Ibid., 7.

59. It was originally proposed that the GSA administer regulations since the ABA dealt specifically with newly constructed public buildings financed by the federal government.

60. This is reflected in the proposed 1968 Vocational Rehabilitation Act Amendments in Subsection 8 of Section 5, where it defined part of the role of vocational rehabilitation agencies to assist in making places of employment accessible.

61. *Building Design for the Physically Handicapped: Comprehensive Plan for the U.S. Capitol Grounds*, 90th Cong. 38 (1968).

62. *Accessibility of Public Buildings to the Physically Handicapped*, 1.

63. Baumgartner and Jones, *Agendas*, 35.

64. When Kennedy was elected president in 1960, Speaker of the House Sam Rayburn (D-TX), who was responsible for ensuring the passage of the president's legislative agenda, believed he had to act on what was seen as a House that was "inhospitable" for a legislative agenda such as Kennedy's. See Polsby, *How Congress Evolves*, 31.

65. Ibid., 45–48.

66. Baumgartner and Jones's work on agenda setting illustrates how, between the late 1950s and late 1970s with increasing government attention to social policy (broadly defined), various social welfare policy issues expanded from the focus on cities, to child abuse, to traffic safety. See Baumgartner and Jones, *Agendas*.

67. I am using the Policy Agendas Project topic codes to identify policy domains. There are nineteen major topic codes identified in the data (see the Chapter 3 section in the appendix for more information).

68. Hearing-days refer to the total number of days Congress dedicated to disability-related issues. Joel Aberbach notes that some committee chairs might prefer to hold fewer multiple-day hearings, while others prefer more, but shorter, hearings. Aberbach, *Keeping a Watchful Eye*. I also show in Figure 3.6 that number and length of hearings may be inversely related.

69. See King, *Turf Wars*.

70. Committees have formal jurisdictions determined by Congress, which made many committees far removed from disability (for example, Agriculture). Formal or statutory jurisdictions of a committee are based on my content analysis of committee descriptions published in *Rule X of the Rules of the House of Representatives* and *Rule XXV of the Standing Rules of the Senate*. See ibid. I assign a value of 1 for each committee, using the following criteria: handicap/disease discrimination/rights (employment, education, etc.); access/physical barriers; mental health/retardation; long-term care/rehabilitation services; special education; social welfare/housing/community services for "vulnerable" groups; social security/disability insurance; work programs/vocational services. This variable therefore ranges from 0 (e.g., Agriculture Committee) to 7 (Senate Committee on Health, Education, Labor, and Pensions).

71. Between 1960 and 1964 (the year the Urban Mass Transportation Act was passed), these committees held hearings regarding urban mass transit during which disability was only briefly mentioned. These hearings include *Urban Mass Transportation—1961*, 87th Cong. (1961); *Urban Mass Transportation Act of 1962*, 87th Cong. (1962); and *Urban Mass Transportation Act of 1963*, 88th Cong. (1963).

72. Pub. L. 88-365.

73. *Urban Mass Transportation—1961*, 75.

74. *Urban Mass Transportation Act of 1962*, 85.

75. Brown v. Board of Education of Topeka, 347 U.S. 483 (1954).

76. *Building Design for the Physically Handicapped*, 20. Disability public transportation was barely raised in the one hearing held on the issue in 1968.

77. Recall that transit accessibility per se was not the original intent of Bartlett's bill.

78. *Building Design for the Physically Handicapped*, 20.

79. They advocated for access to the buildings, such as the stations, but not the transit system itself.

80. *Building Design for the Physically Handicapped*, 45.

81. Importantly, conference committees convene only when there is disagreement between House and Senate versions of a bill. Thus, discussions and amendments that occur here are done so after the fact and only before senior members of Congress.

82. *Design and Construction of Federal Facilities to Be Accessible to the Physically Handicapped*, 91st Cong. 3 (1969).

83. Others facilitating disability entrepreneurs' efforts in the 1960s and 1970s included John Volpe (R-MA), Charles Percy (R-IL), George H. Fallon (D-MD), Henry C. Schadeberg (R-WI), John McFall (D-CA), Burton Phillip (D-CA), Paul Sarbanes (D-MD), Patricia Schroeder (D-CO), and Silvio Conte (R-MA).

84. The title is taken from King, *Turf Wars*.

85. See the 1970 Urban Mass Transportation Assistance Act (Pub. L. 91-453), Section 16. The Biaggi Amendment amended H.R. 18185 and was accepted by voice on the House floor. "Urban Mass Transportation."

86. Biaggi was considered a conservative Democrat. He later ran for New York City mayor in 1973 as a conservative "law-and-order" candidate. He finished in fourth place.

87. Bennett strongly supported rehabilitation efforts. In 1957, he testified before the House Committee on Education and Labor in support of H.R. 9171, which would establish a committee to improve rehabilitation personnel and personnel involved in job placement. See *Welfare of the Physically Handicapped*, 85th Cong. 6 (1957).

88. *Mass Transportation Assistance to Meet Needs of Elderly and Handicapped Persons*, 95th Cong. 183 (1977).

89. John Wright Patman (D-TX) was a self-described populist who developed a reputation for attacking the banking industry.

90. 116 Cong. Rec. 34,183 (September 1970).

91. *Federal-Aid Highway Act, 1970*, 91st Cong. 18 (1970).

92. Pub. L. 91-453: "SEC. 16. (a) It is hereby declared to be the national policy that elderly and handicapped persons have the same right as other persons to utilize mass transportation facilities and services; that special efforts shall be made in the

planning and design of mass transportation facilities and services so that the avail-ability to elderly and handicapped persons of mass transportation which they can effectively utilize will be assured; and that all Federal programs offering assistance in the field of mass transportation (including the programs under this Act) should contain provisions implementing this policy." See https://www.govinfo.gov/content/pkg/STATUTE-84/pdf/STATUTE-84-Pg962.pdf.

93. *To Consider Accommodations for Handicapped on Metro System*, 92nd Cong. 46 (1972).

94. Ibid., 44.

95. Pub. L. 93-643.

96. Pub. L. 93-503 and bill S. 662, respectively.

97. After a reluctant Kennedy made civil rights for African Americans a more central priority, as outlined in his June 1963 address to Congress ("Message to Congress"), growing party realignments on this and other social issues accelerated. See Carmines and Stimson, *Issue Evolution*. Liberal Democrats increasingly supported involvement in civil rights and social welfare, while many Republicans and Dixiecrats would side with "states' rights." Baumgartner and Jones show that the amount of civil rights attention hit a high in the early 1970s. See Baumgartner and Jones, *Agendas*; on attention to civil rights issues, see also Skrentny, *The Minority Rights Revolution*; and King, Bentele, and Soule, "Protest and Policymaking."

98. Bill H.R. 12154.

99. In 1971, the House and Senate Judiciary Committees also held hearings re-garding the Equal Rights Amendment (ERA). Analogizing black civil rights to dis-ability was restricted to certain entrepreneurs and venues that did not include the Judiciary Committees. Thus, in the early 1970s, the Judiciary Committees had no pretext for viewing disability as part of their mandate in civil rights.

100. Percy and Marlow Cook (Cook was a Republican from Kentucky elected around the same time as Percy) earlier that year proposed a concurrent resolution calling for a declaration of rights for the physically and mentally disabled. Both men, interested in hunger and malnutrition, had served together on the recently created Senate Select Committee on Nutrition and Human Needs. Marlow was considered a liberal to moderate Republican. In 1968, he hired current senate majority leader Mitch McConnell as his campaign's state youth chairman.

101. Bill S. 3044.

102. 118 Cong. Rec. 525 (January 1972).

103. *Rehabilitation Act of 1972, Part 1*, 92nd Cong. 1 (1972).

104. Ibid.

105. *Rehabilitation Act of 1972, Part 2*, 92nd Cong. 1400 (1972).

106. Bill S. 3987.

107. According to the *Congressional Quarterly Almanac*, Nixon criticized provisions of H.R. 8395 that would have authorized "activities that have no vocational element . . . or are essentially medical in character." New programs for people who were confined to their homes or institutionalized and those with spinal-cord injuries or end-stage renal disease—as well as several commissions to study employment, transportation, and housing problems encountered by disabled people—would have been set up under the vetoed measure. "Presidential Veto Message."

108. *Rehabilitation Act, 1973*, 93rd Cong. 1 (1973).

109. Randolph's 1973 bill S. 7 was virtually identical to the 1972 S. 3987.

110. *Rehabilitation Act, 1973*, 1.

111. Ibid., 77.

112. "Senate Backs Compromise on Vetoed Vocational Bill."

113. Bill H.R. 8070.

114. "Senate Backs Compromise on Vetoed Vocational Bill," 38.

115. Paul Starr distinguished between three related forms of policy entrenchment: power entrenchment that ensures members supporting policies remain in power, rules entrenchment that preserve policies, and structural entrenchment that make policies meaningful in everyday life. See Starr, "Three Degrees of Entrenchment."

116. Momentum generated positive-feedback effects such that hearings led to more hearings, and policy proposals led to more policy proposals. For a discussion of agenda-setting processes, see Baumgartner and Jones, *Agendas*. Additionally, the number of actors and venues addressing disability and transportation expanded. The Subcommittee on Urban Mass Transportation under the House Committee on Banking and Currency, the House Committee on Public Works, and the Senate Committee on Labor and Public Welfare, which contained the Senate Subcommittee on the Handicapped, now all had a stake in the game.

117. The Subcommittee on Urban Mass Transportation had an average CC score of 45 in 1973.

118. The Subcommittee on Public Buildings and Grounds had an average CC score of 53 in 1973.

119. The Urban Mass Transportation Act eventually became Pub. L. 95-599, the Federal-Aid Highway Act of 1978.

120. *Urban Mass Transportation, 1975*, 94th Cong. 4 (1975).

121. The PCEH was concerned that many with severe disabilities could never be accommodated by equal access to mainstream public transit.

122. Walker and Humphreys worked on S. 3987 and H.R. 3395, the Rehabilitation Act of 1972. See 118 Cong. Rec. 32,279 (September 1972).

123. The Rehabilitation Act Amendments of 1974 made it clear that Section 504 applied not just to employable disabled individuals (akin to the "educable" and "trainable" espoused by rehabilitationists) but to all people with disabilities. Pub. L. 93-651.

124. Cong. Rec. 36,822 (November 1974).

125. *Education for All Handicapped Children, 1973–74, Part 1*, 93rd Cong. 625 (1973).

126. Disabled children were a part of this broader bill that also addressed bilingual education, among other topics that Williams and Ted Kennedy were working on at the time. See Cong. Rec. 15,283–15,343, (May 1974).

127. Bill S. 3378, Section 215, Part D.

128. 121 Cong. Rec. 16,515 (June 1975).

129. Ibid.

130. *Rehabilitation of the Handicapped Programs, 1976, Part 3*, 94th Cong. 1519 (1976).

131. Scotch, *From Goodwill to Civil Rights*, 64.

132. *Rehabilitation of the Handicapped Programs, 1976, Part 3*, 1492.

133. Eventually, under the Carter administration and to HEW secretary Joseph Califano's chagrin, the agency was divided into the Department of Health and the Department of Education.

134. *Rehabilitation of the Handicapped Programs, 1976, Part 3*, 1509.

135. Ibid., 1496.

136. In a similar vein, Jeb Barnes and Thomas Burke argue in *How Policy Shapes Politics* that criticism toward the expansion of Social Security Disability Insurance (SSDI) was largely warded off by a subgovernment comprising members in the Social Security Administration (SSA) as well as key congressional committees and organized labor. They also alluded to the important role of the Executive Branch in protecting and expanding its jurisdiction over various aspects of developing social policies.

137. Note that outsiders are likely to make claims on issues if they understand that a subset, usually the periphery, of a policy domain can realistically be defined within their jurisdiction. In other words, the Judiciary Committee or the Agricultural Committee is unlikely to engage in a turf war with the House Education and Labor Committee over rehabilitation.

138. See Lawrence, Suddaby, and Leca, "Institutional Work."

139. Based on Richard Scotch's interview with Senate staffer Nik Edes. See Scotch, *From Good Will to Civil Rights*, 57.

140. Auslander, "Cultural Opportunities for the Handicapped," WC13.

141. No doubt, establishing effective Civil Rights Act enforcement took years and often lacked resources, but by the 1970s, efforts to implement civil rights were bolstered by strong support by forces inside and outside government. See White, "The EEOC"; Reskin, "Employment Discrimination and Its Remedies"; and Burstein, "Intergroup Conflict."

142. The characterization of disability policy as bipartisan was widespread. Cranston used those terms in referring to the 1972 Rehabilitation Act Amendments. See

118 Cong. Rec. 32,279 (September 1972). Bennett claimed that Section 504 was not a "controversial matter," and both Cranston and Biaggi repeatedly argued that equal rights for the disabled was a "bipartisan issue." Bipartisanship was even used to characterize the UN Convention on Disability Rights discussed in Chapter 1 that the Senate failed to ratify.

Chapter 4

1. In the social movements literature, "mobilizing structures" is an "encompassing" term defining macro-, meso- and/or microlevel formal or informal networks and relationships that contribute to participation in goal-oriented, strategic, collective action. McAdam, McCarthy, and Zald, *Comparative Perspectives on Social Movements*.

2. The density of disability organizations is the number of existing active organizations at the end of a given year plus the number of new organizations minus those that became inactive or defunct. See Minkoff, "Sequencing of Social Movements," 787.

3. Skocpol, "Government Activism," 45.

4. Tarrow, *Power in Movement*.

5. For an account of the ways in which policy created new opportunities for groups like the American Association of Retired Persons (AARP) to become more political in mobilizing senior citizens, see Campbell, *How Policies Make Citizens*.

6. Minkoff, *Organizing for Equality*, 119.

7. *Accessibility of Public Buildings to the Physically Handicapped*, 90th Cong. 70 (1967).

8. Ibid., 84.

9. *Mental Retardation and Other Developmental Disabilities, 1969*, 91st Cong. 273 (1969).

10. The document was referred to in the 1984 *Pennhurst v. Halderman* Supreme Court case upholding a lower-court ruling requiring the state to adopt the "least restrictive environment" approach for the care of the mentally retarded. Pennhurst State Sch. v. Halderman, 465 U.S. 89 (1984).

11. Ralph Yarborough, a Texas Democrat considered to be a leader of the progressive wing of the Democratic Party (he was among the few Southerners to vote favorably on all civil rights bills during his time in the Senate between 1957 and 1971), chaired both the Senate Subcommittee on Health and its parent Senate Committee on Labor and Public Welfare. The subcommittee included key Senate disability rights entrepreneurs like Randolph, Williams, Javits, and Cranston in addition to Kennedy and Pell.

12. *Mental Retardation and Other Developmental Disabilities, 1969*, 167.

13. Ibid., 169.

14. Ibid., 197.

15. Randolph, "Developmentally Disabled Assistance and Bill of Rights Act."

16. Ibid., 39.

17. *Vocational Rehabilitation Services to the Handicapped*, 92nd Cong. 32 (1972).

18. Ibid.

19. Ibid., 160. The speaker was referring to early twentieth-century policies meant to encourage employers to hire people with disabilities at subminimum wages. The practice was recently criticized in the 2016 presidential campaign—a topic rarely addressed by presidential candidates. In a speech about the Supreme Court nomination, Hillary Clinton said, "There should not be a tiered wage, and right now there is a tiered wage when it comes to facilities that do provide opportunities but not at a self-sufficient wage that enables people to gain a degree of independence as far as they can go." Quoted in Fournier, "Clinton's Case Against the Subminimum Wage."

20. Scotch, *From Good Will to Civil Rights.*

21. Debra Minkoff found that forty-two women's and ethnic-racial organizations transitioned to advocacy between 1955 and 1985. See Minkoff, "Bending with the Wind," 1681.

22. *Oversight Hearings on the Rehabilitation Act of 1973*, 95th Cong. 727 (1978).

23. *Implementation of Section 504, Rehabilitation Act of 1973*, 95th Cong. 32 (1977).

24. For a discussion of "public moods," see Stimson, *Tides of Consent.*

25. Paul Pierson documents a similar strategy in the Reagan administration's attempts to dismantle the welfare state. See Pierson, *Dismantling the Welfare State?*

26. *Vocational Rehabilitation Services to the Handicapped*, 161.

27. There was mention of educational opportunities for people with disabilities in terms of educational cost sharing with states. See "Presidential Statement to Congress: Nixon on Funds for Education."

28. "Presidential Statement to Congress: Nixon's 1970 Economic Report."

29. 120 Cong. Rec. 36,850 (November1974).

30. *Vocational Rehabilitation Services to the Handicapped*, 60.

31. Ibid., 55.

32. Recently elected representative Chris Dodd (D-CT; part of the so-called Watergate babies), whose sister was blind, found the inability and unwillingness of Ford and the Executive Branch to act on Section 504 "disturbing and disheartening." He also suggested greater linkages between the Civil Rights Act and Section 504 to allow the law to right wrongs. 122 Cong. Rec. 4852 (March 1976).

33. *Rehabilitation of the Handicapped Programs, 1976, Part 3*, 94th Cong. 1495 (1976).

34. Ibid., 1511. As outgoing OCR head in 1977, Gerry admitted certain failures in HEW's addressing enforcement of civil rights more generally. See Halpern, *On the Limits of the Law.*

35. *Implementation of Section 504, Rehabilitation Act of 1973*, 214.

36. *Department of Transportation and Related Agencies Appropriations for 1979, Part 6*, 95th Cong. 765 (1978).

37. 119 Cong. Rec. 16,402 (May 1973).

38. *Equal Employment Opportunity for the Handicapped Act of 1979*, 96th Cong. 187 (1979) (statement of Mainstream).

39. I am borrowing the term from Costain, *Inviting Women's Rebellion*.

40. Barnartt and Scotch, *Disability Protests*, 62.

41. *Implementation of Section 504, Rehabilitation Act of 1973*, 209.

42. A key debate in the late 1970s revolved around how and whether all facilities in public transit had to be made accessible to people with disabilities. According to APTA, O'Neil stated in a 1977 letter in regard to Section 504 that it did not mean "every part of a facility must be accessible." *Department of Transportation and Related Agencies Appropriations for 1979, Part 6*, 778.

43. *Implementation of Section 504, Rehabilitation Act of 1973*, 2.

44. This argument by detractors would resurface in the 1980s to fight against the inclusion of communicable diseases such as HIV/AIDS under Section 504 and, later, the ADA. In terms of education, this rationalization would be echoed in the late 1990s against IDEA by Sen. Jeff Sessions (R-AL), President Trump's former attorney general.

45. *Implementation of Section 504, Rehabilitation Act of 1973*, 13–14.

46. Ibid., 14.

47. Ibid., 35. The hearing was interrupted frequently by a simultaneous roll-call vote in the House.

48. Keeping its "house clean" referred to entities receiving federal money.

49. *Implementation of the Rehabilitation, Comprehensive Services, and Developmental Disabilities Amendments, 1979*, 96th Cong. 49 (1979).

50. Ibid., 51.

51. Ibid., 8.

52. *Implementation of Section 504, Rehabilitation Act of 1973*, 299–300.

53. *Implementation of the Rehabilitation, Comprehensive Services, and Developmental Disabilities Amendments, 1979*, 7.

54. Robert Katzmann referred to this as an "institutional disability" on the part of government because it generated confusion rather than intended policy outcomes. See Katzmann, *Institutional Disability*.

55. By the middle of the decade, groups turned to members of the Subcommittee on the Handicapped in 1976 to pressure HEW and OCR. Groups like PVA were already looking to the 1964 Civil Rights Act as an alternative policy strategy. See *Rehabilitation of the Handicapped Programs, 1976, Part 1*, 94th Cong. 49 (1976).

56. *Equal Employment Opportunity for the Handicapped Act of 1979*, 1.

57. Ibid., 186.

58. Ibid., 9.

59. Protections from discrimination in the private sector would have to wait another decade, when the ADA was enacted.

60. *Equal Employment Opportunity for the Handicapped Act of 1979*, 70.

61. Trageser v. Libbie Rehab. Center, Inc./Convalescent Home, 442 U.S. 947 (1979). The court found that victims of employment discrimination did not have private cause of action. As Milk testified, "Unfortunately, the promise of section 505.B has been painfully denied by the decision in the case of Trageser v. Libbie Rehabilitation. As you know, the judge not only found against the right to file suit, but against the employment protection under section 504 totally. The Supreme Court's refusal to review the Trageser decision may have no legal impact, but it certainly has impact on other courts considering employment cases and on the belief of disabled people in their rights to exercise employment generally." *Implementation of the Rehabilitation, Comprehensive Services, and Developmental Disabilities Amendments, 1979*, 49.

62. *Implementation of the Rehabilitation, Comprehensive Services, and Developmental Disabilities Amendments, 1979*, 48.

63. *Equal Employment Opportunity for the Handicapped Act of 1979*, 12.

64. *Waiver of Section 402(a) of the Congressional Budget Act with Respect to Consideration of S.446*, 96th Cong. 1 (1980).

65. Ibid.

66. *Field Hearings on the Education for All Handicapped Children Act*, 96th Cong. 122 (1980).

67. *Implementation of the Rehabilitation, Comprehensive Services, and Developmental Disabilities Amendments, 1979*, 172.

68. *Field Hearings on the Education for All Handicapped Children Act*, 2.

69. *Implementation of the Rehabilitation, Comprehensive Services, and Developmental Disabilities Amendments, 1979*, 102, 166–172, 186, 201.

70. "Going Wrong with Disability Rights," 16.

71. *Oversight on Education for All Handicapped Children Act, 1980, Part 2*, 96th Cong. 130 (1980).

72. Ibid., 35.

73. Williams, Stafford, Randolph, and Kennedy were still members. Patricia Forsythe served as the minority professional staff member (she was Randolph's aide and developed specific interests in children with learning disabilities while working on the Education for All Handicapped Children Act).

74. *Care for the Retarded, 1981*, 97th Cong. 1 (1981).

75. See Riley, *Disability and the Media*.

76. "The purpose of the DD Council is to promote, through systemic change, capacity building, and advocacy activities . . . the development of a consumer and

family-centered, comprehensive system and a coordinated array of culturally competent services, supports, and other assistance designed to achieve independence, productivity, and integration and inclusion into the community for individuals with developmental disabilities." National Transition Network, "Developmental Disabilities Assistance and Bill of Rights Act Amendments of 1994."

77. *Care for the Retarded, 1981,* 47.

78. Ibid., 6.

79. Ibid., 11.

80. *Oversight on Education for All Handicapped Children Act, 1982,* 97th Cong. 1 (1982).

81. In 1982, member groups were American Association on Mental Deficiency, American Coalition of Citizens with Disabilities, American Occupational Therapy Association, American Speech-Language-Hearing Association, Association for Children with Learning Disabilities, Association for Retarded Citizens, Council for Exceptional Children, Epilepsy Foundation of America, National Association of Private Residential Facilities for the Mentally Retarded, National Easter Seal Society, National Mental Health Association, National Rehabilitation Association, National Society for Autistic Children, and Adults United Cerebral Palsy Associations, Inc. Nonmember groups were the Children's Defense Fund, Disability Rights and Education Defense Fund, National Education Association, National Parents and Teachers Association, and the Parents' Campaign for Handicapped Children and Youth.

82. This law introduced the term "developmental disabilities" into disability politics.

83. *Oversight on Education for All Handicapped Children Act, 1982,* 49.

84. While the Carter administration was far from enthusiastic about implementing disability rights law, Califano did finally sign Section 504 regulations, which DOT had to adopt. His successor, John Adams, required the production of accessible buses (Transbus). Unlike other sections of the Rehabilitation Act, 504 applied to both services and employment, and administrators noted that "it does not lend itself as readily to a single regulation" because services from agency to agency differ so widely. See *Department of Transportation and Related Agencies Appropriations for 1979, Part 6,* 117, 171, 248, 314–315.

85. *Transit Assistance Act of 1981,* 97th Cong. 1 (1981); Bill 97 S. 1160. Williams and Cranston served on the Subcommittee on Housing and Urban Affairs.

86. "Conservative Alliance Votes Less Often, More Effectively."

87. *Transit Assistance Act of 1981,* 2.

88. Lewis noted this in a report titled "Transportation and the Disadvantaged" submitted to the committee. See *Transit Assistance Act of 1981,* 11.

89. Ibid., 250.

90. *Examining the Nation's Immediate and Long-Term Surface Transportation Capital Needs*, 97th Cong. 1714 (1981).

91. *Equal Employment Opportunity for the Handicapped Act of 1979*, 168–171.

92. *Field Hearings on the Education for All Handicapped Children Act*, 96th Cong. 542 (1981).

93. *Urban Mass Transportation, 1975*, 94th Cong. 13 (1975).

94. Although the Subcommittee on DOT Appropriations did not have direct experience addressing disability-related issues, committee member Massachusetts Republican Silvio Conte supported Biaggi's push for full equal access. Apparently, while Califano allowed the protest at HEW offices, he did not allow protesters to return if they left the sit-in.

95. *Equal Employment Opportunity for the Handicapped Act of 1979*, 66.

96. *Rehabilitation of the Handicapped Programs, 1976, Part 2*, 94th Cong. 685 (1976).

97. *Equal Employment Opportunity for the Handicapped Act of 1979*, 66 (statement of B. Richmond Dudley Jr.).

98. See Pettinicchio, "Elites, Policy and Social Movements."

Chapter 5

1. Quoted in Pierre-Pierre, "Disrupting Sales at Greyhound."

2. *Implementation of the Rehabilitation, Comprehensive Services, and Developmental Disabilities Amendments, 1979*, 96th Cong. 51 (1979).

3. Sweeney, "Handicapped Protest High Court Ruling on Education," A26.

4. Ibid.

5. Richardson, "In Wheelchairs and on Crutches, Some Disabled Protest a Telethon," B2.

6. For a discussion of black activism and the threat to existing policy interests, see Platt, "Participation for What?"; on the effects of countermovement threat on mobilizing pro-choice groups, see Staggenborg, "Consequences of Professionalization" and *The Pro-choice Movement*.

7. For a discussion of threat and political opportunity structures, see Kriesi, "Political Opportunity Structure"; Van Dyke, "Crossing Movement Boundaries"; and Meyer, "Protest and Political Opportunities."

8. Nella Van Dyke and Sarah Soule discussed the role of reactive mobilization in mobilizing groups that historically had access to resources. However, the case of the disability rights movement concerns a group reacting to threats to recent policies meant to improve social, political, and economic conditions among Americans with disabilities. See Van Dyke and Soule, "Structural Social Change."

9. Gregg, "Physically Handicapped Protest Cuts in Services," C5.

10. Scott, "Marchers Protest Federal Cutbacks," A22. The original slogan had been, "War is unhealthy for children and other living things."

11. "Handicapped in Protest of 'Federalism' Policy," 1.14. New federalism refers to the devolution of federal government responsibilities to state and local jurisdictions. Critics saw Reagan's "new federalism" as an excuse to end federal social programs while justifying lax enforcement of regulations, including Section 504 regulations.

12. Ibid.

13. *Oversight on Education for All Handicapped Children Act, 1982*, 97th Cong. 49 (1982).

14. "Parents of Handicapped Protest on U.S. Plan," A21.

15. Jordan, "Civil Rights."

16. The hearing began with a complaint by Republicans Lungren and Sensenbrenner because these organizations apparently had violated a rule about the submission of prepared testimony and documents forty-eight hours before the hearing. Sensenbrenner made an opening statement to the chair: "Mr. Chairman, I did have an opening statement, but I think it is absolutely useless to conduct kangaroo-court committee hearings when the minority is not given the testimony of two of the witnesses until at the close of business, or considerably thereafter, on the day preceding the morning hearing." See *Civil Rights Enforcement in the Department of Education*, 97th Cong. 4 (1982).

17. Ibid., 6.

18. Laxalt was regarded as one of Ronald Reagan's closest friends in politics. See Roberts, "Reagan's First Friend."

19. *Civil Rights Enforcement in the Department of Education*, 54. The letter refers to a memo dated December 3, 1981, from Deputy Assistant Secretary of Civil Rights Michael A. Middleton to Thomas. Mattox also drew attention to the so-called hold categories that preclude complaints based on Section 504 from being processed as well as the OCR letters of finding claiming that compliance involved few corrective action plans.

20. Smith v. Robinson, 468 U.S. 992 (1984).

21. 130 Cong. Rec. 20,597 (July 1984).

22. *Transit Assistance Act of 1981*, 97th Cong. 1 (1981).

23. Quoted in Pierre-Pierre, "Disrupting Sales at Greyhound."

24. "Disabled Block Trolleys in S.F.," C3.

25. Marika, "Excluded from Vehicles," D3.

26. *Americans with Disabilities Act of 1988*, 100th Cong. 2 (1988).

27. 134 Cong. Rec. 9542 (April 1988).

28. *Americans with Disabilities Act of 1988*, 9.

29. Kessler, "Buses 'Captured' in Demonstration by Handicapped," B1.

30. Cooley, "Disabled People Block Bus at Terminal."

31. Tarrow, *Power in Movement*, 6. Policy and organizational transformations in the 1970s did much to invigorate numerous social movements, including the women's and environmental movements. See Costain, *Inviting Women's Rebellion*; Minkoff, *Organizing for Equality*; Soule et al., "Protest Events"; Olzak and Soule, "Cross-cutting Influences"; and Johnson, "Social Movement Size."

32. Fahrenthold, "Disability Group Makes Point," B3A.

33. The average number of groups to event in the disability rights movement is lower than other constituencies, with usually a single organization coordinating a given protest. Sarah Soule and Jennifer Earl found that in 1960, the average number of groups at a protest was slightly fewer than 2 and reached a high of 2.5 in the early 1970s, declining to about 1.5 in the 1980s. See Soule and Earl, "A Movement Society Revisited."

34. On protest diffusion, see Pfaff and Kim, "Exit-Voice Dynamics in Collective Action"; Pfaff, *Exit-Voice Dynamics*; Koopmans, "Dynamics of Protest Waves"; and Opp, *Political Protest and Social Movements*.

35. See Groch, "Oppositional Consciousness."

36. This evidence corroborates other accounts of disability protest. See, for example, Scotch, *From Good Will to Civil Rights*; and Barnartt and Scotch, *Disability Protests*.

37. David King, Keith Bentele, and Sarah Soule compared activism across issues and constituencies by plotting where protest for each group exceeds the overall (moving) average. In addition to different timing of protest waves, race, rights to privacy, choice, LGBT, gender, human rights, and free speech, all had numerous instances when their respective protest levels exceed the average, whereas disability had only once exceeded the average. Disability protests surpassed the average once in the late 1970s just when average overall protest levels were at their lowest point.

38. Maroto and Pettinicchio, "Limitations of Disability Antidiscrimination Legislation."

39. Note that "medium" is also the modal category in Pamela Oliver and Daniel Myers's analysis of protest. See Oliver and Myers, "How Events Enter the Public Sphere."

40. Soule and Earl's analysis of protest across different constituencies between 1961 and 1983 finds that about 16 percent of protests led to arrests, which is roughly the same result that my analysis reveals for disability (although several key protest centers had low arrest rates, and arrest rates tended to be highest in particular time periods and with particular issues). See Soule and Earl, "A Movement Society Revisited."

41. Holmes, "Militant Advocacy Group for Disabled Revels in Role of Agitator," B17.

42. Stein, "Disabled Stage Protest Parade; 8 Arrested," B1.

43. Ibid.

44. Himmel, "Bus Protest Stops Traffic," 25.

45. Fahrenthold, "Protest Shuts Constitution Ave.," B7.

46. Lyman, "Protesters with Hearts on Sleeves and Anger on Signs," A15.

47. "Paralyzed Veterans Declare War Against ADAPT," 4.

48. 134 Cong. Rec. 23,684 (September 1988).

49. Rep. Gus Yatron submitted Reich's statement for inclusion in the *Congressional Record*. As chair of the House Foreign Affairs Subcommittee on Human Rights and International Organizations, Yatron was instrumental in organizing the UN Decade of Disabled Persons.

50. 134 Cong. Rec. 23,684 (September 1988).

51. As Stephen Percy described, the DOJ was composed of young conservative lawyers. David Stockman, considered the father of Reaganomics, ran the OMB from 1981 to 1985. He helped pass Reagan's budget in the hope that it would undermine the welfare state. See Percy, *Disability, Civil Rights, and Public Policy*, 90. For more insight on Stockman, see Greider, "The Education of David Stockman."

52. Pear, "U.S. Agencies Vary on Rights Policy," 1.

53. Some in Congress, including William Dannemeyer (R-CA), argued that inclusion of people with communicable diseases under the Rehabilitation Act was inappropriate. See 132 Cong. Rec. E2338 (October 1986).

54. Reagan, "Statement on Signing the Handicapped Children's Protection Act of 1986."

55. Department of Transportation v. Paralyzed Veterans of America, 477 U.S. 597 (1986). The courts ruled that Section 504 did not apply to commercial air carriers because they did not directly receive federal funding through airports.

56. School Bd. of Nassau County v. Arline, 480 U.S. 273 (1987).

57. Grove City Coll. v. Bell, 465 U.S. 555 (1984).

58. *AIDS Issues (Part 2)*, 101st Cong. 78 (1989).

59. See Pelka, *What We Have Done*, 316.

60. Ibid.

61. 135 Cong. Rec. 8506 (May 1989).

62. Dart's father was also a major player in the Republican Party. See Pelka, *What We Have Done*.

63. 134 Cong. Rec. H2894 (September 1988).

64. 134 Cong. Rec. 9542 (April 1988).

65. Gunderson was the first openly gay Republican representative and the only Republican in Congress to later vote against the Defense of Marriage Act.

66. 136 Cong. Rec. 2 (1990).

67. "Conservative Coalition: Still Alive, but Barely."

68. The term "silent army" referred to the vast number of people connected to disability usually unbeknown to most and often working quietly behind the scenes to effect change. Sometimes the term is used interchangeably or in conjunction with "hidden army" and "passionate insiders," although these terms refer more directly to institutional activism.

69. Reagan and others in his administration sought to make statistical discrimination ineligible under Title VII.

70. *AIDS Issues (Part 1)*, 101st Cong. 2 (1989).

71. 136 Cong. Rec. 6692–6693 (April 1990).

72. The amendment was named for Jim Chapman (D-TX). Before joining the House, Chapman was considered a tough law-and-order prosecutor. Chapman was a centrist or moderate Democrat on the basis of the bills he sponsored. See "Rep. Jim Chapman."

73. "Questions and Answers About the Chapman Amendment."

74. 136 Cong. Rec. 11 (1990). Many disability organizations voiced their opposition to policy makers, as Dole noted in his records on the Chapman Amendment, including Easter Seals, National Multiple Sclerosis Association, UCP, and DREDF, as well as several labor unions and religious groups. See "Questions and Answers About the Chapman Amendment."

75. However, employers still had to provide alternative employment as part of an accommodation.

76. *Housing for Elderly and Handicapped Persons*, 101st Cong. 42–60, 141–162, 214–244 (1990).

77. 134 Cong. Rec. 9787 (May 1988).

78. 136 Cong. Rec. 5603 (March 1990).

79. *Americans with Disabilities Act of 1989*, 101st Cong. 147 (1989).

80. "ADAPT Rides Again in Phoenix," n.p.

81. *Americans with Disabilities Act of 1989*, 125.

82. Chung, "Cops Bust Disabled Protesters," A4.

83. For example, Henderson, "Transit Policy Protested."

84. *Department of Transportation and Related Agencies Appropriations for 1991, Part 3*, 101st Cong. 340 (1990).

85. The amendments undermined the commitment to make all new rail cars accessible.

86. 136 Cong. Rec. 11,432 (May 1990).

87. Rep. Jim Sensenbrenner (R-WI) generally supported the ADA and would later actively support ADARA.

88. 136 Cong. Rec. 11,426 (May 1990).

89. 156 Cong. Rec. S6131–S6144 (2010).

90. 136 Cong. Rec. 11,467 (1990).

91. Democrats and Republicans adopted the Hatch Amendment instead. Seen as a compromise, a yearly list compiled by HHS of communicable diseases (which would not include HIV) that could be transmitted via food handling could then be used by restaurant operators to potentially dismiss an employee.

92. "The Disabled Protest and Clinton Yields," A6.

93. Levy, "Protesters in Wheelchairs Block Clinton Headquarters in S.F.," A15.

94. Spayd, "Disabled Meet Clinton, Stage March."

95. "Disabled Protesters Are Arrested After Blockading Building," B.04.

96. "Protesting Home Care Laws," B1.

97. See On the Issues, "03n-APHA on Dec 31, 2003."

98. *Community-Based Care for Americans with Disabilities*, 105th Cong. 3 (1998).

99. Ibid.

100. Ibid., 78.

101. Ibid., 17.

102. Ibid., 92.

103. "Protest on Wheels," C7.

104. 148 Cong. Rec. 15,280 (July 2002).

105. He had a 100 percent approval rating from the Christian Coalition, did not believe in humankind's contribution to climate change, and supported President Trump's "Muslim Ban" in 2017.

106. 148 Cong. Rec. 15,280 (July 2002).

107. *Strategies to Improve Access to Medicaid Home- and Community-Based Services*, 108th Cong. 13 (2004).

108. Ibid.

109. Riley, "Rally Calls for More Aid for the Disabled," B1.

110. *Strategies to Improve Access to Medicaid Home- and Community-Based Services*, 32.

111. Ibid., 14.

112. For a discussion of "satisficing"—the combination of the words "satisfying" and "sufficing"—see Simon, *Administrative Behavior*, 118–120.

113. *Home- and Community-Based Care: Expanding Options for Long-Term Care*, 110th Cong. 4 (2007).

114. Ibid., 1.

115. *Helping Families with Needed Care: Medicaid's Critical Role for Americans with Disabilities*, 110th Cong. 50 (2008).

116. *Departments of Labor, Health and Human Services, and Education, and Related Agencies Appropriations for Fiscal Year 2010*, 111th Cong. 1 (2009).

117. "Community Choice Act National Kickoff Draws Thousands," n.p.

118. Ibid.

119. *The ADA and Olmstead Enforcement: Ensuring Community Opportunities for Individuals with Disabilities*, 111th Cong. 5 (2011).

120. Obamacare also extended the MFP demonstration grants until September 2016 and expanded eligibility.

121. See Boatman, "News Analysis."

122. 134 Cong. Rec. 23,684 (September 1988).

123. Kessler, "Buses 'Captured' in Demonstration by Handicapped," B1.

124. Cooley, "Disabled People Block Bus at Terminal."

125. "Disabled Protesters Achieve a Partial Victory in Atlanta," A18.

126. Abromowitz, "Dozens of Groups Protest Spending Cuts," B9.

127. Roderick, "Group of Disabled Assail Bradley," 3.

Chapter 6

1. *Joint Hearing on H.R. 2273, the Americans with Disabilities Act of 1989*, 101st Cong. 1 (1988).

2. In *Ironies of Affirmative Action*, concerning the role of political elites and social movements in expanding group inclusion in affirmative action, John Skrentny reminded us that initially, policy makers did not view women's equal rights struggles similar to those of ethnoracial groups.

3. On the role of policy in changing negative stereotypes about disability and work, see Maroto and Pettinicchio, "Limitations of Disability Antidiscrimination Legislation."

4. Dimond, "The Constitutional Right to Education." See also Abeson and Zettell, "The End of Quiet Revolution."

5. For how political opportunities may differently shape mobilization across different groups, issues, and constituencies, see Meyer and Minkoff, "Conceptualizing Political Opportunity."

6. Campbell, "Universalism, Targeting, and Participation," 124.

7. Shapiro, *No Pity*; and Fleisher and Zames, *The Disability Rights Movement*.

8. Barnartt and Scotch, *Disability Protests*.

9. Charlton, *Nothing About Us Without Us*; Gill, *Already Doing It*.

10. 163 Cong. Rec. S4227 (2017).

11. Ruiz, "How Disability Rights Activists Plan to Take Down the GOP Health Care Bill."

12. Calfas, "Video Shows Disability Advocates Forcibly Removed from Senate Protest."

13. 163 Cong. Rec. S4227 (July 2017).

14. 163 Cong. Rec. S4253 (July 2017).

15. Pettinicchio, "Public and Elite Policy Preferences."

16. Tarrow, *Power in Movement.*

17. See King, Bentele, and Soule, "Protest and Policymaking."

18. 136 Cong. Rec. 6328 (April 1990); 136 Cong. Rec. H11,427 (May 1990).

19. 136 Cong. Rec. 10,415 (May 1990).

20. 136 Cong. Rec. 12,592 (June 1990).

21. "Transcript of Statement by the President."

22. 135 Cong. Rec. 22,733 (October 1989).

23. 145 Cong. Rec. 29,862 (September 1989).

24. *Americans with Disabilities Act of 1989,* 101st Cong. 7 (1989).

25. 134 Cong. Rec. 9543 (April 1988).

26. *Americans with Disabilities Act of 1989,* 226.

27. Ibid., 6.

28. 136 Cong. Rec. 4420 (March 1990).

29. 136 Cong. Rec. 3657 (March 1990).

30. See Kriesi, "Political Opportunity Structure"; and Kitschelt, "Political Opportunity Structures." The open political structure has been described as "federal, functionally differentiated, directly democratic, and with a relatively incoherent system of public administration—which promotes assimilative strategies and higher mobilization overall." See Amenta and Young, "Democratic States and Social Movements," 154.

31. For an analysis linking agenda setting to policy proposals and policy outcomes, see Burstein, "Policy Domains."

32. 136 Cong. Rec. 17,656 (July 1990). Note that this was done in the context of Congress's recent attempts to restore the *Griggs v. Duke Power Co.* ruling, which was overturned by *Wards Cove Packing Co. v. Atonio* and addressed by the Civil Rights Restoration Act of 1990.

33. See Colker, "The ADA's Journey Through Congress."

34. Colker, "ADA Title III," 379.

35. *Oversight Hearing on H.R. 4498, Americans with Disabilities Act of 1988,* 100th Cong. 2 (1988).

36. *Roundtable Discussion: Determining the Proper Scope of Coverage for the Americans with Disabilities Act,* 110th Cong. 3 (2008).

37. *Restoring Congressional Intent and Protections Under the Americans with Disabilities Act,* 110th Cong. 81 (2007).

38. For a discussion of ADA implementation and employment and earnings outcomes, see Maroto and Pettinicchio, "Limitations of Disability Antidiscrimination Legislation."

39. 136 Cong. Rec. 17 (1990).

40. *ADA Restoration Act of 2007,* 110th Cong. 60 (2007).

41. According to a statement on its website, the US Chamber of Commerce continues to oppose more stringent regulations to make existing spaces accessible. US Chamber of Commerce, "Americans with Disabilities Act (ADA)."

42. *Roundtable Discussion: Determining the Proper Scope of Coverage for the Americans with Disabilities Act*, 28–29.

43. *Restoring Congressional Intent and Protections Under the Americans with Disabilities Act*, 73.

44. *Roundtable Discussion: Determining the Proper Scope of Coverage for the Americans with Disabilities Act*, 27–28.

45. *ADA Restoration Act of 2007*, 60.

46. *H.R. 3195, ADA Restoration Act of 2007*, 110th Cong. 3 (2008).

47. Constangy, Brooks, Smith, and Prophete, "News and Analysis."

48. *H.R. 3195, ADA Restoration Act of 2007*, 2.

49. *ADA Restoration Act of 2007*, 3.

50. For detailed analyses of court rulings, see Maroto and Pettinicchio, "Limitations of Disability Antidiscrimination Legislation."

51. Rosenbaum, "Ruling on Disability Rights Called a Blow by Advocates."

52. "U.S. Supreme Court Handicaps the Disabled."

53. Sutton v. United Air Lines, Inc., 527 U.S. 471 (1999); Murphy v. United Parcel Service, Inc., 527 U.S. 516 (1999); Albertson's, Inc. v. Kirkingburg, 527 U.S. 555 (1999).

54. *Americans with Disabilities Act: Sixteen Years Later*, 109th Cong. 102 (2006).

55. *Restoring Congressional Intent and Protections Under the Americans with Disabilities Act*, 68.

56. Board of Trustees of Univ. of Ala. v. Garrett, 531 U.S. 356 (2001).

57. Epstein, "Courts and Interest Groups."

58. This information is based on my analysis of Collins's *Friends of the Supreme Court* data. The data set contains information about amicus curiae briefs filed by organizations between 1978 and 2001. A very small number of cases with positive outcomes are associated with disability groups' filing briefs.

59. Rosenbaum, "Ruling on Disability Rights Called a Blow by Advocates."

60. However, there is little evidence that this strategy led to especially positive outcomes for disability rights. For a discussion of organizational use of legal mobilization, see Wasby, *Race Relations Litigation*; and Collins, "Friends of the Court."

61. Chevron U.S.A. Inc. v. Echazabal, 536 U.S. 73 (2002).

62. *H.R. 3195, ADA Restoration Act of 2007*, 12.

63. Magee v. Coca-Cola Refreshments USA, Inc., 143 F. Supp. 3d 464 (2015).

64. N. E. v. Seattle School District, 15-35910 (9th Cir. 2016). As the Ford Law Firm, which worked on the Ninth Circuit case, commented, "The Ninth Circuit Appellant Court turned *stay put* on its head" by requiring a student be left in whatever

setting is indicated on the Individualized Education Program (IEP), even if that setting had never been used (a placement not agreed on by the parents). Stay put, which was meant to protect parents, is being "weaponized" by school districts, and the court's ruling has further legitimized this. Ford Law Firm, "IDEA's Stay Put Provision."

65. Frieden, "The Current State of Transportation."

66. American Public Transportation Association, "2013 Public Transportation Fact Book."

67. Bureau of Transportation Statistics, "Data Analysis."

68. Sandra Rosenbloom's analysis of public-transit use suggests that the kinds of travel barriers people with disabilities face today are not necessarily the kinds of problems policy debates are addressing, including broader issues related to the intersection of social class and disability in limiting accessibility. See Rosenbloom, "Transportation Patterns."

69. *Curbside Operators: Bus Safety and ADA Regulatory Compliance*, 109th Cong. 11 (2006) (statement of Mike Sodrel of Indiana). Sodrel, who served in the House for two years (2005–2007), ultimately lost the Republican nomination in Indiana's ninth district to Todd Young. He was considered very conservative, with a 92 percent rating from the American Conservative Union.

70. *Curbside Operators*, 5. While regulations were implemented by DOT in 1991 following enactment of the ADA, regulations extending to over-the-road buses were put in place only in 1998 (affecting over-the-road bus operators). The administrator then pointed to enforcement problems: "Companies are supposed to report to the Department of Transportation on whether they are meeting the accessibility requirements. I can tell you that up to this point, the reporting has been very poor across the industry." Ibid.

71. Peter Pan Bus Lines, Inc. v. FMCSA, 05-1436 (D.C. Cir. 2006).

72. *Improving and Reforming the Nation's Surface Transportation Programs*, 112th Cong. 121 (2011).

73. Ibid., 82.

74. Federal Transit Administration, "Enhanced Mobility for Seniors and Individuals with Disabilities."

75. Zola, "Toward the Necessary Universalizing of a Disability Policy."

76. National Center for Education Statistics, "Fast Facts." Note that these figures vary considerably by type of disability. Students who are deaf or blind and those with multiple disabilities are more likely to be in separate institutions, and those with autism and specific learning disabilities among the least likely.

77. For example, because IDEA relies heavily on the expertise and decisions of local districts about individual education plans, 2004 amendments sought to ensure that the procedural rights of parents were safeguarded.

78. The meeting's title was "Learning Disabilities and Early Intervention Strategies: How to Reform the Special Education Referral and Identification Process."

79. The Tancredo Amendment, which sought to define learning disability to mean a disorder due to a medically detectable and diagnosable physiological condition relying on physical and scientific evidence and not based on subjective evidence, failed the recorded vote 54–367. However, the Shadegg Amendment, which ensured that only those diagnosed by a medical professional were considered disabled under IDEA, succeeded by voice vote.

80. Wrightslaw, "Alert!"

81. Schemo, "Senate Panel Approves Bill for Students with Disability."

82. Ibid.

83. 152 Cong. Rec. H1606 (April 2006).

84. Since the 1980s, individuals filing suit under IDEA have been able to recover attorney fees.

85. Levenson, "Boosting the Quality and Efficiency of Special Education," 2. While it acknowledged their importance in the early history of IDEA to ensure necessary support by the states, the organization has generally taken a position against maintenance of effort requirements (MOEs).

86. The focus throughout Obama's second term shifted more directly to granting local jurisdictions more flexibility, especially in regard to the federal MOE demanding that states provide financial support to special education at the same level each year.

87. Association of Educational Service Agencies, "Maintenance of Effort Requirements in Title I and IDEA."

88. National Down Syndrome Congress, "Every Student Succeeds Act."

89. See Himmelstein, *To the Right*; and Crutchfield and Pettinicchio, "Cultures of Inequality."

90. Hill, "Whither the Disability Rights Movement?" Hill also served as deputy assistant attorney general for civil rights at the DOJ in the Obama administration.

91. On criminal victimization of the elderly, see Cook and Skogan, "Congressional Attitudes and Voting Behavior"; on abortion, see Linders, "Victory and Beyond."

92. Blumer, "Collective Behavior"; Tilly, *From Mobilization to Revolution*. On abeyance, also see Hopper, "The Revolutionary Process"; Della Porta and Diani, *Social Movements*; Staggenborg, "Consequences of Professionalization"; and Taylor, "Social Movement Continuity." See Zald and Ash, "Social Movement Organizations," on organizational decline; and Karstedt-Henke, "Theorien zur Erklärung terroristischer Bewegungen," on institutionalization and co-optation.

93. Coy and Hedeen, "A Stage Model of Social Movement Co-optation."

94. Goldstone, *States, Parties, and Social Movements*, 22.

95. Colignon, *Power Plays*, 6; see also Selznick, *TVA and the Grass Roots*. On forms of co-optation, see Naples, "Materialist Feminist Discourse Analysis"; Gamson, *The*

Strategy of Social Protest; Meyer and Tarrow, *The Social Movement Society*; and Auerbach, *Justice Without Law?*

96. See Hedeen and Coy, "Community Mediation and the Court System."

97. On the link between nonprofit advocacy and access to the policy-making process, see Skocpol, "Voice and Inequality."

98. Campbell, "Policy Feedbacks and the Impact of Policy Designs on Public Opinion," 969.

99. See Sulkin, *Issue Politics in Congress*.

100. *Roundtable Discussion: Determining the Proper Scope of Coverage for the Americans with Disabilities Act*, 4.

101. Erik Johnson, Jon Agnone, and John McCarthy pointed this out in their work on environmental advocacy. See Johnson, Agnone, and McCarthy, "Movement Organization," 2285.

102. See Zald and Ash, "Social Movement Organizations"; and Taylor, "Social Movement Continuity."

103. One specific and notable example involved Carter's reorganization of HEW. Elizabeth Boggs, founder of NARC, who had become a member of the National Council on the Handicapped, criticized the administration's proposal to separate handicap issues from general housing, education, and health issues, arguing that this "would be contrary to the concept of integration." *Developmental Disabilities Assistance and Bill of Rights Act, 1981*, 97th Cong. 28 (1981).

104. Social movement scholars have increasingly recognized the importance of social movements in setting the policy agenda. See King, Bentele, and Soule, "Protest and Policymaking"; Olzak and Soule, "Cross-cutting Influences"; Johnson, "Social Movement Size"; and Johnson, Agnone, and McCarthy, "Movement Organization."

105. Hill, "Whither the Disability Rights Movement?"

106. Patashnik and Zelizer, "The Struggle to Remake Politics," 1071.

107. 156 Cong. Rec. S6144 (July 2010).

108. See Secret, "Disabilities Act Prompts Flood of Suits Some Cite as Unfair"; and Pettinicchio, "'Ambulance Chasing' as Legal Mobilization?"

109. Savransky, "Trump Admin."

110. For a discussion of how policy development influences downstream reversal, see Patashnik and Zelizer, "The Struggle to Remake Politics," 1083.

111. For a discussion of the limits placed on disability rights legislation by enforcement and compliance mechanisms, see Maroto and Pettinicchio, "The Limitations of Disability Antidiscrimination Legislation."

112. McCubbins, Noll, and Weingast, "Administrative Procedures as Instruments of Political Control," 255.

Appendix

1. "Conservative Coalition Tables."
2. See Polsby, *How Congress Evolves.*
3. See Jones and Baumgartner, *The Politics of Attention.*
4. Ibid., 4. See also Baumgartner and Jones, *Agendas,* on their seminal analysis of punctuated equilibrium in agenda setting.
5. See Pettinicchio, "Strategic Action Fields."
6. Burstein and Hirsh, "Interest Organizations."
7. Auerbach, *Justice Without Law?*
8. Sheingate, "Structure and Opportunity," 844.
9. See King, *Turf Wars.*
10. Minkoff, *Organizing for Equality.*
11. See Minkoff, "The Sequencing of Social Movements," 787.
12. Johnson, "Social Movement Size," 975.
13. Minkoff, *Organizing for Equality.*
14. See Barnartt, "The Globalization of Disability Protests, 1970–2005."
15. See King, Bentele, and Soule, "Protest and Policymaking."
16. Oliver and Myers, "How Events Enter the Public Sphere."
17. Maroto and Pettinicchio, "The Limitations of Disability Antidiscrimination Legislation."
18. Ibid.; Maroto and Pettinicchio, "Twenty-Five Years After the ADA"; Pettinicchio and Maroto, "Employment Outcomes Among Men and Women with Disabilities"; Maroto, Pettinicchio, and Patterson, "Hierarchies of Categorical Disadvantage."

Bibliography

Aberbach, Joel. *Keeping a Watchful Eye: The Politics of Congressional Oversight*. Washington, DC: Brookings Institution Press, 1990.

Abeson, Alan, and Jeffrey Zettel. "The End of Quiet Revolution: The Education for All Handicapped Children Act of 1975." *Exceptional Children* 44, no. 2 (1977): 114–128.

Abrams, Abigail. "'Our Lives Are at Stake': How Donald Trump Inadvertently Sparked a New Disability Rights Movement." *Time*, February 26, 2018. http://time.com/5168472/disability-activism-trump.

Abromowitz, Michael. "Dozens of Groups Protest Spending Cuts Proposed for D.C. Human Services." *Washington Post*, March 3, 1988, p. B9.

Adams, Gordon. *The Politics of Defense Contracting: The Iron Triangle*. Piscataway, NJ: Transaction, 1981.

Adams, Gordon, and Stephen Alexis Cain. "Defense Dilemmas in the 1990s." *International Security* 13, no. 4 (1989): 5–15.

"ADAPT Rides Again in Phoenix." *Incitement* 3, no. 2 (1987): n.p.

Altman, Barbara M., and Sharon N. Barnartt. "Moral Entrepreneurship and the Promise of the ADA." *Journal of Disability Policy Studies* 4 (1993): 21–40.

Amenta, Edwin, and Michael P. Young. "Democratic States and Social Movements: Theoretical Arguments and Hypotheses." *Social Problems* 57 (1999): 153–168.

American Public Transportation Association. "2013 Public Transportation Fact Book." October 2013. http://www.apta.com/resources/statistics/Documents/FactBook/2013-APTA-Fact-Book.pdf.

Association of Educational Service Agencies. "Maintenance of Effort Requirements in Title I and IDEA." 2014. https://www.aesa.us/conferences/2014_eca_talking_points/Maintenance_of_Effort_Requirements_in_Title_I_and_IDEA.pdf.

Auerbach, Jerold S. *Justice Without Law?* Oxford: Oxford University Press, 1984.

Auslander, Susan. "Cultural Opportunities for the Handicapped." *New York Times*, June 11, 1978, p. WC13.

Barnartt, Sharon. "The Globalization of Disability Protests, 1970–2005: Pushing the Limits of Cross-Cultural Research?" *Comparative Sociology* 9, no. 2 (2010): 222–240.

Barnartt, Sharon N., and Richard K. Scotch. *Disability Protests: Contentious Politics, 1970–1999*. Washington, DC: Gallaudet University Press, 2001.

Barnes, Jeb, and Thomas F. Burke. *How Policy Shapes Politics: Rights, Courts, Litigation, and the Struggle over Injury Compensation*. New York: Oxford University Press, 2015.

Baumgartner, Frank R., and Bryan D. Jones. *Agendas and Instability in American Politics*. Chicago: University of Chicago Press, 1993.

Baumgartner, Frank R., Bryan D. Jones, and Michael C. Macleod. "The Evolution of Legislation Jurisdictions." *Journal of Politics* 62 (2000): 321–349.

Berkowitz, Edward D. *Disabled Policy: America's Programs for the Handicapped; A Twentieth Century Fund Report*. Cambridge: Cambridge University Press, 1987.

Berkowitz, Edward D., and Larry DeWitt. *The Other Welfare: Supplemental Security Income and U.S. Social Policy*. Ithaca, NY: Cornell University Press, 2013.

Berry, Jeffrey, and Clyde Wilcox. *The Interest Group Society*. New York: Longman, 1997.

Blumer, Herbert. "Collective Behavior." In *Principles of Sociology*, edited by Alfred McClung Lee, 165–222. New York: Barnes and Noble, 1953.

Boatman, Mark. "News Analysis: The Obama Administration and Community Choice." *New Mobility*, February 2, 2013. http://www.newmobility.com/2013/02/news-analysis-the-obama-administration-and-community-choice.

Bourdieu, Pierre. *Distinction: A Social Critique of the Judgement of Taste*. Cambridge, MA: Harvard University Press, 1984.

Bullock, Charles S. "Freshman Committee Assignments and Re-election in the United States House of Representatives." *American Political Science Review* 66, no. 3 (1972): 996–1007.

Burden, Barry C. *Personal Roots of Representation*. Princeton, NJ: Princeton University Press, 2007.

Bureau of Transportation Statistics. "Data Analysis." May 20, 2017. https://www.bts.gov/archive/publications/freedom_to_travel/data_analysis.

Burns, James MacGregor. *The Deadlock of Democracy: Four-Party Politics in America*. Englewood Cliffs, NJ: Prentice-Hall, 1963.

Burstein, Paul. "Intergroup Conflict, Law, and the Concept of Labor Market Discrimination." *Sociological Forum* 5 (1990): 459–476.

———. "Policy Domains: Organization, Culture, and Policy Outcomes." *Annual Review of Sociology* 17 (1991): 327–350.

Burstein, Paul, and C. Elizabeth Hirsh. "Interest Organizations, Information, and Policy Innovation in the U.S. Congress." *Sociological Forum* 22, no. 2 (2007): 174–199.

Calfas, Jennifer. "Video Shows Disability Advocates Forcibly Removed from Senate Protest." *Time*, June 22, 2017. http://time.com/4829103/mitch-mcconnell-protest-senate-health-care-bill.

Califano, Joseph A., Jr. *Governing America: An Insider's Report from the White House and the Cabinet*. New York: Simon and Schuster, 2007.

Campbell, Andrea Louise. *How Policies Make Citizens: Senior Political Activism and the American Welfare State*. Princeton, NJ: Princeton University Press, 2003.

———. "Policy Feedbacks and the Impact of Policy Designs on Public Opinion." *Journal of Health Politics, Policy and Law* 36, no. 6 (2011): 961–973.

———. "Universalism, Targeting, and Participation." In *Remaking America: Democracy and Public Policy in the Age of Inequality*, edited by Joe Soss, Jacob S. Hacker, and Suzanne Mettler, 121–140. New York: Russell Sage Foundation, 2007.

Carmines, Edward G., and James A. Stimson. *Issue Evolution: Race and the Transformation of American Politics*. Princeton, NJ: Princeton University Press, 1989.

Charlton, James I. *Nothing About Us Without Us: Disability Oppression and Empowerment*. Berkeley: University of California Press, 1998.

Chung, L. A. "Cops Bust Disabled Protesters." *San Francisco Chronicle*, September 29, 1987, p. A4.

Clapp, Charles L. *The Congressman: His Work as He Sees It*. Washington, DC: Brookings Institution, 1964.

Cohen, Stanley. *Visions of Social Control*. Cambridge, UK: Polity, 1985.

Colignon, Richard A. *Power Plays: Critical Events in the Institutionalization of the Tennessee Valley Authority*. Albany: State University of New York Press, 1997.

Colker, Ruth. "ADA Title III: A Fragile Compromise." *Berkeley Journal of Employment and Labor Law* 21 (2000): 377–412.

———. "The ADA's Journey Through Congress." *Wake Forest Law Review* 39, no. 1 (2004): 1–48.

Collins, Paul M., Jr. "Friends of the Court: Examining the Influence of Amicus Curiae Participation in U.S. Supreme Court Litigation." *Law and Society Review* 38, no. 4 (2004): 807–832.

———. *Friends of the Supreme Court: Interest Groups and Judicial Decision Making*. Oxford: Oxford University Press, 2008.

"Community Choice Act National Kickoff Draws Thousands." *Incitement* 22, no. 8 (2009): n.p.

"Congress Enacts New Mental Health Programs." In *CQ Almanac, 1963*, 19th ed., 222–228. Washington, DC: Congressional Quarterly, 1964.

"Congress Extends Vocational Rehabilitation Act." In *CQ Almanac, 1967*, 23rd ed., 06-366–06-367. Washington, DC: Congressional Quarterly, 1968.

"Conservative Alliance Votes Less Often, More Effectively." In *CQ Almanac, 1980*, 36th ed., 34-C–39-C. Washington, DC: Congressional Quarterly, 1981.

"Conservative Coalition: Still Alive, but Barely." In *CQ Almanac, 1988*, 44th ed., 42-B. Washington, DC: Congressional Quarterly, 1988.

"Conservative Coalition Tables." In *Congressional Quarterly Almanac*, 66th ed., edited by Jan Austin. Washington, DC: CQ Press. http://library.cqpress.com/cqalmanac/toc .php?mode=cqalmanac-appendix&level=2&values=Conservative+Coalition+Tables.

Constangy, Brooks, Smith, and Prophete. "News and Analysis: ADA Amendments Act to Take Effect January 1." October 2, 2008. https://www.constangy.com/newsroom -newsletters-185.

Cook, F. L., and W. G. Skogan. "Congressional Attitudes and Voting Behavior: An Examination of Support for Social Welfare." *Legislative Studies Quarterly* 16 (1990): 375–392.

Cooley, Kathleen H. "Disabled People Block Bus at Terminal." *Los Angeles Times*, February 10, 1985. https://www.latimes.com/archives/la-xpm-1985-02-10-me-3451-story .html.

Costain, Anne N. *Inviting Women's Rebellion: A Political Process Interpretation of the Women's Movement*. Baltimore: Johns Hopkins University Press, 1992.

Costain, Anne N., and Steven Majstorovic. "Congress, Social Movements and Public Opinion: Multiple Origins of Women's Rights Legislation." *Political Research Quarterly* 47, no. 1 (1994): 111–135.

Cowen, Tyler. "Don't Mistake This for Gridlock." *New York Times*, December 21, 2013. https://www.nytimes.com/2013/12/22/business/dont-mistake-this-for-gridlock .html.

Coy, Patrick G., and Tim Hedeen. "A Stage Model of Social Movement Co-optation: Community Mediation in the United States." *Sociological Quarterly* 46, no. 3 (2005): 405–435.

Crutchfield, Robert, and David Pettinicchio. "'Cultures of Inequality': Ethnicity, Welfare Beliefs, and Criminal Justice." *Annals of the American Academy of Political and Social Science* 623 (2009): 134–147.

Della Porta, Donatella, and Mario Diani. *Social Movements: An Introduction*. Malden, MA: Blackwell, 2006.

DiMaggio, Paul J., and Walter W. Powell. "The Iron Cage Revisited: Institutional Isomorphism and Collective Rationality in Organizational Fields." *American Sociological Review* 48, no. 2 (1983): 147–160.

Dimond, Paul R. "The Constitutional Right to Education: The Quiet Revolution." *Hastings Law Journal* 24 (1972–1973): 1087–1127.

Disability Rights Education and Defense Fund. "The ADA Is Under Serious Attack! Urgent Action Needed." April 17, 2017. https://dredf.org/2017/04/17/ada-serious -attack-urgent-action-needed.

"Disabled Block Trolleys in S.F.: Protesters Demand Special Streetcars." *Los Angeles Times*, July 13, 1978, p. C3.

"The Disabled Protest and Clinton Yields." *San Francisco Chronicle*, January 1, 1992, p. A6.

"Disabled Protesters Achieve a Partial Victory in Atlanta." *Washington Post*, September 27, 1989, p. A18.

"Disabled Protesters Are Arrested After Blockading Building." *Washington Post*, May 18, 1995, p. B4.

Economic Report of the President, 1961–1970. Washington, DC: US Government Printing Office, 1961–1970.

Eisenhower, Dwight D. "Special Message to the Congress on the Health Needs of the American People." January 8, 1954. In *Public Papers of the Presidents of the United States: Dwight D. Eisenhower, 1954*, 69–78. Washington, DC: US Government Printing Office.

Encyclopedia of Associations. 3rd–43rd ed. Detroit: Gale Research, 1961–2006.

Epstein, Lee. "Courts and Interest Groups." In *The American Courts: A Critical Assessment*, edited by John Gates and Charles Johnson, 335–371. Washington, DC: Congressional Quarterly Press, 1991.

Fahrenthold, David A. "Disability Group Makes Point: Demonstrations at AMA and Cuomo's Home Spur Meetings." *Washington Post*, June 20, 2000, p. B3A.

———. "Protest Shuts Constitution Ave.; Activists Disperse After Meeting Justice Official." *Washington Post*, May 13, 2003, p. B7.

Federal Transit Administration. "Enhanced Mobility for Seniors and Individuals with Disabilities: Proposed Circular." *Federal Register*, July 11, 2013. https://www.federal register.gov/documents/2013/07/11/2013-16624/enhanced-mobility-for-seniors -and-individuals-with-disabilities-proposed-circular.

Feldblum, Chai R. "Definition of Disability Under Federal Anti-discrimination Law: What Happened? Why? And What Can We Do About It?" *Berkeley Journal of Employment and Labor Law* 21, no. 1 (2000): 91–165.

Fiorina, Morris P., Samuel J. Abrams, and Jeremy Pope. *Culture War? The Myth of a Polarized America*. Boston: Longman, 2010.

Fleischer, Doris Zames, and Frieda Zames. *The Disability Rights Movement: From Charity to Confrontation*. Philadelphia: Temple University Press, 2011.

Fligstein, Neil, and Doug McAdam. *A Theory of Fields*. Oxford: Oxford University Press, 2012.

Ford Law Firm. "IDEA's Stay Put Provision: Once a Shield for Parents, Now a Weapon for School Districts." August 25, 2017. https://www.fordlawfirmpllc.com/news-blog/ ?category=Special+Education.

Fournier, Ron. "Clinton's Case Against the Subminimum Wage." *The Atlantic*, March 29, 2016. https://www.theatlantic.com/politics/archive/2016/03/clinton-subminimum -wage/475863.

Frieden, Lex. "The Current State of Transportation for People with Disabilities in the United States." National Council on Disability. June 13, 2005. https://www.ncd.gov/ publications/2005/current-state-transportation-people-disabilities-united-states.

Gamson, William A. *The Strategy of Social Protest.* Belmont, CA: Wadsworth Press, 1975.
———. *The Strategy of Social Protest.* 2nd ed. Belmont, CA: Wadsworth Press, 1990.
Gill, Michael Carl. *Already Doing It: Intellectual Disability and Sexual Agency.* Minneapolis: University of Minnesota Press, 2015.
Givel, Michael. "Punctuated Equilibrium in Limbo: The Tobacco Lobby and U.S. State Policymaking from 1990 to 2003." *Policy Studies Journal* 34, no. 3 (2006): 405–418.
"Going Wrong with Disability Rights." *New York Times,* July 19, 1980, p. 16.
Goldstone, Jack A., ed. *States, Parties, and Social Movements.* New York: Cambridge University Press, 2003.
Gottweiss, Herbert. "Rhetoric in Policy Making: Between Logos, Ethos, and Pathos." In *Handbook of Public Policy Analysis: Theory, Politics, and Methods,* edited by Frank Fischer, Gerald J. Miller, and Mara S. Sidney, 237–250. Boca Raton, FL: CRC Press, 2007.
Grant, Philip A. "Senator Hoke Smith, Southern Congressmen, and Agricultural Education, 1914–1917." *Agricultural History* 60, no. 2 (1986): 111–122.
Gregg, Sandra R. "Physically Handicapped Protest Cuts in Services." *Washington Post,* September 10, 1981, p. C5.
Greider, William. "The Education of David Stockman." *The Atlantic,* December 1, 1981. https://www.theatlantic.com/magazine/archive/1981/12/the-education-of-david-stockman/305760.
Groch, Sharon A. "Oppositional Consciousness: Its Manifestation and Development; The Case of People with Disabilities." *Sociological Inquiry* 64, no. 4 (1994): 369–395.
Halpern, Stephen C. *On the Limits of the Law: The Ironic Legacy of Title VI of the 1964 Civil Rights Act.* Baltimore: Johns Hopkins University Press, 1995.
"Handicapped in Protest of 'Federalism' Policy." *New York Times,* East Coast late edition, May 1, 1982, p. 1.14.
Hannan, Michael T., and Glenn R. Carroll. *Dynamics of Organizational Populations: Density, Legitimation and Competition.* New York: Oxford, 1992.
Hannan, Michael T., and John Freeman. *Organizational Ecology.* Cambridge, MA: Harvard University Press, 1989.
Hechter, Michael. "The Role of Values in Rational Choice Theory." *Rationality and Society* 6, no. 3 (1994): 318–333.
Hechter, Michael, Lynn Nadel, and Richard E. Michod. *The Origin of Values.* New York: Aldine de Gruyter, 1993.
Hedeen, Timothy, and Patrick G. Coy. "Community Mediation and the Court System: The Ties That Bind." *Mediation Quarterly* 17, no. 4 (2000): 351–367.
Henderson, Nell. "Transit Policy Protested: Disabled Seek Increase in Wheelchair Lifts." *Washington Post,* March 15, 1988, p. D3.
Hill, Eve. "Whither the Disability Rights Movement? The Future of Disability Rights Law." *Human Rights Magazine,* June 27, 2017.

Himmel, Nieson. "Bus Protest Stops Traffic: Disabled Group Wants Access on Greyhound." *Los Angeles Times*, August 13, 1988, p. 25.

Himmelstein, Jerome L. *To the Right: The Transformation of American Conservatism.* Berkeley: University of California Press, 1990.

Holmes, Steven. "Militant Advocacy Group for Disabled Revels in Role of Agitator." *New York Times*, October 10, 1991, p. B17.

Hopper, R. D. "The Revolutionary Process: A Frame of Reference for the Study of Revolutionary Movements." *Social Forces* 28, no. 3 (1950): 270–279.

Howard, Christopher. *The Welfare State Nobody Knows: Debunking Myths About U.S. Social Policy.* Princeton, NJ: Princeton University Press, 2007.

Hughes, Jonathan. *The Vital Few.* London: Oxford University Press, 1973.

Johnson, Erik W. "Social Movement Size, Organizational Diversity and the Making of Federal Law." *Social Forces* 86, no. 3 (2008): 967–993.

Johnson, Erik W., Jon Agnone, and John D. McCarthy. "Movement Organization, Synergistic Tactics and Environmental Public Policy." *Social Forces* 88, no. 5 (2010): 2267–2292.

Jones, Bryan D., and Frank R. Baumgartner. *The Politics of Attention: How Government Prioritizes Problems.* Chicago: University of Chicago Press, 2005.

Jordan, Vernon E., Jr. "Civil Rights: Revolution and Counter-revolution." *Columbia Human Rights Law Review* 14 (1982–1983): 1, 8.

Karstedt-Henke, Suzanne 1980. "Theorien zur Erklärung terroristischer Bewegungen" [Theories for the explanation of terrorist movements]. In *Politik der inneren Sicherheit* [Internal security policy], edited by Erhard Blankenberg, 198–234. Frankfurt am Main: Suhrkamp, 1980.

Katzmann, Robert A. *Institutional Disability: The Saga of Transportation Policy for the Disabled.* Washington, DC: Brookings Institution, 1986.

Kaufman, Ted. "News Journal: The Senate Refuses to Lend Support for People with Disabilities." March 2014. http://tedkaufman.com/ted_kaufman_on/News-Journal -The-Senate-refuses-to-lend-support-for-people-with-disabilities.

———. "Time to Ratify the Global Disabilities Convention." *Huffington Post*, November 4, 2013. https://www.huffpost.com/entry/time-to-ratity-the-global_b_4212503.

"Kennedy's Key Votes in House and Senate Since 1947." In *CQ Almanac, 1960*, 16th ed., 11-837–11-839. Washington, DC: Congressional Quarterly, 1960.

Kentucky Career Center. "Carl D. Perkins Vocational Training Center." https://kcc.ky.gov/ vocational-rehabilitation/cdpvtc/pages/default.aspx (accessed February 18, 2019).

Kessler, Ronald. "Buses 'Captured' in Demonstration by Handicapped: Handicapped Protesters Block Buses." *Washington Post*, September 28, 1984, p. B1.

King, Brayden G., Keith G. Bentele, and Sarah A. Soule. "Protest and Policymaking: Explaining Fluctuation in Congressional Attention to Rights Issues, 1960–1986." *Social Forces* 86, no. 1 (2007): 137–164.

King, David C. *Turf Wars: How Congressional Committees Claim Jurisdiction*. Chicago: University of Chicago Press, 1997.

Kingdon, John W. *Agendas, Alternatives, and Public Policies*. New York: Longman, 1995.

———. "A House Appropriations Subcommittee: Influences on Budgetary Decisions." *Southwestern Social Science Quarterly* 47 (1966): 68–78.

Kitschelt, Herbert. "Political Opportunity Structures and Political Protest: Anti-nuclear Movements in Four Democracies." *British Journal of Political Science* 16 (1986): 57–85.

Koopmans, Ruud. "The Dynamics of Protest Waves: West Germany, 1965–1989." *American Sociological Review* 58 (1993): 637–658.

Kriesi, Hanspeter. "The Political Opportunity Structure of New Social Movements: Its Impact on Their Mobilization." In *The Politics of Social Protest*, edited by Craig Jenkins and Bert Klandermans, 167–198. Minneapolis: University of Minnesota Press, 1995.

Lawrence, Thomas, Roy Suddaby, and Bernard Leca. "Institutional Work: Refocusing Institutional Studies of Organization." *Journal of Management Inquiry* 20, no. 1 (2011): 52–58.

Levenson, Nathan. "Boosting the Quality and Efficiency of Special Education." Thomas B. Fordham Institute, September 2012. https://fordhaminstitute.org/national/research/boosting-quality-and-efficiency-special-education.

Levitan, Sar A., and Robert Taggart. *The Promise of Greatness*. Cambridge, MA: Harvard University Press, 1976.

Levy, Dan. "Protesters in Wheelchairs Block Clinton Headquarters in S.F." *San Francisco Chronicle*, October 20, 1992, p. A15.

Linders, Annulla. "Victory and Beyond: A Historical Comparison of the Outcomes of the Abortion Movements in Sweden and the United States." *Sociological Forum* 19, no. 3 (2004): 371–404.

Lundqvist, Lennart J. *The Hare and the Tortoise: Clean Air Policies in the United States and Sweden*. Ann Arbor: University of Michigan Press, 1980.

Lyman, Rick. "Protesters with Hearts on Sleeves and Anger on Signs." *New York Times*, March 28, 2005, p. A15.

Maass, Arthur. *Muddy Waters: The Army Engineers and the Nation's Rivers*. New York: Da Capo Press, 1951.

"Major Investigations Undertaken by 86th Congress." In *CQ Almanac, 1960*, 16th ed., 11-688–11-696. Washington, DC: Congressional Quarterly.

Marika, Gerrard. "Excluded from Vehicles Because of Faulty Lifts: 20 in Wheelchairs Protest at Bus Stop." *Los Angeles Times*, March 12, 1981, p. D3.

Maroto, Michelle, and David Pettinicchio. "The Limitations of Disability Antidiscrimination Legislation: Policymaking and the Economic Well-Being of People with Disabilities." *Law and Policy* 36, no. 4 (2014): 370–407.

———. "Twenty-Five Years After the ADA: Situating Disability in America's System of Stratification." *Disability Studies Quarterly* 35, no. 3 (2015): 1–34.

Maroto, Michelle, David Pettinicchio, and Andrew C. Patterson. "Hierarchies of Categorical Disadvantage: Economic Insecurity at the Intersection of Disability, Gender, and Race." *Gender and Society* 33 (2019): 54–93.

Marshall, Alfred T. *Citizenship and Social Class and Other Essays.* London: Cambridge University Press, 1950.

McAdam, Doug, and Hilary Boudet. *Putting Social Movements in Their Place: Explaining Opposition to Energy Projects in the United States, 2000–2005.* New York: Cambridge University Press, 2012.

McAdam, Doug, John D. McCarthy, and Mayer N. Zald. *Comparative Perspectives on Social Movements: Political Opportunities, Mobilizing Structures, and Cultural Framings.* Cambridge: Cambridge University Press, 1996.

McCarthy, John D. "Velcro Triangles: Elite Mobilization of Local Antidrug Issues Coalitions." In *Routing the Opposition: Social Movements, Public Policy, and Democracy,* edited by David S. Meyer, Helen S. Ingram, and Valerie Jenness, 87–116. Minneapolis: University of Minnesota Press, 2005.

McCarthy, John D., and Mayer N. Zald. "Resource Mobilization and Social Movements: A Partial Theory." *American Journal of Sociology* 82, no. 6 (1977): 1212–1241.

McCubbins, Mathew D., Roger G. Noll, and Barry R. Weingast. "Administrative Procedures as Instruments of Political Control." *Journal of Law, Economics, and Organization* 3, no. 2 (1987): 243–277.

"Message to Congress: Kennedy on Health Care, Other Problems of the Aged." In *CQ Almanac, 1963,* 19th ed., 962–966. Washington, DC: Congressional Quarterly, 1964.

Meyer, David S. "Protest and Political Opportunities." *Annual Review of Sociology* 30, no. 1 (2004): 125–145.

———. "Social Movements: Creating Communities of Change." In *Feminist Approaches to Social Movements, Community, and Power,* vol. 1, *Conscious Acts and the Politics of Social Change,* edited by Robin L. Teske and Mary Ann Tetreault, 35–55. Columbia: University of South Carolina Press, 2000.

Meyer, David S., and Debra C. Minkoff. "Conceptualizing Political Opportunity." *Social Forces* 82, no. 4 (2004): 1457–1492.

Meyer, David S., and Sidney Tarrow. *The Social Movement Society.* Lanham, MD: Rowman and Littlefield, 1998.

Meyer, John W., and Brian Rowan. "Institutionalized Organizations: Formal Structure as Myth and Ceremony." *American Journal of Sociology* 83, no. 2 (1977): 340–363.

Miller, Warren E., and Donald E. Stokes. "Constituency Influence in Congress." *American Political Science Review* 57, no. 1 (1963): 45–56.

Minkoff, Debra C. "Bending with the Wind: Strategic Change and Adaptation by Women's and Racial Minority Organizations." *American Journal of Sociology* 104, no. 6 (1999): 1666–1703.

———. "From Service Provision to Institutional Advocacy: The Shifting Legitimacy of Organizational Forms." *Social Forces* 72, no. 4 (1994): 943–969.

———. *Organizing for Equality: The Evolution of Women's and Racial-Ethnic Organizations in America, 1955–1985.* New Brunswick, NJ: Rutgers University Press, 1995.

———. "The Sequencing of Social Movements." *American Sociological Review* 62, no. 5 (1997): 779–799.

Moyers, Bill, and Michael Winship. "Do-Nothing Congress Gives Inertia a Bad Name." *BillMoyers.com,* April 26, 2013. https://billmoyers.com/2013/04/26/do-nothing-congress-gives-inertia-a-bad-name.

Munger, Frank J., and Richard F. Fenno. *National Politics and Federal Aid to Education.* Syracuse, NY: Syracuse University Press, 1962.

Naples, Nancy. "Materialist Feminist Discourse Analysis and Social Movement Research: Mapping the Changing Context for Control." In *Social Movements: Identity, Culture, and the State,* edited by David S. Meyer, Nancy Whittier, and Belinda Robnett, 226–246. New York: Oxford University Press, 2002.

National Center for Education Statistics. "Fast Facts: Students with Disabilities, Inclusion of." https://nces.ed.gov/fastfacts/display.asp?id=59 (accessed February 19, 2019).

National Down Syndrome Congress. "Every Student Succeeds Act: Frequently Asked Questions and IEP Tips." 2016. https://www.ndsccenter.org/wp-content/uploads/ESSA-FAQs-and-IEP-Tips.pdf.

National Transition Network. "Developmental Disabilities Assistance and Bill of Rights Act Amendments of 1994: Its Impact on Transition Services." *Policy Update,* Fall 1994.

"New Vocational Rehabilitation Program Established." In *CQ Almanac, 1968,* 24th ed., 07-391–7-393. Washington, DC: Congressional Quarterly, 1969.

Oleszek, Walter J. *Congressional Procedures and the Policy Process.* Washington, DC: CQ Press, 2007.

Oliver, Pamela E., and Daniel J. Myers. "How Events Enter the Public Sphere: Conflict, Location, and Sponsorship in Local Newspaper Coverage of Public Events." *American Journal of Sociology* 105 (1999): 38–87.

Olzak, Susan, and Sarah A. Soule. "Cross-cutting Influences of Environmental Protest and Legislation." *Social Forces* 88, no. 1 (2009): 201–225.

On the Issues. "03n-APHA on Dec 31, 2003." http://www.ontheissues.org/Notebook/Note_03n-APHA.htm (accessed February 18, 2019).

Opp, Karl-Dieter. *Political Protest and Social Movements: A Multidisciplinary Introduction, Critique and Synthesis.* London: Routledge 2009.

Orloff, Ann Shola. "The Political Origins of America's Belated Welfare State." In *The Politics of Social Policy in the United States*, edited by Margaret Weir, Ann S. Orloff, and Theda Skocpol, 37–80. Princeton, NJ: Princeton University Press, 1988.

"Paralyzed Veterans Declare War Against ADAPT." *Incitement* 3, no. 2 (1987): 4.

"Parents of Handicapped Protest on U.S. Plan." *New York Times*, East Coast late edition, September 9, 1982, p. A21.

Patashnik, Eric M., and Julian E. Zelizer. "The Struggle to Remake Politics: Liberal Reform and the Limits of Policy Feedback in the Contemporary American State." *American Political Science Association* 11, no. 4 (2013): 1071–1087.

Patterson, James T. *America's Struggle Against Poverty in the Twentieth Century*. Cambridge, MA: Harvard University Press, 2000.

Pear, Robert. "U.S. Agencies Vary on Rights Policy." *New York Times*, November 16, 1981, p. 1.

Pelka, Fred. *What We Have Done: An Oral History of the Disability Rights Movement*. Amherst: University of Massachusetts Press, 2012.

Percy, Stephen L. *Disability, Civil Rights, and Public Policy: The Politics of Implementation*. Tuscaloosa: University of Alabama Press, 1989.

Peterson, Mark A. "Institutional Change and the Health Politics of the 1990s." *American Behavioral Scientist* 36, no. 6 (1993): 782–801.

Pettinicchio, David. "'Ambulance Chasing' as Legal Mobilization?" *Mobilizing Ideas*, April 27, 2012. https://mobilizingideas.wordpress.com/2012/04/27/ambulance -chasing-as-legal-mobilization.

———. "Elites, Policy and Social Movements." In *Research in Political Sociology*, vol. 24, edited by Barbara Wejnert and Paolo Parigi, 155–190. Bingley, UK: Emerald, 2017.

———. "Institutional Activism: Reconsidering the Insider/Outsider Dichotomy." *Sociology Compass* 6, no. 6 (2012): 499–510.

———. "Public and Elite Policy Preferences: Gay Marriage in Canada." *International Journal of Canadian Studies* 42, no. 2 (2010): 125–153.

———. "Strategic Action Fields and the Context of Political Entrepreneurship: How Disability Rights Became Part of the Policy Agenda." *Research in Social Movements, Conflicts and Change* (2013): 79–106.

Pettinicchio, David, and Michelle Maroto. "Employment Outcomes Among Men and Women with Disabilities: How the Intersection of Gender and Disability Status Shapes Labor Market Inequality." In *Factors in Studying Employment for Persons with Disability*, edited by Barbara M. Altman, 3–33. Bingley, UK: Emerald, 2017.

Pfaff, Steven. *Exit-Voice Dynamics and the Collapse of East Germany: The Crisis of Leninism and the Revolution of 1989*. Durham, NC: Duke University Press, 2006.

Pfaff, Steven, and Hyojoung Kim. "Exit-Voice Dynamics in Collective Action: An Analysis of Emigration and Protest in the East German Revolution." *American Journal of Sociology* 109, no. 2 (2003): 401–444.

Pierre-Pierre, Garry. "Disrupting Sales at Greyhound, Disabled Protest Bus Access." *New York Times*, August 9, 1997. https://www.nytimes.com/1997/08/09/nyregion/disrupting-sales-at-greyhound-disabled-protest-bus-access.html.

Pierson, Paul. *Dismantling the Welfare State? Reagan, Thatcher, and the Politics of Retrenchment.* Cambridge: Cambridge University Press, 1994.

———. "When Effect Becomes Cause: Policy Feedback and Political Change." *World Politics* 45, no. 4 (1993): 595–628.

Pierson, Paul, and Theda Skocpol, eds. *The Transformation of American Politics: Activist Government and the Rise of Conservatism.* Princeton, NJ: Princeton University Press, 2007.

Platt, Matthew B. "Participation for What? A Policy-Motivated Approach to Political Activism." *Political Behavior* 30, no. 3 (2008): 391–413.

"Political and Legislative Highlights of 1960." In *CQ Almanac, 1960,* 16th ed., 11-844–11-847. Washington, DC: Congressional Quarterly, 1960.

Polsby, Nelson W. *How Congress Evolves: Social Bases of Institutional Change.* New York: Oxford University Press, 2004.

Posner, Paul L. *The Politics of Unfunded Mandates: Whither Federalism?* Washington, DC: Georgetown University Press, 1998.

Pratt, Henry J. *The Gray Lobby.* Chicago: University of Chicago Press, 1976.

"President Eisenhower Presents Largest Peacetime Budget." In *CQ Almanac, 1957,* 13th ed., 09-49–09-54. Washington, DC: Congressional Quarterly, 1958.

"Presidential Statement to Congress: Nixon on Funds for Education." In *CQ Almanac, 1971,* 27th ed., 11-79-A–11-81-A. Washington, DC: Congressional Quarterly, 1972.

"Presidential Statement to Congress: Nixon's 1970 Economic Report." In *CQ Almanac, 1970,* 26th ed., 11-16-A–11-18-A. Washington, DC: Congressional Quarterly, 1971.

"Presidential Veto Message: Nixon Vetoes Nine Bills, Oct. 27." In *CQ Almanac, 1972,* 28th ed., 11-80-A–11-81-A. Washington, DC: Congressional Quarterly, 1973.

"President's 'War on Poverty' Approved." In *CQ Almanac, 1964,* 20th ed., 208–229. Washington, DC: Congressional Quarterly, 1965.

"Protesting Home Care Laws." *Washington Post*, June 17, 1997, p. B1.

"Protest on Wheels." *Washington Post*, November 4, 1998, p. C7.

Pulzl, Helga, and Oliver Treib. "Implementing Public Policy." In *Handbook of Public Policy Analysis: Theory, Politics, and Methods,* edited by Frank Fischer, Gerald J. Miller, and Mara S. Sidney, 89–108. Boca Raton, FL: Taylor and Francis, 2007.

"Questions and Answers About the Chapman Amendment." Robert J. Dole Senate Papers—Legislative Relations, 1969–1996. Robert J. Dole Archive and Special Collections. University of Kansas, Lawrence. http://dolearchivecollections.ku.edu/collections/ada/files/s-leg_749_003_all.pdf.

Randolph, Jennings. "Developmentally Disabled Assistance and Bill of Rights Act: Senate Report on Public Bills 93 S. 3378 and S. 427." CIS number 74-S543-30.

Reagan, Ronald. "Statement on Signing the Handicapped Children's Protection Act of 1986." August 5, 1986. https://www.reaganlibrary.gov/research/speeches/080586d.

"Record of 84th Congress." In *CQ Almanac, 1955*, 11th ed., 44–47. Washington, DC: Congressional Quarterly, 1956.

"Rep. Jim Chapman." *GovTrack*. https://www.govtrack.us/congress/members/jim_chapman/402454 (accessed May 7, 2019).

Reskin, Barbara F. "Employment Discrimination and Its Remedies." In *Labor Markets: Evolving Structures and Processes*, edited by Ivar Berg and Arne L. Kalleberg, 567–599. Boston: Springer, 2001.

Richardson, Lynda. "In Wheelchairs and on Crutches, Some Disabled Protest a Telethon." *New York Times*, East Coast late edition, September 7, 1993, p. B2.

Riley, Charles A. *Disability and the Media: Prescriptions for Change*. Hanover, NH: University Press of New England, 2005.

Riley, Marianna. "Rally Calls for More Aid for the Disabled." *St. Louis Post-Dispatch*, September 18, 2003, p. B1.

Roberts, Steven V. "Reagan's First Friend." *New York Times*, March 21, 1982. http://www.nytimes.com/1982/03/21/magazine/reagan-s-first-friend.html.

Roderick, Kevin. "Group of Disabled Assail Bradley; 6 Quit as Advisers." *Los Angeles Times*, April 22, 1988, p. 3.

Roe, Emery. *Narrative Policy Analysis: Theory and Practice*. Durham, NC: Duke University Press, 1994.

Rose, Richard, and Phillip L. Davies. *Inheritance in Public Policy: Change Without Choice in Britain*. New Haven, CT: Yale University Press, 1994.

Rosenbaum, David E. "Ruling on Disability Rights Called a Blow by Advocates." *New York Times*, February 22, 2001. http://www.nytimes.com/2001/02/22/us/ruling-on-disability-rights-called-a-blow-by-advocates.html.

Rosenbloom, Sandra. 2007. "The Transportation Patterns and Needs of People with Disabilities." In *The Future of Disability in America*, edited by Marilyn J. Field and Alan M. Jette, 519–560. Washington, DC: Institute of Medicine of the National Academies, National Academic Press.

Ruiz, Rebecca. "How Disability Rights Activists Plan to Take Down the GOP Health Care Bill." *Mashable*, June 30, 2017. http://mashable.com/2017/06/30/disability-rights-activists-medicaid-health-care-bill/#u6DnFoOIGPqa.

Sabatier, Paul A. "Top-Down and Bottom-Up Approaches to Implementation Research: A Critical Analysis and Suggested Synthesis." *Journal of Public Policy* 6, no. 1 (1986): 21–48.

Savransky, Rebecca. "Trump Admin Rolling Back Use of Fines Against Nursing Homes." *The Hill*, December 26, 2017. http://thehill.com/policy/healthcare/366497-trump-admin-rolling-back-use-of-fines-against-nursing-homes.

Schemo, Diana Jean. "Senate Panel Approves Bill for Students with Disability." *New York Times*, June 26, 2003. https://www.nytimes.com/2003/06/26/us/senate-panel-approves-bill-for-students-with-disabilty.html.

Schneider, Mark, and Paul Teske. "Toward a Theory of the Political Entrepreneur: Evidence from Local Government." *American Political Science Review* 86, no. 3 (1992): 737–747.

Scotch, Richard K. *From Good Will to Civil Rights: Transforming Federal Disability Policy.* Philadelphia: Temple University Press, 2001.

Scott, Austin. "Marchers Protest Federal Cutbacks." *Los Angeles Times*, May 9, 1981, p. A22.

Secret, Mosi. "Disabilities Act Prompts Flood of Suits Some Cite as Unfair." *New York Times*, April 16, 2012. https://www.nytimes.com/2012/04/17/nyregion/lawyers-find-obstacles-to-the-disabled-then-find-plaintiffs.html.

Selznick, Philip. *TVA and the Grass Roots: A Study in the Sociology of Formal Organization.* Berkeley: University of California Press, 1949.

"Senate Backs Compromise on Vetoed Vocational Bill." *New York Times*, July 19, 1973, p. 38.

Shakespeare, Tom. "The Social Model of Disability." In *The Disability Studies Reader,* edited by Lennard J. Davis, 2–197. New York: Routledge, 2006.

Shapiro, Joseph P. *No Pity: People with Disabilities Forging a New Civil Rights Movement.* New York: Three Rivers Press, 1994.

Sheingate, Adam D. "Political Entrepreneurship, Institutional Change, and American Political Development." *Studies in American Political Development* 17, no. 2 (2003): 185–203.

———. "Structure and Opportunity: Committee Jurisdiction and Issue Attention in Congress." *American Journal of Political Science* 50, no. 4 (2006): 844–859.

Simon, Hebert A. *Administrative Behavior: A Study of Decision-Making Processes in Administrative Organization.* 4th ed. New York: Free Press, 1997.

———. "Rational Choice and the Structure of the Environment." *Psychological Review* 63, no. 2 (1956): 129–138.

Skocpol, Theda. "Government Activism and the Reorganization of American Civic Democracy." In *The Transformation of American Politics: Activist Government and the Rise of Conservatism,* edited by Paul Pierson and Theda Skocpol, 39–67. Princeton, NJ: Princeton University Press, 2007.

———. *Protecting Soldiers and Mothers.* Cambridge, MA: Harvard University Press, 1995.

———. "State Formation and Social Policy in the United States." *American Behavioral Scientist* 35, no. 4–5 (1992): 559–584.

———. "Voice and Inequality: The Transformation of American Civic Democracy." *Perspectives on Politics* 2, no. 1 (2004): 1–18.

Skrentny, John David. *The Ironies of Affirmative Action: Policies, Culture, and Justice in America.* Chicago: University of Chicago Press, 1996.

———. *The Minority Rights Revolution.* Cambridge, MA: Belknap Press of Harvard University Press, 2002.

Smith, Steven Rathgeb, and Michael Lipsky. *Nonprofits for Hire: The Welfare State in the Age of Contracting.* Cambridge, MA: Harvard University Press, 1993.

Soule, Sarah A., and Jennifer Earl. "A Movement Society Revisited: The Character of American Social Protest." *Mobilization: An International Quarterly* 10, no. 3 (2005): 345–364.

Soule, Sarah A., Doug McAdam, John McCarthy, and Yang Su. "Protest Events: Cause or Consequence of State Action? The U.S. Women's Movement and Federal Congressional Activities, 1956–1979." *Mobilization: An International Quarterly* 4, no. 2 (1999): 239–256.

Spayd, Liz. "Disabled Meet Clinton, Stage March." *Washington Post*, May 3, 1994. https://www.washingtonpost.com/archive/1994/05/03/disabled-meet-clinton-stage-march/5cd475a3-3bbb-4320-9909-9b9c28b6a590.

Staggenborg, Suzanne. "The Consequences of Professionalization and Formalization in the Pro-choice Movement." *American Sociological Review* 53, no. 4 (1988): 585–605.

———. *The Pro-choice Movement: Organization and Activism in the Abortion Conflict.* New York: Oxford University Press, 1991.

Starr, Paul. "Three Degrees of Entrenchment: Power, Policy, Structure." Lecture for Berkeley Sociology Colloquium Series, Berkeley, CA, September 15, 2014.

Stein, George. "Disabled Stage Protest Parade; 8 Arrested." *Los Angeles Times*, October 7, 1985, p. B1.

Steinhauer, Jennifer. "Dole Appears, but G.O.P. Rejects a Disabilities Treaty." *New York Times*, December 4, 2012. https://www.nytimes.com/2012/12/05/us/despite-doles-wish-gop-rejects-disabilities-treaty.html.

Stimson, James A. *Tides of Consent: How Public Opinion Shapes American Politics.* Cambridge: Cambridge University Press, 2004.

Sulkin, Tracy. *Issue Politics in Congress.* New York: Cambridge University Press, 2005.

Sweeney, Joan. "Handicapped Protest High Court Ruling on Education." *Los Angeles Times*, August 18, 1979, p. A26.

Tarrow, Sidney. *Power in Movement: Social Movements, Collective Action and Politics.* Cambridge: Cambridge University Press, 1994.

Taylor, Verta. "Social Movement Continuity: The Women's Movement in Abeyance." *American Sociological Review* 54, no. 5 (1989): 761–775.

TenBroek, Jacobus, and Floyd W. Matson. *Hope Deferred: Public Welfare and the Blind.* Watertown, MA: Howe Memorial Press, 1959.

Thornburgh, Dick. "Respecting the Convention on the Rights of Persons with Disabilities." Testimony before the U.S. Senate Foreign Relations Committee, July 12, 2012. https://www.foreign.senate.gov/imo/media/doc/Dick_Thornburgh_Testimony.pdf.

Tilly, Charles. *From Mobilization to Revolution*. Reading, MA: Addison-Wesley, 1978.

"Transcript of Statement by the President." July 26, 1990. National Archives. https://www.archives.gov/research/americans-with-disabilities/transcriptions/naid-6037493-statement-by-the-president-americans-with-disabilities-act-of-1990.html.

True, James L., and Glenn H. Utter. "Saying 'Yes,' 'No,' and 'Load Me Up' to Guns in America." *American Review of Public Administration* 32, no. 2 (2002): 216–241.

"Urban Mass Transportation." In *CQ Almanac, 1970*, 26th ed., 09-329–09-333. Washington, DC: Congressional Quarterly, 1971.

US Chamber of Commerce. "Americans with Disabilities Act (ADA)." August 4, 2010. https://www.uschamber.com/americans-disabilities-act-ada.

"U.S. Supreme Court Handicaps the Disabled." *Los Angeles Times*, August 19, 1979.

Van Dyke, Nella. "Crossing Movement Boundaries: Factors That Facilitate Coalition Protest by American College Students, 1930–1990." *Social Problems* 50, no. 2 (2003): 226–250.

Van Dyke, Nella, and Sarah A. Soule. "Structural Social Change and the Mobilizing Effect of Threat: Explaining Levels of Patriot and Militia Mobilizing in the United States." *Social Problems* 49, no. 4 (2002): 497–520.

van Eeten, M. J. "Narrative Policy Analysis." In *Handbook of Public Policy Analysis: Theory, Politics, and Methods*, edited by Frank Fischer, Gerald J. Miller, and Mara S. Sidney, 251–288. Boca Raton, FL: CRC Press, 2007.

"Vocational Rehabilitation." In *CQ Almanac, 1954*, 10th ed., 04-213–04-215. Washington, DC: Congressional Quarterly, 1955.

Wasby, Stephen L. *Race Relations Litigation in an Age of Complexity*. Charlottesville: University Press of Virginia, 1995.

White, Rebecca H. "The EEOC, the Courts, and Employment Discrimination Policy: Recognizing the Agency's Leading Role in Statutory Interpretation." *Utah Law Review* 51 (1995): 51–107.

Wilensky, Harold L. *The Welfare State and Equality: Structural and Ideological Roots of Public Expenditures*. Berkeley: University of California Press, 1975.

Wrightslaw. "Alert! IDEA Threatened—Kids Need Our Help on April 29." *Special Ed Advocate Newsletter*, April 21, 2003. http://www.wrightslaw.com/nltr/03/al.0421.htm.

Zald, Mayer N., and Roberta Ash. "Social Movement Organizations, Growth, Decay and Change." *Social Forces* 44, no. 3 (1966): 327–341.

Zald, Mayer N., and Michael A. Berger. "Social Movements in Organizations: Coup d'Etat, Insurgency, and Mass Movements." *American Journal of Sociology* 83, no. 4 (1978): 823–861.

Zippel, Kathrin S. *The Politics of Sexual Harassment: A Comparative Study of the United States, the European Union, and Germany*. New York: Cambridge University Press, 2006.

Zola, Irving Kenneth. "Toward the Necessary Universalizing of a Disability Policy." *Milbank Quarterly* 83, no. 4 (2005). https://www.ncbi.nlm.nih.gov/pmc/articles/PMC2690291.

Index

Page numbers in italics indicate material in figures or tables.

AAPD (American Association of People with Disabilities), 133, 152

ABA (Architectural Barriers Act), 2, 59–61, 65–67, 81, 109, 202n59

Abzug, Bella, 51, *173*

ACCD (American Coalition of Citizens with Disabilities): and Civil Rights Act Amendment, 96; and "disability rebellion," 91; and Frank Bowe testimony, 86, 96; Judy Heumann and, 11; member of CCDD, 212n81; as monitoring employment discrimination, 96; protests by, 104, 105, 109, 111–114, *112*, 151; and Reese Robrahn testimony, 103; and Rehabilitation Act, 97; and Section 504, 76, 88, 92, 95, 103; and Vincent Macaluso testimony, 103

ACLD (Association for Children and Adults with Learning Disabilities), 90, 100, 107

ACT UP, *112*, 116, 119, 122

ADA (Americans with Disabilities Act): ADA Education and Reform Act (H.R. 620), 15, 163; bipartisanship on, 120–121, 142, 145, 159; as "emancipation proclamation," xiii, 120, 125; enforcement issues of, 14–15, 121, 133, 146, 149, 154, 157; as Handicapped Bill of Rights, 3; introduction and passage of, 110, 118–119; John McCain and, 120; protests regarding, 114–117; Reagan administration and, 120–121; Ted Kennedy and, 101, 121–122, 145; Tom Harkin and, 12, 14, 101, 110, 120, 133, 161; Trump administration and, 137, 139–141, 163. *See also* Section 504 of Rehabilitation Act

ADAAA (Americans with Disabilities Act Amendments Act), 152–153, 158, 181

Adams, John, 92, 94, 212n84

ADAPT (Americans Disabled for Attendant Programs Today), xiv, *112*, 161; in Bay Area, 113–114; and Bill Clinton, 126; and Bob Casey, 139–140; and court cases, 151–152; and Dawn Russell statement, 140; and DC Metro, 134; differences of, with APTA, 124; friction of, with PVA, 116; and in-home care issue, 126–130; and MiCASSA, 131; and Mitch McConnell, 140; and Obama, 133; in Phoenix, 124; politicians' acknowledgment of, 123; protest actions by, 16, 109–111, 123; public sympathy for, 110; as seeking arrest, 115; in St. Louis, 131; targets of, 114–116; and Tom Harkin, 132

adapting citizens or society, 20

ADARA (Americans with Disabilities Act Restoration Act of 2008, S. 1881), 15, 146–152

AFDC (Aid to Families with Dependent Children), 58

Affordable Care Act (ACA, a.k.a. Obamacare), 15, 44, 133, 219n120

AFL-CIO, 98

agenda stability, 28–31, 195–196n42
AIDS, 121–123, 210n44
Aiken, George, 19
Albertson's v. Kirkingburg, 151
Alexander Graham Bell Association for the
   Deaf, 34
Allen, James R., 46
Allen, Robert S., 46
Altman, Barbara, 1
"Amendments Act" (ADAAA), 152–153, 158,
   181
American Association of People with
   Disabilities (AAPD), 133, 152
American Association on Intellectual and
   Developmental Disabilities, 6
American Coalition of Citizens with
   Disabilities. *See* ACCD (American
   Coalition of Citizens with Disabilities)
American Council of the Blind, 86, 96–97
American Federation for the Blind, 56
American Federation of the Physically
   Handicapped, 19, 36–38
American Foundation for the Blind, 83, 87
American Institute of Architects, 65
American Instructors of the Deaf, 35
American Medical Association, 35, 118
American Nurses Association, 35
American Printing House for the Blind, 26,
   33
American Psychiatric Association, 35
Americans Disabled for Attendant Programs
   Today. *See* ADAPT (Americans Disabled
   for Attendant Programs Today)
American Servicemen's Union, 111
"America's rights revolution," 3
AMVETS (American Veterans), 58, 202n52
APTA (American Public Transit
   Association), 11, 74, 92, 103, 109,
   124–125, 153
Architectural Barriers Act (ABA), 2, 59–61,
   65–67, 81, 109, 202n59
Arneson, Kathleen, 59–60
assisted suicide, 13, 105, 116, 128
Association for Children and Adults with
   Learning Disabilities (ACLD), 90, 100, 107
Association for the Blind, 35
Auberger, Michael, 128–129, 134
Autism Society of America, 6

backlash: "backlash reverse," 94; as causing
   hesitation, 89; against civil rights, 107;
contemporary, 141; cycles of, 14–15, 77,
   108; mobilizing against, 106
Bankhead, William, 19–20
Barden, Graham, 24, 26–27, 29, 195n24,
   196n52
Baring, Walter, 38, 198n72
Barnartt, Sharon, 1, 91, 178, 189n3
Barrier Free Anaheim, 112
Barry, Marion, 134
Bartlett, Bob, 50, 59–60, 66, *173*, 204n77
Baucus, Max, 131–132
Baumgartner, Frank, 47, 168, 195–196n42,
   203n66
Bay Area of California, 113, 178
Beall, John Glenn, Jr., 71
Bell, T. H., 106–107
Bennett, Charles, 60, 67, 204n87, 207–
   208n142
Bentele, Keith, 215n37
Berg, Gregg, 115
Berkowitz, Edward, 1, 190n6
Biaggi, Mario, 50, 92, *173*; addition of rights
   language to Urban Mass Transportation
   Act by, 66–67; Biaggi "special efforts"
   Amendment, 68, 73, 81, 109, 204n85;
   as conservative Democrat, 204n86;
   on disabled rights as bipartisan issue,
   207–208n142; on "present day realities,"
   99; and Section 504, 99; on transit
   discrimination, 9
Biden, Joseph, 73
Bilirakis, Michael, 128–129
bipartisanship, 5, 207–208n142; on ABA,
   59–60; on ADA, 120–121, 142, 145, 159;
   breakdown in, 7, 121, 127; Clinton-
   Gingrich bipartisanship on MiCASA,
   128; fetishization of, 162; funding issues
   as hampering, 56, 156, 158; and Harkin
   and Money Follows proposal, 131; on
   IDEA, 156; among liberals, 29; Malloy
   on, 77; Ted Kennedy on, 152
black lung disease, 106
Blank, Wade, 109, 129
blind community: Chris Dodd and, 209n32;
   contrasted with the deaf, 20; federal
   laws regarding, 43; and Gallaudet
   College, 26; Jacobus TenBroek on, 46;
   Kennedy and, 200n3; monitoring court
   cases, 97; monitoring discrimination,
   96; Nixon cutting program for, 87;
   "normality" of, 199n104; organizations

of/for, 26, 33–36, *34*, 38, 56, 85–86, 91,
96; as part of "the disabled," 44–45;
poor work opportunities for, 83–84;
protests by, 105, 110; public spending
on, 53; Randolph-Sheppard Act,
195n33; as a resource, 46; and right of
self-expression, 38; Subcommittee to
Promote the Education of the Blind,
30, 34
Blumer, Herbert, 159
*Board of Trustees of the University of
Alabama v. Garrett*, 151–153
Boggs, Elizabeth, 37, 82, 224n103
BOLD (Building on Local District Flexibility
in IDEA Act of 2015), 157
Boudet, Hilary, 7, 191n26
Bowe, Frank, 86, 89, 96–97
Brademas, John, *173*; and Carter
administration, 92; on committee chair,
75; as disability rights entrepreneur, 50,
55; and Nixon administration, 86–88;
and Rehabilitation Act Amendments, 74;
and role of disability organizations, 75,
83; and Section 504, 72, 94, 99
Bristol, Stanley, 98
Brooke, Edward, 73
Brown v. Board of Education of Topeka, 64,
133, *169*
Building on Local District Flexibility in
IDEA Act of 2015 (BOLD), 157
Burgdorf, Robert, 11, 121, 151
Burns, James MacGregor, 22
Burton, Dan, 144
Bush, George H. W., 4, 13, 121–123, 125, 130,
133, 143–144
Bush, George W., 13, 131, 155–156, 162
Bush, Neil, 121

Califano, Joseph, 10, 89, *90*, 94, 104, 207n133,
212n84, 213n94
Campbell, Andrea, 7, 139, 160–161
Cannon, Chris, 163
Carey, Hugh L., 53–55
Carroll, Thomas P., 87, 94–95
Carter, Jimmy: activists' disappointment
with, 10–11, 105, 109, 161; and disability
rights, 9–11; and HEW reorganization,
207n133, 224n103; Reagan rollback after,
102; and Section 504 implementation,
9–10, 89, 92, 117, 212n84; and Social
Security, 58

Casey, Bob, xiv, 139, 141
Catholic Guild for All the Blind, 83
CC (Conservative Coalition), 23, 28, 121. *See
also* CC scores
CCA (Community Choice Act), 132–133,
162
CCDD (Consortium Concerned with the
Developmentally Disabled), 102, 107
CC scores, 24, 29, *29*, 70, 73, 167; Barry
Goldwater, 195n32; Carl Elliot, 195n25;
David Durenberger, 121; Dick Lugar,
103; Graham Barden, 195n24; H.
Alexander Smith, 26; John Sherman
Cooper, 195n32; Lister Hill, 26; Michael
Bilirakis, 128; Paul Douglas, 195n34
Celebrezze, Anthony, 56, 201n29
Center for Independent Living, 11, 111, 113,
132, 199n98
Chabot, Steve, 151
Chapman Amendment, 122, 125, 145, 217n72
Chevron v. Echazabal, 152
Civil Rights Act (1964), 94–98; amendment
to add disability to, 8–9, 69, 96–98, 137;
bypassing of, 77; compared to disability
rights laws, 144, 148; Danny K. Davis
on, 130; and EEOC, 97; and infectious
disease, 122–123; opportunities created
by, 81; Sections 601 and 605 of, 69, 94; on
statistical discrimination, 121; support
for and opposition to, 31, *169*, *173*,
198n72, 200n106, 207n141, 210n55. *See
also* minority rights for disabled
Civil Rights Act (1990), 125
civil rights and disability rights, 3–5
Civil Services Act, 46
client-service models, 2, 8; ABA and, 60,
62; Mary Switzer on, 55; as merging
with rights paradigm, 51; as monopoly,
28–31; origins and growth of, 19–23;
as paternalistic, 113; and political
advocacy, 85; political elites and, 33, 35;
and welfare state, 42
Clinton, Bill, 13, 126, 128
Clinton, Hillary, 209n19
Coelho, Tony, 4, 12, 14, 110, 135, 142,
144–145
Cohen, Stanley, 194n12
Cohen, Wilber, 58
Colker, Ruth, 145
Committee on Aging and Disabled for
Welfare, 113

Committee on Education and Labor/
    Workforce (U.S. House): and AAPD on
    ADA Restoration Act, 152; under Carl
    Perkins, 75; and IDEA, 155; ideology
    within, *24, 25*, 26, 28, *29*; jurisdiction of,
    52, 62; as main committee for disability,
    23; under Samuel McConnell, *169*; and
    Section 504 issues, 99; testimony before,
    34–35, 41, 200n10, 204n87; turnover in
    1961, 50; and Vocational Rehabilitation
    Act Amendments (1967), 56–57
Committee on Labor and Public Welfare
    (U.S. Senate), 168–172, *169, 170, 171*,
    206n116; under Harrison Williams, 70;
    ideology within, 26, 28; jurisdiction
    of, 52, *53*, 62; as main committee for
    disability, 23; Section 504 and, 72;
    testimony before, 34–35; and Vocational
    Rehabilitation Act Amendments (1967),
    56–57, 70; work of staff on, 75
Committee on Mental Retardation, 81
Community Choice Act (CCA), 132–133, 162
Conference of Executives of American
    Schools for the Deaf, 35
Congressional Quarterly (*CQ*), 29, *30*, 167
Consortium Concerned with the
    Developmentally Disabled (CCDD),
    102, 107
Conte, Silvio, 12, 213n94
Convention on the Rights of Persons with
    Disabilities, 13, 14
Cooper, John Sherman, 195n32
Council for the Retarded, 94
Council of Chief State School Officers, 92
Council of State Administrators of
    Vocational Rehabilitation, 91
Cowen, Tyler, 15
Coy, Patrick, 160
Cranston, Alan, *173*; on bipartisanship,
    207–208n142; on Nixon veto, 87; and
    OCR, 75; promoting civil rights, 51;
    and Section 604, 94; and Sections 503
    and 504, 94–95; and Sections 600 and
    705, 71; on Subcommittee on Health,
    208n11; on Subcommittee on Housing
    and Urban Affairs, 103, 212n85; on
    Subcommittee on the Handicapped, 70,
    73; as thanking staffers, 74

Dallas Morning News, 178
Daniels, Dominick, 30, 57, *169*

Dannemeyer, William, 143, 148, 216n53
Dart, Justin, 1, 3, 11–12, 120–121, 128, 130,
    142
Davis (*Southeastern Community College v.
    Davis*), 7, 97, 118, 149
Davis, Danny K., 130, 132
"deadlock of democracy," 22
deaf community: contrasted with blind
    people, 20, 44; Department of the
    Deaf and Dumb, 20; and education
    institutions, 222n76; federal laws
    regarding, 43; and Gallaudet College/
    University, 26, 53; organizations of/
    for, *34*, 34–35, 85–86, 90–91, 107,
    118; as part of "the disabled," 44–45;
    and rehabilitation programs, 54; as a
    resource, 46; and Television Decoder
    Circuitry Act, 125; training teachers
    for, 56
Deafpride, 86
DeFazio, Peter, 154
DeGette, Diana, 129
De Mint, Jim, 157
"deserving" individuals, groups, 2, 44, 50,
    57, 102, 190n7
Developmental Disabilities Assistance, 83,
    101, 118, 125, 127
Developmental Disabilities Services and
    Facilities Construction Act, 74, 81, 102
Dhillon, Surinder, 104
DIA (Disabled in Action), 151; amicus curiae
    briefs by, 151; in coalitions, 114; as
    congressional watchdog, 11; on disabled
    as productive and employable, 82, 116;
    Dole statement on, 90–91; founding of,
    75; and lawsuit over Baltimore buses,
    9; Lincoln Memorial vigil by, 9, 90; as
    political/legal advocacy group, 6, 10;
    public protests by, 105, 108, 111–113,
    112, 116; and Section 504, 76, 92; sit-ins
    by, 104
Dimond, Paul R., 138
Disability Employment Incentive Act, xiv
disability insurance, 43, *57*, 172, 192–193n48,
    203n70, 207n136
Disability Integration Act (2017), xiii
disability organizational sector, 14, 37, 44,
    80, 106
disability policy network: activists outside,
    50; expansion of, 37, 62–63, 138; in-
    fluence of, 55, 60; members of, 29, 32;

motivations of, 3–5; and Nixon, 87; and Rehabilitation Act, 3; relationship of, with Congress, 38–39, 82; and Section 504, 72, 87, 93–94, 114; social welfare emphasis of, 51, 53; and transportation issues, 65. *See also* nonprofit sector
Disability Rights Center, 10, 86
disabled. *See* minority rights for disabled
Disabled American Veterans (DAV), 37, 80, 97
Disabled in Action (Disabled in Action). *See* DIA
Dodd, Chris, 127, 209n32
Dole, Bob, 3–4, 90–91, 101, 118, 120–123, 135, 145
DOL Section 501, 97
Douglas, Paul, 26, 30, *169*, 195n34
Drach, Ronald, 97
DREDF (Disability Rights and Education Defense Fund), 12, 16, 91, 107–108, 118, 155, 163
Dudley, B. Richmond, Jr., 79–80, 91, 104
Dukakis, Michael, 133
Durenberger, David, 120–121

Eagleton, Thomas F., 71
Earl, Jennifer, 40, 215n33
Easter Seals, 35, 76, 91; and architectural barriers, 81; Bob Casey on, 140; called "derelict," 84–85; and Chapman Amendment, 217n74; in congressional hearings, 154; fund-raising campaigns by, 46; magazine ad by, 44, *45*; response to H.R. 1350 by, 156
Economic Opportunity Act 1964 (War on Poverty), 50–52, 56, 76, 81, *169*, 196n46
Edes, Nik, 74–75
"The Edge of Change," 81
Education Amendments (1972, 1974), 74, 94
Education for All Handicapped Children Act (1975). *See* IDEA
Edwards, Don, 107
EEOC, 97, *173*
Eisenhower, Dwight D., 23, 27, 40, 202n45
Elliot, Carl, 26, 30–31, 38, 47, *169*, 195n25
enforcement issues, 3, 153–154, 163–164; ADA, 14–15, 121, 133, 146, 149, 154, 157; as civil rights issues, 77, 107; and cost issues, 7, 69, 108; and Education for All Handicapped Children Act, 100; and Fair Housing Amendments Act, 118;

G. H. W. Bush and, 121; Harkin and, 133, 138; as leading to "disability rebellion," 91; out of public view, 108; Reagan and, 117, 120; and Section 501 issues, 97; and Section 504 issues, 9–10, 75, 88–89, 92, 99, 108, 111, 117; Trump and, 163. *See also* protests
entrepreneurship: disability rights entrepreneurs, 8–11, 13–14, 68–69, 120, 136–137; elite, 8, 154; political, 6, 8, 11, 13, 16, 76, 137–138, 141, 189n3, 190n8; within Republican Party, 120
Enzi, Mike, 146
Epilepsy Foundation of America, 90, 95, 118, 163, 212n81
Equal Employment Opportunity Act (1972), 77
Equal Employment Opportunity for the Handicapped Act (S. 446), 79, 96–98
ESSA (Every Student Succeeds Act), 157
evolution versus devolution, 7
Ewing, Oscar R., 32

Fair Housing Act, 101
Federal-Aid Highway Acts (1970, 1973, 1974), 67–69
Federal Services Administration (FSA), 22, 32, 39
Fess, Simeon, 20–21, 194n6. *See also* Smith-Fess Act (1920)
Fiorina, Morris, 23
Ford, Gerald, 11, 74–75, 88–89, 209n32
Forsythe, Patricia, 74–75, 211n73
Fossett, Katherine S., 65
Frelinghuysen, Peter, 29, 196n46
French, Jocey, 111
Frieden, Lex, 121

Gallaudet College/University, 26, 53, 114
Gamson, William, 35, 197n64
Garrett (*Board of Trustees of the University of Alabama v. Garrett*), 151–153
Garrett, Scott, 157
Gashel, James, 96
Gerry, Martin, 75–76, 84–85, 88–89, 209n34
Gingrich, Newt, 127–128, 132
global human rights initiative, 13
Goldwater, Barry, 195n32
Goodel, Charles, 51
Goodling, Franklin, 142, 143
Goodwill Industries, 33, 35–36, 46, 76, 88, 91

grassroots activism, 6–7, 78, 116, 134, 139, 142, 159
Gray, Kenneth, 50, 65–66, 68, 73, *173*
Great Society, 4, 28, 50–52, 55, 76, 87, *173*
Green, Edith, 30–31, 55, *169*
Greenwood, Ernest, 31, *169*
Griffith, Kenneth, 47
Griggs v. Duke Power Co., 220n32
Grove City College v. Bell, 119–120
Gunderson, Steven, 120, 216n65
Gwinn, Ralph, 35

Hancock, Mel, 143
Handicapped Bill of Rights, ADA as, 3
Handicapped Children's Protection Act (1986), 108, 118
Harkin, Tom, 135; and ADA, 12, 14, 101, 110, 120, 133, 161; and ADAPT, 132; and ADARA, 149–150; and CCA, 132; as chairman of Senate Subcommittee on Handicapped, 127; and Developmental Disabilities Assistance, 125; frustration of, with lack of progress, 146–147, 150–151, 161; on future, 162; and IDEA Fairness Restoration Act, 157; and MiCASSA, 130–132; other bills sponsored by, 118; and paratransit services, 123; on "quiet revolution," 138
Hatch, Orrin, 4, 100–101, 122, 127, 144–145, 161, 218n91
Hawkes, Teresa, 101–102
Hedeen, Timothy, 160
Helms, Jesse, 144
Heumann, Judy, 11, 16, 74–75
HEW (Department of Health, Education, and Welfare), 58, 88, 92; and ABA regulations, 66; and Anthony Celebrezze, 56, 201n29; and architectural barriers, 60; in Carter administration, 224n103; conflict of, with DOT and PCEH, 73; disability groups monitoring, 39; and disability insurance, 43; dissemination of information by, 76; and F. David Matthews, 84; funding shortfalls of, 56; and Harrison Williams, 73, 75; and HHS, 101; and Joseph Califano, 89, 104, 207n133, 213n94; jurisdictional disputes regarding, 75; in Kennedy administration, 56; as "liberal bureaucracy," 57–58; and Martin Gerry, 209n34; and Mary Switzer, 58;

in Nixon administration, 58; and OCR, 75; Office of the Handicapped, 71; and Oveta Culp Hobby, 40; proposals to decentralize, 76; role of, 22, 32, 34, 40; and Roswell D. Perkins, 43; and Section 504 implementation, 10, 73, 75–76, 88–94, *93*; sit-ins at, 10, 104, 179, 213n94; Special Staff on Aging, 58; Subcommittee on the Handicapped, 210n55; and Vocational Rehabilitation, 55; and Wilbur Cohen, 58
Hill, Beatrice, 39, 41
Hill, Eve, 158, 162
Hill, Lister, 26, 52, 57
HIV/AIDS, 121–123, 210n44
Hobby, Oveta Culp, 40, 43
House of Representatives, U.S., *24*, *174*, *175*; Ad Hoc Subcommittee on the Handicapped, 53; Committee on Banking and Currency, 206n116; Committee on Education, 19; Committee on Education and Labor, 52; Committee on Public Works, 65, 72, 206n116; Select Subcommittee on Education, 1, 10, 60, 67, 75, 83, 86, 136; Special Subcommittee for Establishing a Federal Commission for Physically Handicapped, 46; Special Subcommittee on Education, 55; Special Subcommittee on Employment and Manpower, 52; Special Subcommittee on Problems of the Aged and Aging, 52–53; Subcommittee on Civil and Constitutional Rights, 107; Subcommittee on DOT Appropriations, 104, 213n94; Subcommittee on Education Reform, 155; Subcommittee on Employment Opportunities, 67; Subcommittee on Health, 26; Subcommittee on Health and the Environment, 119, 128; Subcommittee on Public Buildings and Grounds, 66; Subcommittee on Roads, 67; Subcommittee on Special Education, 26, 39, 42, 49; Subcommittee on Surface Transportation, 144; Subcommittee on the Constitution, 151; Subcommittee on Urban Mass Transportation, 72, 206n116; Subcommittee on War on Poverty Programs, 51; Subcommittee to Promote the Education of the Blind, 30, 34, 196n48
Housing Act (1954), 64

Howard, Christopher, 199n93
Hoyer, Steny, 123, 125, 135, 145, 149
Hughes, Jonathan, 58
humanitarianism, 7, 39–40, 47
Humphrey, Hubert, 3–4, 50, 69, 96, 136–137, *173*, 190n14
Humphreys, Bob, 74–75

iatrogenesis, 194n12
Iddings, Wendell B., *93*
IDEA (Individuals with Disabilities Education Act): attorney fee reimbursement under, 223n84; and BOLD Act, 157; criticisms of, 87; as Education for All Handicapped Children Act (1975), 4–5, 74, 81, 99–100, 108; Harkin and, 147; and IDEA Funding Coalition, 157; Jeff Sessions and, 210n44; and *N. E. v. Seattle School District*, 153; and parental rights, 222n77; Patricia Wright and, 108; and "quiet revolution," 138; Reagan attempts to eliminate, 106–108; reauthorization of, 127, 155–156; results of, 155; and Shadegg Amendment, 223n79; and *Smith v. Robinson*, 108, 118; "stay put rule" of, 153, 156; Weicker and, 106–108
Imparato, Andrew, 152
independent living movement: Carl Perkins and, 28; Center for Independent Living, 11, 111, 113, 132, 199n98; and civil rights protection, 152; disability policy network and, 53; Ed Roberts and, 16, 105, 113, 199n98; and in-home care, 127–128; Jacobus TenBroek and, 71; Martin Mahler and, 38; National Council on Independent Living, 140; and social welfare, 53; threats to, 44; varying needs for, 129; and vocational rehabilitation, 40–43
institutional isomorphism, 37, 139, 197n67
International Association of Parents of the Deaf, 107
"iron triangle," 31, 189n2
Issa, Darrell, 148
issue salience, 30, *30*, 47, 110, 158, 167

Jackson, Jesse, 119
Javits, Jacob, 26, 51, 56, 70–71, 98, *173*, 208n11

Jeffords, Jim, *90*, 91–92, 94, 101, 121, 127
jelly beans, 106
Jerry Lewis Telethons, 46, 105, 116
Johnson, Erik, 176, 224n101
Johnson, Leroy, 40
Johnson, Lyndon, 26, 51, 54, 57, 81, 87
Johnson, Mark, 124
Jones, Bryan D., 47, 168, 195–196n42, 203n66
Jones, Roger W., 32, 197n59
Jordan, B. Everett, 59, 61
Jordan, Vernon E., 107
Joseph P. Kennedy Jr. Foundation, 49

Kaplan, Debbie, 10
Katzmann, Robert, 66, 210n54
Keith, Raymond, 75
Kelley, Augustine B., 30–31, *169*, 197n56
Kennedy, Edward (Ted): and ADA, 101, 121–122, 145; and ADARA, 148, 152; and Developmental Disabilities Assistance and Bill of Rights Act Amendments, 101; and Developmental Disabilities Services and Facilities Construction Act, 81–82; and Education Amendments, 207n126; on HIV/AIDS epidemic, 121–122; on Subcommittee on Health, 208n11; on Subcommittee on the Handicapped, 211n73; and Vocational Rehabilitation Act, 70–71
Kennedy, John F.: and bills on mental health/cognitive disability, 197n56, 200n6; budget issues blocking agenda of, 56; and employment of the handicapped issue, 202n45; House blocking agenda of, 23; and mandate on needs of disabled, 64; and Panel on Mental Retardation, 37, 49; personal interest of, in disability issues, 49, 51; and Sam Rayburn, 203n64; as supporting civil rights, 205n97
Kennedy, Joseph P., Jr., 49
Kennedy, Rosemary, 49
King, David, 215n37
Klobuchar, Amy, xiii

Lantos, Tom, 13
Laxalt, Paul, 107
Lazio, Rick, 128
Leadership Conference on Civil Rights, 96, 98, 107, 118
League of Special Education Voters, 156

Lebanon School Board, 92, *93*
Lee, John J., 40–41
Lee, Sheila Jackson, 156
Lehman, Herbert H., 27, 30, 51, *169*
Lehman, Mayer, 195n35
Levitan, Sar, 52
Lewis, Drew, 103
Lewis, Jerry, 46, 105, 116
Lincoln, Abraham, 49–50
Lincoln Center, 59
Lincoln Memorial, 9, 90
Lipinski, Bill, 142, 143
Lipsky, Michael, 33
Little, R. M., 47
Lorber, Lawrence, 149
Los Angeles Times, 105, 109, 115, 150–151, 178
Lugar, Dick, 103, 108
Lungren, Daniel, 214n16
Lynch, Ed, 75

Macaluso, Vincent, 103
Madigan, Edwin, 118
Magee v. Coca-Cola, 153
Mahler, Martin, 19, 38
Mainstream, Inc., 95, 105
mainstreaming education, 5, 13, 74, 99–100, 134, 138, 147, 155–156. *See also* IDEA
Malloy, Larry, 77
MAP-21 (Moving Ahead for Progress in the 21st Century Act), 154
Marchand, Paul, 102, 107
March of Dimes, 33, 46
Mass Transit Amendments (Proposed), 103
Mathews, F. David, 84
Mattox, Nancy, 108, 214n19
McAdam, Doug, 7, 191n26, 199n102
McCain, John, 4, 12, 14, 110, 120, 135, 144
McConnell, Mitch, 140, *140*, 205n100
McConnell, Samuel K., 30–31, *169*
McCutcheon, Stephen, 150
McGovern, George B., 21
McKeon, Howard (Buck), 149, 157
McNamara, Pat, 52
medical models of disability, 1, 189n5
Mental Disability Legal Resource Center, 86
mental health, 35, 43, 51, 56, 123, 131, 170, 172
mental retardation, 37, 45, 49–51, 56, 81, 170, 172

Messner, Sherwood, 82
Milk, Leslie, 95, 97, 105, 211n61
Miller, George, 9
Minkoff, Debra, 35, 81, 175–177, 191n21, 197n65, 209n21
minority rights for disabled, xiv, 136; in Britain and Australia, 192–193n48; and client-service model, 19, 62; and collective minority concept, 42–43; "first wave" of demonstrations for, 111; Harrison Williams on, 49; language of, 61; as largest minority, 134; as last frontier, 162; Lowell Weicker on, 96, 101–102; no organized resistance to, 77; political elite support for, 4, 80–82; to promote good citizenship, 46; school administrators' opposition to, 95; through Section 504 tactic, 8–9; Supreme Court on, 150. *See also* Civil Rights Act (1964); Section 504 of Rehabilitation Act
model citizen, 40
Mondale, Walter, 70–71
Morrison, James Hobson, 200n106
Morton, Thurston, 26, 29
Mothers of Young Mongoloids (a.k.a. Parents of Down Syndrome Children), 85
Moving Ahead for Progress in the 21st Century Act (MAP-21), 154
Moyers, Bill, 14
Murphy v. UPS, 151
Murray, James E., 27
Murray, Patty, 141
Muscular Dystrophy Association, 37
Myers, Daniel, 179, 215n39
Myers, John, 92, *93*

NAACP (National Association for the Advancement of Colored People), 107, 118, 132
Nader, Ralph, 86
Nadler, Jerrold, 150
Nagel, John F., 71
NARC (National Association of Retarded Children), 91, 94; amicus curiae briefs by, 151; as coordinating protest actions, 105, 111, 113; on disabled as minority group with rights, 82; and Elizabeth Boggs statement, 82–83; founding of, 36–37; and HEW, 39, 224n103;

membership of, 80; as monitoring rights violations, 96, 129; and Orrin Hatch, 100–101; and Reagan, 100; and vocational training, 56, 71

National Advisory Committee on Education of the Deaf, 53

National Alliance of Blind Students, 86

National Art and Handicapped Information Service, 77

National Association for Mental Health, 35

National Association of College and University Business Officers, 92

National Association of Retarded Children. See NARC (National Association of Retarded Children)

National Association of Social Workers, 35

National Association of the Deaf, 35, 90–91

National Association of the Physically Handicapped, 36–37, 65, 70

National Center for Law and the Handicapped, 86–87, 91, 94

National Commission on Architectural Barriers, 59–60

National Council of the Blind, 91

National Council on the Handicapped, 11, 120, 224n103

National Employ the Physically Handicapped Week, 47, 202n45

National Epilepsy League, 36–37

National Federation of the Blind. See NFB (National Federation of the Blind)

National Foundation for Neuromuscular Disease, 37

National Health Program and National Program to Combat Mental Retardation, 49

National Legislative Council for the Handicapped, 86

National Mass Transportation Assistance Act, 69

National Multiple Sclerosis Society, 37, 80

National Organization for Mentally Ill Children, 39

National Paraplegia Foundation, 36, 39, 104

National Parkinson Foundation, 37

National Recreation Association, 39, 41

National Rehabilitation Association. See NRA (National Rehabilitation Association)

National Rehabilitation Institute, 39

National Restaurant Association, 122

National Society for Autistic Children, 85, 100, 191n20, 212n81

National Spinal Cord Injury Association, 103, 125

National Tay-Sachs Association, 37

National Technical Institute for the Deaf Act, 53

National Women's Law Center, 107, 118

Nationwide Action for a Fair Budget, 106

NCLB (No Child Left Behind Act), 155–157

neoliberalism, 6, 9

Nerney, Tom, 101

N. E. v. Seattle School District, 153, 221–222n64

"new federalism," 106, 214n11

New York Times, 99–100, 178

NFB (National Federation of the Blind): coordination of, with other groups, 105, 111, 114; founding and purpose of, 36, 46, 199n104; increasing membership of, 80; statements by, 71, 81, 83–84, 96

Nixon, Richard: and cuts to rehabilitation programs, 84, 87; and HEW, 58; and Rehabilitation Act, 5, 71–72, 87, 104, 113, 197n56, 206n107; as supporting deinstitutionalization, 71

nonprofit sector: AAPD, 152; as advocates, 85, 85; and co-optation, 160; deaf and blind organizations in, 85–86; as experts, 1; in 1960s, 56; as part of "iron triangle," 31–35, 41; and rehabilitation goals, 21–22; and rights-oriented policies, 5; school officials and, 92; as service providers, 2; shifts in, 80, 80–81. See also disability policy network

No Pity (Shapiro), 123, 199n99

Not Dead Yet, 112, 116

NRA (National Rehabilitation Association), 37, 91, 212n81; and Congress, 32, 35, 39, 56, 83; creation of, 33; increasing membership of, 80; and Section 504, 76

Nugent, Timothy, 65

OASDI (Old-Age and Survivors Insurance), 43, 56, 57

Obama, Barack, 13, 132–133, 154, 156–157, 162, 223n86

Obamacare, 15, 44, 133, 219n120

Oberstar, Jim, 154

OCR (Office of Civil Rights): as criticized for inaction, 88–89; as disseminator of information, 76; and enforcement issues, 117, 209n34; and Gerry on disability rights, 84; jurisdiction of, 75; letters of finding by, 214n19; morale within, 108; and narrow interpretation of rights, 92; pressure on, 210n55; and Section 504, 92, 95; as supporting sit-ins, 10. *See also* HEW (Department of Health, Education, and Welfare)

Office of Disability Policy Act, xiv

Office of Vocational Rehabilitation (OVR), 22, 31–32, 38–39

Old-Age and Survivors Insurance (OASDI), 43, 56, *57*

Oliver, Pamela, 178, 215n39

Olmstead v. L.C., 118, 129–130, 133, 151

O'Neil, David, 92, 210n42

open political structure, 145, 220n30

oppositional consciousness, 113, 139, 141

Orloff, Ann, 22, 189n1

Over-the-Road Bus Transportation Accessibility Act, 154, 222n70

Owens, Bill, 123

Owens, Robert Odell, 12, 14, 136, 145–146, 192n35

Pain Relief Promotion Act (1999), 128

Panel on Mental Retardation, 37, 49

Parks, Rosa, 105, 108

participation-policy cycle, 7

Patashnik, Eric, 162

Patman, John, 67, 204n89

Patterson, James, 57

PCEH (President's Committee on Employment of the Handicapped), 58, 60, 73, 99, 103, 202n45, 206n121

Pell, Claiborne, 70–71, 98, 101, 208n11

Percy, Charles (Chuck), 69, 204n83

Percy, Stephen, 216n51

Perez, Thomas E., 133

Perkins, Carl D., 28, 30, 31, 57, 75, 92, 99, *169*

Perkins, Roswell D., 43

Peter Pan Bus Lines, Inc. v. FMCSA, 154

Petri, Tom, 144

Phillips, John, 26

Pierson, Paul, 22, 191n23, 209n25

pity as motivator, 13, 35, 44–46, *45*, 105, 116, 123

policy "hare," U.S. as, 15, 164

political elites, xiv, 28; and ABA and Section 504, 61; and civil rights, 8, 50; and client-service models, 33, 35; and deaf and blind issues, 35; disability activists working with and against, 9–11, 17–18, 77, 85, 104, 111, 123–125, 155–157; and disability empowerment policy, 4; and jurisdictional issues, 63; measures of success for, 2, 22, 40, 155, 164; paternalism concerns by, 38; as pushing government to lead social services, 33, 50, 118; rehabilitation goals of, 22, 43, 70; and "Repeal and Replace" issue, 139–142; as seeking bipartisanship, 40, 50, 63, 152, 161; as seeking compromise, 70, 137, 156, 161; and transportation issues, 65, 157

political entrepreneurship, 6, 8, 11, 13, 16, 76, 137–138, 141, 189n3, 190n8

political opportunity structure, 145, 220n30

Polsby, Nelson, 24, 61, 167, 196n43

President's Panel on Mental Retardation, 49

professional associations, 1, 34–35

Promoting Wellness for Individuals with Disabilities Act, 132

protests: by ACCD, 104, 105, 109, 111–114, *112*, 151; by ADAPT, 16, 109–111; coordinated by NARC, 105, 111, 113; by DIA, 105, 108, 111–113, *112*, 116; sit-ins, 10, 104, 179, 213n94; against Trump, 133

Public Law 94-142, 99, 102

PVA (Paralyzed Veterans of America): and AIDS issues, 123; and architectural barriers, 59, 123; and Civil Rights Act, 210n55; congressional testimony by, 79, 95, 104, 192n30; and *DOT v. PCA*, 118, 216n55; friction of, with ADAPT, 116; and public transportation, 123; rights approach of, 73

Quenstedt, Warren, 68

Quie, Al, 95

Rainbow Alliance of the Deaf, 86

Raker, John E., 19–20

Randolph, Jennings: and Committee on Public Works, 60; as cosponsor of S. 446, 98; and Developmental Disabilities Assistance and Bill of Rights Act, 83; and hearings on regulatory delays, 11; and HEW jurisdiction, 75–76; and investigation of manpower problems,

52; as liberal voice in Senate, 26; and
Randolph-Sheppard Act, 195n33; and
Rehabilitation Act, 74; and Section
504 legislation, 71–72, 76, 92, 99; and
Subcommittee on Health, 208n11; and
Subcommittee on the Handicapped, 70,
88, 211n73; work by staff of, 74
Rauh, Joseph, 107
Rayburn, Sam, 203n64
Reagan, Ronald: as abandoning affirmative
action, 117; ADA support within
administration of, 120–121; Disabled for
Reagan campaign, 120; on government
as the problem, 99, 108; mobilization
against, xiv, 12, 106–107, 114; NARC
and, 100–101; as opposing accessibility
regulation, 7, 9, 11, 144; as opposing
retroactive awards, 118; as opposing
statistical discrimination standard,
121; and Section 504, 91, 96, 117; as
supporting UMTA administrators,
102–103; veto of CRRA by, 119; and
welfare state, 209n25, 216n51
reasonable accommodations, 7, 146, 151, 163
Reed, Daniel, 43
Regional Center for Independent Living, 132
Rehabilitation Act (1973), 3, 48, 80–81, 158,
180; ACCD on, 97; and ADA, 148–149;
amendments to (1974), 74; Bob Dole
and, 145; communicable diseases
and, 216n53; compliance issues with,
95–96; G. H. W. Bush on, 143; Harrison
Williams on, 97–99; as impossible
law, 11; Nixon's veto and signing of, 5,
71–72, 87, 104, 113; reauthorization of,
127; Section 503 of, 98; will of Congress
regarding, 12. See also Section 504 of
Rehabilitation Act
Rehabilitation, Inc., 104
rehabilitation policy paradigm: and architectural barriers, 59; and client-service
policy, 85; and disability policy network, 51; helping disabled help themselves, 19–20, 33, 36, 36, 41–42, 55–56;
and in-home care issue, 127–128; and
mainstreaming, 1–2; and rights framework, 44; and vocational programs, 21
Rehabilitative Services Administration
(RSA), 21, 41, 87, 120, 170, 171
Rehnquist, William, 118
Reich, Alan A., 13, 117, 162, 192n41, 216n49

Reid, Harry, 14
Reid, Stuart F., 21
Retzinger, Jynny, 109
Reynolds, William Bradford, 117, 120
Riley, Charles A., 121
Roberts, Ed, 16, 105, 113, 199n98
Robrahn, Reese, 103
Robsion, John, 34
Rockwell, Norman, 36, 36, 42
Rosenbaum, Edward E., 42
Rosenbloom, Sandra, 222n68
RSA (Rehabilitative Services Administra-
tion), 21, 41, 87, 120, 170, 171
Rusk, Howard, 47, 59
Russell, Dawn, 140
Russell, Harold, 52, 58–60, 99, 103–104,
202n46
Ryan, William F., 67

Sandberg, Annette, 154
San Diego, CA, 108, 111–112
San Francisco Chronicle, 124, 178
"satisficing," 131, 218n112
Scalia, Antonin, 118
Schiavo, Terry, 116
Schloss, Irvin P., 87
School Board of Nassau County v. Arline, 118
Schumer, Chuck, 132
Scotch, Richard, 75, 91, 139, 189n1, 193n60
Seaborn, Jimmy, 41–42
Sears, William J., 19
Section 501 (DOL), 97
Section 503 of Rehabilitation Act, 94, 98
Section 504 of Rehabilitation Act, 8, 72, 84;
ACCD and, 76, 88, 92, 95, 103; ADA and,
15; Adams and, 212n84; Amendments
of 1974 on, 206n123; APTA and, 92;
Bennett and, 207–208n142; Biaggi and,
99, 207–208n142; Brademas and, 72, 94,
99; Califano and, 10, 89, 90, 212n84;
Carroll and, 87, 94; Carter and, 9–10,
89, 92, 117, 212n84; and Civil Rights
Act, 8–10, 72, 93–95, 119–120, 209n32;
claims of bipartisanship regarding,
207–208n142; and compliance concerns,
92–96, 93; court cases involving, 97,
108, 118, 149, 211n61, 216n55; Cranston
and, 94–95, 207–208n142; DIA and, 10,
76, 92; disability policy network and, 2,
61, 72, 87, 93–95, 114; and diseases and
infections, 119, 210n44; DOJ limiting,

Section 504 of Rehabilitation Act (*continued*)
117; and enforcement issues, 9; Ford
and, 89, 209n32; Gerry and, 75–76,
84, 88–89; G. H. W. Bush and, 121;
HEW implementation of, 10, 73, 75–76,
88–94, *93*; and HIV/AIDS, 210n44; hold
categories regarding, 214n19; Jeffords
on, 94; Jesse Jackson on, 119–120;
Kaplan and, 10; Keith and, 75–76; lax
enforcement of, 111, 113, 137; Lebanon
School Board on, 92, *93*; Lynch and,
75–76; merging rights and client-service
paradigm in, 51; Nixon and, 5, 72, 87;
NRA and, 76; OCR and, 75–76, 84, 88,
92, 95; O'Neil on, 210n42; public transit
and, 103; Randolph and, 71–72, 76, 92,
99; Reagan and, 91, 96, 106, 117, 214n11;
results of, 2, 87–88, 99; Richard Scotch
on, 193n60; schools opposing, 92, *93*,
99; signing of regulations for, 10; state
laws patterned after, 114; and technical
issues, 210n42; Williams and, 73, 76,
88, 92, 98–99; Wodatch and, 75. *See also*
Rehabilitation Act (1973); Vocational
Rehabilitation Act Amendments
Selznick, Philip, 160
Senate, U.S.: Committee on Banking,
Housing, and Urban Affairs, 73;
Committee on Education and Public
Welfare, 26; Committee on Health,
Education, Labor, and Pensions, 133,
147, 152, 155, 172; Committee on
Labor and Human Resources, 122;
Committee on Labor and Public
Welfare, 52; Committee on Public
Works, 68; Subcommittee on Health,
56, 59, 81–82, 208n11; Subcommittee
on Housing and Urban Affairs, 73–74,
103; Subcommittee on Public Buildings
and Grounds, 59; Subcommittee on
the Handicapped (Disability Policy),
4, 11, 75–76, 88, 99–102, 106, 127,
174, 206n116, 210n55; Subcommittee
on Vocational Rehabilitation of the
Physically Handicapped, 19, 26, 30,
196n48. *See also* Committee on Labor
and Public Welfare (U.S. Senate)
Sensenbrenner, Cheryl, 152
Sensenbrenner, James, xiv, 125, 145, 149–150,
214n16, 217n87
Sessions, Jeff, 156, 210n44

Shadegg Amendment, 223n79
Shanker, Albert, 100
Shapiro, Joseph, 44, 123, 199n99
Shapiro, Sieglinde A., 10, 192n30
Shepherd, Vivian, 39
Shimkus, John, 130
"silent army," 121, 217n68
sit-ins, 10, 104, 179, 213n94. *See also* protests
Skocpol, Theda, 22, 79, 189n1, 190n7
Smith, H. Alexander, 26
Smith, Hoke, 194n6
Smith, Steven, 33
Smith, Wint, 30, *169*
Smith-Fess Act (1920), 20, 26, 33. *See
also* Vocational Rehabilitation Act
Amendments
Smith-Hughes Act (1917), 194n4, 196n51
Smith-Sears Act (1918), 19, 194n4
Smith v. Robinson, 108, 118
Social Security Act (1935), 43, 56, 58, 127,
199n104
Sodrel, Mike, 222n69
Soule, Sarah, 37, 40, 213n8, 215n33
Southeastern Community College v. Davis, 7, 97
Southern Democrats, 23–24, 26, 28, 31, 50,
57, 194n6, 200n106
Sparkman, John, 73
Specter, Arlen, 149
Stafford, Robert, 51, 69–71, 94–95, 102, 135,
173, 211n73
"stay put rule," 153, 156
Stevenson, Adlai, 70–71
Stockman, David, 216n51
subminimum wages, 209n19
Sutton v. United Airlines, 151
Switzer, Mary, 21, 41, 55, 58–60, *170–171*
sympathy versus rights, 3

Taft, Robert, 29
Taft, Robert, Jr., 71
Taggart, Robert, 52
Tancredo Amendment, 223n79
Tarrow, Sydney, 111, 141, 191n26
Telecommunications Accessibility
Enhancement Act, 120
Television Decoder Circuitry Act, 125
TenBroek, Jacobus, 46, 71, 104, 199n103
"third wave" of civil rights activism, xiv,
117, 133
Thomas, Clarence, 108
Thomas B. Fordham Institute, 157

Thornburgh, Richard (Dick), 13, 151
Tilly, Charles, 159
Title IX (Education Amendments), 94
Tobin, Maurice, 19
tortoise-and-hare analogy, 15, 164
Trageser v. Libbie Rehabilitation Center, 97, 211n61
"Transbuses," 102
transit accessibility, 11, 102, 108, 114–117, 123–124, 126, 154
Transit Assistance Act (1981), 102, 108
Trump, Donald, xiv; effects of, on courts, 153; and Muslim ban, 218n105; protests against, 133; as undermining ADA, 137, 139–141, 163

UCP (United Cerebral Palsy), 91; amicus curiae briefs by, 151; creation of, 36; and Lincoln Memorial vigil, 9; political advocacy by, 6, 100, 103–104, 118, 156, 217n74; and Sherwood Messner statement, 82; and "stay put rule," 156
Udall, Stewart, 26
UMTA (Urban Mass Transportation Administration), 102–103, 110
United Nations, xiii, 13–14, 207–208n142
Urban Mass Transportation Act (1964), 64, 66
Urban Mass Transportation Assistance Act (1970), 2, 64, 66, 68, 72–73, 123, 125, 206n119

Van Dyke, Nella, 213n8
Vanik, Charles, 50, 69–71, 75, 96, 137, *173*
Velde, Harold, 29
Vento, Bruce, 136–137
Vocational Rehabilitation Act Amendments, 26 27; of 1954, 13, 72, 77, 86, 202n15; of 1956, 26–27, 43; of 1965, 59–60; of 1967 and 1968, 55, 56, 66–67, 202n60; of 1972, 8, 70; Rehabilitation Act of 1973 as replacing, 3. *See also* Section 504 of Rehabilitation Act
vocational training, 20–22, 28, 56, 71, 114
voluntary sector, xiv, 6, 19, 33, 82–83, 86, 106, 191n21

Wainwright, Stuyvesant, 30, *169*
Walberg, Tim, 157
Walker, Lisa, 74–75, 95, 103
Wards Cove Packing Co. v. Atonio, 220n32

War on Poverty (Economic Opportunity Act, 1964), 50, 51, 56, 76, *169*
Washington Post, 178
Weicker, Lowell, xiii, 12, 14, 96, 99–102, 106–108, 121, 135
Weiss, Ted, 99
welfare state: as belated, 22, 79, 189n1; and disability, 1–2, 5, 20, 42; growth of, *54*; myth of, 199n93; nonprofits and, 33; Reagan and, 209n25, 216n51; and rehabilitation, 189n1; and retrenchment, 191n23; in Sweden, 192–193n48
Werdel, Thomas, 29
Wier, Roy W., 30–31, *173*
Williams, Harrison, *173*; and Banking, Housing, and Urban Affairs Committee, 73, 103; and Committee on Education and Public Welfare, 26; and Developmental Disabilities Assistance, 101; and disabled children legislation, 207n126; on equal access and rights, 68; and Equal Employment Opportunity for the Handicapped Act, 96; as including disability groups in process, 88; and Labor and Public Welfare Committee, 70; and legislation versus regulation debate, 73; and National Mass Transportation Assistance Act, 69; and OCR jurisdiction, 75, 88; promotion of Biaggi Amendment by, 73; as quoting Lincoln, 49, 50; and Rehabilitation Act, 97–99; and Section 503, 98–99; and Section 504, 76, 88, 92, 98–99; and Section 604, 71; and Subcommittee on Handicapped, 211n73; and Subcommittee on Health, 208n11; and Urban Mass Transportation Assistance Act, 73; work by staff of, 74; work of, with Brademas and Javits, 55–56
Winship, Michael, 14
Wodatch, John, 75
Wright, Gloria, 71
Wright, Jim, 3, 12, *173*
Wright, Patricia, 12, 108

Yarborough, Ralph, 82, 208n11
Yatron, Gus, 133, 216n49

Zelizer, Julian, 162
Zola, Irving, 154